NO ORDINARY

BOOK

A Bible translator tells his story

Philip Saunders

COPYRIGHT

FOREWORD

It was our first night in a Kouya village. Philip and Heather had invited us to stay in Dema for the weekend. Heather cooked a tasty goat stew for us, but it was the Friday night prayer meeting that I remember most vividly.

Dema was pitch black. Inside the tiny wooden church building we worshipped God by the smoky light of a single paraffin lamp. Face to face we were meeting Kouyas that we previously knew only through prayer letters. We had often prayed back in Belfast for Baï Emile, Kalou Williams and François. That evening we were praying *with* them.

Praying for mission can have unexpected repercussions. Having supported the Saunders from home, we were now in Ivory Coast supporting their work as Wycliffe colleagues, teaching Joy and Rachel at Vavoua International School.

We gradually got to know the Kouya Christians who were working on the translation. We met Baï Laurent whose faithful prayers over several decades were answered when Philip and Heather came to live in a Kouya village.

I was privileged to be present at the first Kouya funeral when the Christians took their stand against traditional customs. My wife Ruth witnessed the first baptisms at Dema reservoir. We watched the Beatitudes come off the solar-powered printer in Gouabafla in Eddie and Sue Arthur's mud bricked, thatch roofed office. I sat in on consultant checking sessions as the whole team worked hard to express the message of Luke's Gospel to the satisfaction of the consultant. We celebrated with the Christians in Bouitafla on the day the new prayer house was opened. We listened as Baï Laurent reminded some old men in the audience that years ago they had stoned him out of the village for preaching the Gospel.

We never did learn more than a few words of Kouya, but we understood better something of the skill and the hard

3

slog required to reduce an unwritten language to writing. We did no translation ourselves, but we saw how God used those first drafts of New Testament books to encourage and grow the Kouya church.

We shared joys and sorrows with Kouya friends. Philip and Heather were great encouragers when we were under pressure at Vavoua School and I hope we were of some help in return.

It was a privilege to live and work alongside the Saunders in Côte d'Ivoire. It is a privilege to write the foreword to this book. "No Ordinary Book" – what a great title for the story of how God brought the Word of Life to a people group where lives continue to be changed as they read the New Testament in the language of their hearts!

This book is to be enjoyed, but it will also challenge. More than 2,700 language groups around the world still do not have a single word of Scripture. Thousands more like Baï Laurent are praying for help to arrive. Will *you* be the answer to their prayers?

John Hamilton
Wycliffe Bible Translators

This book is dedicated to my parents

Eric and Eileen Saunders

ACKNOWLEDGEMENTS

First of all, I would like to acknowledge our Brooklands church family, and the many others who have supported the Kouya translation and literacy project since it began. It was your enthusiasm, generosity, prayer and encouragement that helped to make it all possible.

I want also to thank my brother and sisters, David, Hazel and Pamela, for – well, for being the best siblings you could ever wish for!

Then I must recognise four very important women in my life: my wife Heather, and daughters Joy, Rachel and Hilary. I am grateful to God for each one, and look forward to reading the books *they* will write one day! My thanks to Hilary for many of this book's illustrations, and to my colleague Laurel Miller for the cover photograph.

A number of friends took time to read the original manuscript. I am indebted to all for their feedback and reassurance, but particularly to the following for their invaluable comments: Ronnie Cairns, Paul Drain, Maureen Edmondson, Lisa Leidenfrost, Moyra Martin, Ruth McCormick, David Moore, Lynda Neilands and Stephen Orr. I also appreciated David McFarland's expertise, as we prepared this POD edition together.

Finally, thanks are also due to our countless Kouya friends. Without them there would have been no story to tell.

Baï Laurent, now gone to his reward, pioneered as a Christian among his Kouya people. He once prayed: *'Lord, we thank You that Your Word is not bitter, like malaria medicine. It is sweet, like sugar.'*

The same can be said of friendship too.

CONTENTS

MAPS

Côte d'Ivoire

COTE D'IVOIRE

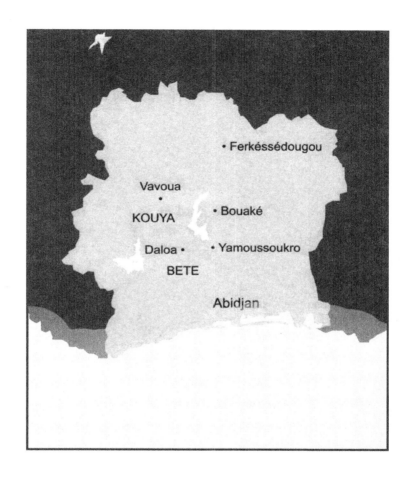

KOUYA VILLAGES

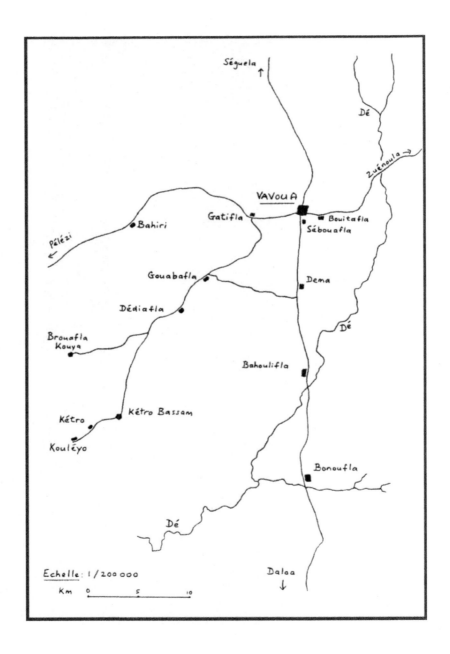

Following our Dream

One day I will hold a book in my hands. It will have a blue cover, and its pages will have golden edges.

And each time I hold it, a memory will come back. An image of a Kouya friend. Of heads thrown back in delighted laughter. Of shoulders bowed in pain. Of villages basking in the red glow of the sinking sun. Of a weary family filing back from their fields after a day's work. Memories of drumming and dancing, danger and death, colour and life.

One day I will hold a book in my hands, and I shall recall that we never thought we would make it. When we went through the mangle of sickness, when stress stretched us beyond our ability to endure, at such times the dream seemed to be out of our grasp.

To accept that we would have to give up, to put the dream away in a drawer, and settle for a second-best to put in the days, the hours, the long minutes of life: this thought was too painful to consider.

But the Lord allowed us to go back. The film had been paused halfway through, but He allowed it to run its course. And there we were, acting out the parts we so deeply yearned to play! The dream that had got stuck was moving again.

One day I will hold a book in my hands. It will have a blue cover, and its pages will have golden edges. A book of memories, yes. Tangible proof of a realised dream, yes. And yet, no ordinary book, for it holds the words of eternal life. It is not for us, but for future generations of Kouyas. Our part may be over, but God acts on.

And I shall sigh, and be glad, so glad that we went back, bore a little more pain, and saw the birth. Others will bring up the child, and we, we will remind ourselves that it is not our baby alone. For our God has given this book an independent Life of its own.

Yes, one day I will hold a book in my hands. And I will take the book, and kneel, and offer it back to Him, for without Him it would not have come about. For it was He who gave us the dream, it was He who produced the pages that rest on my outstretched palms.

CRISIS

March 13th 1990

The African surgeon's hand was shaking as he handed me the consent-form. The long French medical words were a blur, but I took a deep breath and signed my name. I couldn't control the pounding of my heart. Was this really happening? My wife Heather was being hurriedly wheeled out of the intensive care unit towards swing-doors which said 'Theatre' in bold red letters.

And then I was alone. I sat down on the orange plastic seats of the waiting room, struggling to regain composure. My mind was racing yet strangely lucid considering my lack of sleep. The events of the previous days and weeks flitted over an inner screen.

For some weeks Heather had not felt well, so we had packed slowly, and on the morning that she was well enough to travel, we set off from the village for Abidjan, a day's journey by car. Our two-year-old, Hilary, chattered in the back as usual, surrounded by her favourite books and toys. Heather looked well enough, had a healthy colour, but felt very nauseous.

What came next? The events were confused. There was the visit to the French doctor, the suspected miscarriage, hepatitis complications, a minor operation. Finally, she was back with the family for a week, beginning to recover.

Then it happened. Heather woke at one in the morning with a sharp pain in her lower abdomen. She shook me awake. I saw her crawl out from under the mosquito net and head for the bathroom. I knew at once it was serious, for she can normally bear pain well. I knelt down beside her on the tiles, and as I put my arm around her, she broke out in a cold sweat all over, and fainted. With a sickening sense of dread, I lowered her gently to the floor, and ran quickly along to the next apartment. There I roused a colleague, and we carried Heather down four flights of stairs to the car. His wife Jan, a nurse, came with us.

We saw few cars as we sped to the hospital, ignoring red lights. Heather lay on the back seat, her head in Jan's lap, drifting in and out of consciousness. Jan talked to her, calm and reassuring. It was a long ten minutes. The car was full of our silent prayers.

Inside the hospital, it felt cold in the air-conditioning. Heather's blood pressure rose and fell sharply. A succession of people in white coats came to examine her. They thought it was simply the hepatitis. That's why they waited so long. Almost too long...

And that's why the Togolese surgeon's hand was shaking. His face told me that time was short. I saw compassion in his eyes, and urgency. I quickly signed the form. 'It is serious,' he said. 'She has lost a lot of blood.'

I sat there and waited, feeling helpless. It was the longest wait of my life. It wasn't supposed to happen like this. What if Heather were to die? What would I say to Joy and Rachel? They knew nothing, not even that their mummy had been sick! Another day would soon be beginning in their boarding school away up north in Vavoua. Life would be going on as usual for them...

And how could I break it to Heather's parents? I couldn't, I'd need help for that. And we hadn't discussed together where she would be buried, what hymns she wanted... I shook my head, to rid myself of these distressing thoughts.

Hours passed. I tried to find out what was happening, to read the real message behind the reassuring words. At last, the surgeon reappeared. He looked tired, but his eyes were still soft. He knew what I had gone through, for he had been through it himself in those hours. 'Madame a eu de la chance' - 'Madame was lucky' he said. 'She is going to be all right.' I shook his hand slowly and gratefully, knowing that it was not just luck.

They told us later that it had been an ectopic pregnancy. Heather had lost four litres of blood... it hardly seemed possible. They had given her transfusions just in time. She had indeed been very close to death.

Much, much later, when Heather was well enough to describe her experience, this is what she told me:
'I knew I might not make it. But I did not mind for myself. I minded for you and the children. I realised, that if I ever got through, all I wanted to do was to go back to the Kouya people. I wanted to live among them again, I wanted to laugh and cry with them. I just wanted to go back and finish what we had started.'

As for me, I got some priorities sorted out in those hours too. There, standing on the edge of death, I found out that my work and ministry were no longer so very important. What was really important to me, when it came down to it - after God - were my wife, and my family.

The days following her ectopic pregnancy were not the time to let Heather know everything that was on my heart. But for the first time since we had gone to Ivory Coast from Ireland in 1983, seven years ago now, and embarked on the project to translate the New Testament into Kouya, for the very first time a niggling, unwelcome doubt had started to take root deep within me. Up to that point I had been confident: so many hurdles had been surmounted with God's help. But this present crisis was just too much to bear.

Now I seriously began to wonder if we would ever make it.

AN ULSTER CHILDHOOD

'I'm just away to buy some of them wee mandoline oranges!'

Alice bustled out the front door. It was Christmas week, getting dark already, and out on Lurgan High Street she joined the flow of last-minute shoppers heading expectantly, and with some anxiety, for Stewarts and Woolworths.

Heather and her four younger brothers loved Alice. Helping their mother with housework through the years of rearing five young ones, she had become part of the family in the big, rambling Georgian house. She was a character. Invariably she took the children's part, lifting clothes carelessly left by Heather's football-mad brothers, expertly smuggling empty plates from under beds to kitchen-sink without a word to their mother.

And the kids would do Alice favours in return. 'Heather, would you away upstairs and switch on that emergency heater for me?' she would ask. Even now, years later, Heather easily forgets what the more normal expression is! Then Alice would tell them about the sick man who forgot to collect his 'infertility benefit'; or about the woman with the clever son: 'Sure, the world's 'is lobster!' To all five children, Alice was a world of colour, life and interest.

But as they grew older, they realised that there was something different about their friend. She lived in the other part of town, where they hardly ever went. Where the kerbs were painted green, white and gold, instead of red, white and blue. Her people had exciting names like Siobhan, Bertilla, Liam and Seamus. Without fail, she would send round a big bottle of sherry for Christmas, even though Heather's dad was a convinced tee-totaller. Around April, with Christmas forgotten, he would compliment his wife on her tasty trifles. If he knew what made them so tasty, he never let his children suspect it!

And soon the Twelfth of July would come round again, and Alice would squeeze her generous frame down between the Best children on the worn, stone steps between the railings out the front, and together they would watch the bands march past in the sun. It was a pageant of noise and colour. Beads of sweat trickled down the faces of the flute-players. Girls linked arms and danced down the footpath alongside their favourite band, running to keep up. The children would sense Alice shudder too as the giant Lambeg drum shook their bodies to the very core.

Heather's father, Cecil Best, owned clothes shops in Lurgan town. He was in business long before the Troubles came, but when these started, if there had been a peace-line to divide the town, it would probably have run right through the middle of his rows of tailored suits, for his shop was placed smack between the two communities. In a province where names were a dead giveaway as to which 'side' you were on, the Best family name was neither one thing nor the other, so customers from both sides would arrive to get kitted out. Not that there was any secret about their church background, as the family attended High Street Methodist every Sunday. Still, Heather's dad figured that a forty-inch waist was worth concealing on any man, and a pair of Wolsey socks was no respecter of feet, right or left!

Then from the early 1970s came the bombs and the incendiary devices, and he would be called out into the dark like his Catholic shop-owning neighbours, and together they would watch, as temporary repairs were carried out, and the suits and Wolsey socks disappeared behind ugly wooden boards. With a sigh, they would crunch sadly off together through the broken glass, and return to the warmth of their homes. When one of the Best shops was badly bombed in 1975, the blast blew out the shop front and also damaged the Methodist church opposite. It was only two days before our wedding there the following year that the repairers' scaffolding finally came down, to our great relief!

Theirs was a small mid-Ulster town, so when the

bombs and bullets struck, the victims were known by many. Terrorism hit people like Alice, and people like Heather's dad. But there were bright spots. Every year without fail, the Italian owners of the ice-cream parlour sent Catholic ice cream to the Methodist Sunday-school party. Buckets of it, free of charge. Whose 'side' were they on, Heather wondered as a child?

She struggled to understand the whys and wherefores as the troubles dragged on. They lost count of how many times the local golf clubhouse was hit. This was a mystery to Heather. Police stations, army-barracks, even shops she understood. But hard as she tried, she failed to see the sectarian point when it came to golf.

Then one black day, it all came too near home. Outside the Bests' front door, a few yards from where Alice had sat on the Twelfth of July, a policeman was shot dead at the barrier. Heather cried for his family and our poor, beloved country. In spite of herself, she also began to fear the faceless ones, who destroyed but were never seen. Whom she could never talk to, never try to persuade. With so many others, she also shook in her bed, when she heard the distant boom of another bomb.

'Who had got it this time?' Along with most of the town's decent inhabitants, dread took her in its icy grip as the sirens wailed.

But life had to go on, and it did, for the people of Northern Ireland have a resilient, almost stubborn streak.

The Best family usually seemed to have an elderly relative living with them. Alice was convinced that Heather's mother would miss purgatory, because she had already gone through it, caring for the old folks!

'It's straight to heaven for you, Missus Best, after all them uns has put you through!' Mother protested vehemently, but it was true that it was not always easy.

'I'll *never* forgive them,' declared Heather's step-granny, tight-lipped, from her rocking chair beside the Aga stove. She wasn't talking about the bombers this time. This was merely a relative who had committed some trifling fault.

Alice paused in her vigorous scrubbing of the kitchen floor. She drew herself up to her full five feet three inches. *'Did our Lord die in vain?'* she said in reproach, emphasising every word. 'You have to *forgive*, you know,' she added. 'It's in the Lord's Prayer.'

And she was right, Heather figured. Not just right for her granny, but right for our country too. The unconditional forgiveness of Christ, beyond our human ability to achieve, was surely the only solution to the centuries of hatred and strife.

Heather would always be grateful that her parents were 'open' in the right way. No one held more firmly to the doctrines of the Reformation than her father. As a local preacher, he left the people in no doubt as to where he stood. Heather was convinced too, as she accompanied him to the wee country churches, and listened from the hard wooden pews. Yet he also taught his children to see beyond the superficial labels, and to understand that underneath the Union Jacks and the Tricolours beat the hearts of real people.

Warmth, humour and generosity were never far below the surface of Ulster life. Only peace was lacking. Could we not give up our small ambitions for our land, and together strive for something better? Not everyone thought in black and white: there were loyalists who would have liked to learn the Irish language, had it been politically correct. Moreover, Alice was quick to point out that not all good Catholics believed that the Pope was 'inflammable'! Polarised rigidity was certainly rife, but there were some hopeful signs, such as the advent of integrated schools, and an increasing number of cross-community efforts for reconciliation.

But feelings ran very deep. Children so often grew up in Northern Ireland to believe that to be different was a bad, undesirable thing. Heather's upbringing taught her that to be different was often good, interesting, enriching. This insight was to stand her in good stead in later life in West Africa.

OPPOSITES ATTRACT

Heather's family liked to stay in one place. When they moved house in Lurgan, they literally moved next door. They were a family of entrepreneurs, but not all were adventurous travellers.

My own upbringing could not have been more different in this respect. My family moved frequently, making several extended visits overseas, as my father was a civil servant attached to Her Majesty's Forces. During my childhood, we lived several years in Libya and Singapore, three different places in Northern Ireland, and also in England for two years. Yet we were always drawn back to Belfast, where I had been born in 1951. With so much moving about the world, four years was the longest I had spent living in any single location. But sometimes it was painful to have to move again, when our time was up!

Where was "Home"?

The tiny sunbird swooped into my line of vision, in a blur of scarlet, yellow and turquoise.

I sat on the step of our cool veranda, hands cupped under my chin, but suddenly very wide awake. The bird came to hover an inch away from the pink hibiscus flower bordering our pathway, and with a scarcely audible whirr of its wings, remained suspended there. A few seconds spent sipping the nectar through its long slender beak, and then it was off again into the warm humid air.

I sighed. This was our last week in Singapore. Yes, the final, final one. At the end of it, we would be leaving a world I had fallen in love with on our first meeting. We were going "home", and in spite of my doubts, I could sense the quiet excitement of my parents as packing continued, and farewells were said to the many friends, expatriate, Malay, Indian, Chinese, that we had made during three fantastic years.

One of the last items to be packed was our radiogram. As I sat there, behind me, it played Eine kleine Nachtmusik, and for one last time Mozart regaled both our wee family, and reached out through open windows to all the neighbours in their bungalows in Honnington Road, RAF Changi, Singapore.

It was 1963, and it took three weeks to sail back across the Indian Ocean with its flying fish, up the Red Sea and through the Suez Canal, along the Mediterranean with a stop off at Gibraltar, and finally North through the Bay of Biscay and the English Channel to London. The final leg to Northern Ireland via Liverpool seemed short in comparison.

Coleraine Academical Institution was a large boys' school, and I was a very small boy. The pecking order ended at First Form, where I had been placed on arrival back. The skies were grey, classrooms were cold, windows were too high up to see outside. Teachers floated around draughty corridors with their gowns flowing in their wake. To me they seemed dishevelled, remote and stern. I thought back to my Primary School teacher in RAF Changi, Mr Booton, with his starched white shorts and shirt, polished black shoes and ready smile.

I had left a warm, vibrant summer and exchanged it for a harsh, uninviting winter.

But life goes on, a young man must make his way in the world as best he can, so I ignored the constant shouts of "Fight, Fight!" at break time, pretended not to be too clever or interested in lessons, and joined the group of boys playing soccer with a tennis-ball in one corner of the playground. I was different: I spoke differently, I still had a deep tan, and I didn't know who the Blues or Glens were at first. But I was a good goalkeeper, and didn't mind being stuck between the hastily thrown down jackets which were our goals. No matter that my horrified mother saw me wear out my new pair of shoes in six weeks. My schoolmates called me "Sambo" - due to the tan I suppose - and I was accepted.

Accepted, but not happy yet. How I looked forward

each day to bouncing back home to Castlerock in the green double-decker bus. From prison to freedom. As soon as homeworks were over, out I went to the sandhills, and roamed there for hours, gulping in oxygen from the pristine sea air, sometimes coming across a brand-new golf ball hit wildly off course by some rich golfer.

This small seaside village taught me that it is possible to put up with anything life may throw at you. If you are alive, if you can look at the horizon, if you know God is with you, and if you can rest in that, then slowly but surely the yellows, the scarlets and the turquoises of life will gradually seep into, spread through and eventually overcome the blacks, the whites, and the greys.

There will always be a sunbird somewhere in my heart.

Small wonder then, with all this travel, that I grew up with itchy feet, while Heather's were not itchy at all!

Three years after I had returned from Singapore, life as I had known it was to change dramatically. Heather and I were just fourteen years old when we met at 'Carrig Eden', a Christian Endeavour holiday home in Greystones, Southern Ireland. What attracted me to her, besides the chemistry, was her vivacity, and her ease at fitting into a variety of social situations. I was accustomed to a certain deep, quiet, holy joy in the brand of Christianity in which I grew up, whereas Heather's Christian circle displayed a different, bubbly brand, which was strangely attractive. Her group played guitars, and had heart-warming fellowship around beach-barbecues. I was not totally sure of all this at the time, and tended to hover on the fringes, wanting to join in, but lacking confidence in this setting. So what did she see in me? Good question. Potential, perhaps, and a certain mystique as someone who had already travelled the world at fourteen! A social misfit in Northern Ireland at times, my redeeming features were that I could play sport well (important to her brothers), and if I sometimes didn't talk much, I could at least write! In the winning of the lady's heart I was fortunate here, for as teenagers much of our relationship had to be conducted through letters, the twenty-eight miles between Lurgan and Holywood, Co. Down being a very long way in those days!

I grew up with two other passions apart from Heather! One was for languages, and the other was to serve God. The fascination with language probably originated abroad, and was fostered by living there. Heather recently discovered one of my notebooks from Singapore days. She studied it with interest. In pencil, in the big, awkward handwriting of an eight-year-old, were lists of words, Malay words down one side, English translation down the other. Soon after our arrival on the island, I had made friends with Malay people in the local *kampongs*, and loved to escape down there to learn new words in the shade of their *atap* houses under the coconut palms. This was not too different from my job in later life! With Chinese dialects and Indian languages also spoken in Singapore, an insatiable thirst for languages was awakened in me as a boy.

At eleven years of age, I returned to almost monolingual Northern Ireland, but welcomed the opportunity to learn French and German, first in secondary school, and later at Trinity College, Dublin. One important reason for this choice of university was that Heather was intending to study German and French there too!

Dublin, in predominantly Catholic Southern Ireland, was an eye-opener for Heather. In her late teens, although successful academically, she had become aware of her ignorance. Ignorance of Irish history, ignorance of what made the 'other side' tick. She felt ashamed of this. Going to Trinity College in the South was a chance to learn. Between student lectures, she walked the streets and absorbed and tried to understand. And underneath the unfamiliar dialect of English, the laughter from the pubs, the relaxed approach to life, she discovered that there were others like her beloved Alice. She found friends.

So languages were very much part of our lives. Our first letters to each other were written half in French, half in German, and this continued until we realised that some things in life should only be written in the language of the heart. This was to become one of our basic life-principles!

The other big passion in my life was to serve God. I had the privilege of growing up in Open Brethren churches, and committed my life to the Lord Jesus in a meeting for children in Bloomfield Baptist church, Belfast. Our family had got to know many missionaries as we moved around the world. To me they were admirable men and women, but I could not see myself doing the fine work they did. I was not cut out for the up-front ministries of extensive Bible teaching and preaching. It was at the age of seventeen, when I read about the work of Wycliffe Bible Translators in a magazine, that something clicked inside, and I knew that this was for me.

Two of my passions would be satisfied if I were to go in for Bible translation work, so all I had to do was to get my aforementioned passion to agree, first to marry me, and then to accept being married to a Bible translator! I suppose it was all part of the package really.

She said 'Yes'. What a relief! It had been a long process, but that is definitely another story. So at Easter 1976, during our engagement year spent apart while teacher training, we met up at the Wycliffe Centre, Horsleys Green, for a weekend of learning how Wycliffe worked.

'I feel I can be myself,' I remember Heather responding. 'These folks are very spiritual, but they have their feet on the ground.' For my part, I was intrigued by the grammar and translation puzzles based on exotic languages, though a little daunted to learn that they were grossly oversimplified versions we were given to examine!

What touched and captivated both of our hearts was the challenge of reaching the remaining thousands of people-groups which as yet had no Bible in their mother-tongue. As we left the Wycliffe Centre, we knew that it would not be for long. As soon as we possibly could, we would be back to take the linguistic courses which would equip us with the tools for the task.

GETTING READY TO GO

We returned to the Centre three years later, in the summer of 1979. Meanwhile, we had led a packed life, full of changes.

We each completed teacher training, myself in Edinburgh, and Heather in Aberystwyth. For one year I taught languages at Cabin Hill School, Belfast, then after getting married, for four years at Wallace High in Lisburn. Heather taught German, French and Religious Education at the Girls' Model Secondary in Belfast, for three and a half years. Teaching experience was to prove invaluable later on in West Africa, especially for the training of literacy teachers, development of materials, and implementation of a literacy programme.

At that time, Wycliffe courses were held during the summer months, which suited us well being teachers, since we could take the training during the long summer break. One drawback was that the intensity of the courses did not allow our brains much of a rest, but we have fond memories of warm, hazy summers, practising exotic clicks and creaky vowel sounds to the sheep on the beautiful Chiltern Hills surrounding the Centre. Heather helped me get my tongue round some of the more difficult phonetic sounds, while I remember assisting her with the more analytical subjects, like Grammar and Phonemics (the study of sound-systems). We were encouraged to work together mostly, as we would have to cooperate later in a language project, but some assignments had to be done independently.

As we moved into September and towards the end of the course, the weather became cooler and the leaves began to fall from the surrounding beech-trees. I can still picture Heather's doleful expression, as she sat in our bedroom at 1 a.m. with her feet in a basin of hot water, trying to stay warm while completing her independent phonemics assignment for the next morning! 'How can you just lie there, and not *help* me?' she reproached me with a groan.

Translation and literacy principles, anthropology and Biblical exegesis were further courses we were required to take. Sessions on project management and spiritual warfare were to prove so valuable later on.

We spent four consecutive summers (1979-1983) at British S.I.L. (the Summer Institute of Linguistics - Wycliffe's sister organisation), two summers as students, two as teachers. The idea was that if you had to teach the course you had just taken, you might just assimilate it better!

We were accepted as Wycliffe members during our second summer, though the biggest highlight of this summer was the birth of our first daughter Joy on 2nd August!

All that remained after these courses was to return to Belfast for a year of Bible College training at the Irish Baptist College. Here we were able to take some Hebrew, and deepen our knowledge of Greek. This year was fun, we lived close by in our tiny first house on the Old Holywood Road, and our fellow-students were able to practise their budding pastoral skills on Joy during coffee-breaks: during lectures she slept soundly in an adjoining room, a gift she no doubt inherited from myself.

'This has been a *good* year!' we agreed at the end of it.

Between 1981 and 1982 we prepared to leave for long-term service as translators. A New Testament, we knew, would require an investment of at least fifteen years from scratch, if the language had to be reduced to writing first. 'Why are you doing this?' our teaching colleagues had asked us as we were leaving our secular jobs. The simple answer was that we believed that God had called us. We believed He had a mission in mind that He wanted us to complete. Our excitement mounted as we took a few more short courses, learned to type, spent six weeks in France to brush up our fluency, and talked about our proposed future ministry to many people in a variety of settings across Northern Ireland.

Where would we be serving? Because of having French, it seemed sensible to consider the francophone countries with translation needs, so we put out some feelers, writing to francophone Branches of S.I.L.. At the beginning of 1982, we were attracted by a language project in Northern Quebec, Canada, but this door closed. We discussed our situation with John Bendor-Samuel, then Africa Area director, and he (surprise, surprise!) suggested Africa! One quick mental adjustment later, taking off snowshoes and putting on flip-flops, we tried to get used to this new idea.

'Have you any preferences?' John asked.

'We would like to work with an animistic group. Where no basic language analysis has been done yet,' we replied. John pointed to two countries on the big wall-map of Africa behind him: first Zaire, then Ivory Coast. Ivory Coast caught our attention. 'You might consider the Bakwé, or the Kouya. Neither has yet been analysed.' We stored these names away in our minds.

We prayed, asked others to pray, and wrote to John Maire, who was the S.I.L. director in Ivory Coast (Côte d'Ivoire in French). He wisely proposed leaving the final decision until we would arrive and could investigate for ourselves, especially in the light of Heather's asthma. We did not yet know how her breathing would be affected by the extreme heat and humidity of a tropical climate. Although she had suffered from asthma since childhood, she had always lived in a temperate climate, but ninety-degree (F) heat and 90% humidity were routine in the Ivory Coast.

Next, John Maire sent us a copy of a brief survey which had been carried out on the Kouya language. I remember that our wedding anniversary meal out on August 18th 1982, was spent poring excitedly over this document, which had arrived that day in the post. I forget what we ate, though I do recall that we stopped occasionally to gaze romantically into each other's eyes in the candlelight - to mark the occasion!

Just before this, while spending six weeks in France with our missionary friends Derek and Heather Johnston, we had met our first Ivorian, a man called Bernard. He was a Christian, a member of the large Bété people-group. We mentioned the Kouyas to him, thinking he might not know of them, since they numbered only 12,000 or so at that time. But he did!

'*Ah oui, certainement!* I know the Kouya people. They live near Daloa, where I come from. Wait a minute, just hold on, I think I have it here...' He left the room, and came back with a cassette tape in his hand. Smiling, he inserted it into his recorder. To our great astonishment, it was a tape of a Kouya man singing! It was like nothing we had ever heard before. Nasal, chanting, and tonal. We asked Bernard whether he understood the meaning of the words.

'*Oui, oui,*' he replied. 'It's quite like Bété. He's saying that there is no good news. There is no good news today!'

To two apprentice missionaries from Northern Ireland, this seemed to be a sign from above, from the Giver of Good News, that we might just be on the track of His choosing. We would need such encouragements along the way to keep us following that track, especially when the going got tough, and He knew that all too well.

So we kept these thoughts under wraps while we got on with the more pressing business of welcoming a second baby daughter, Rachel, into the world. She arrived on September 16th 1982 in the City Hospital in Belfast.

After that came the task of filling up eight big blue plastic barrels. These stood in a line in the utility room of Heather's family's home in Lurgan. They would be going straight to Ivory Coast, so into them we put what we thought we would need there, which we might not find locally. Unbreakable melloware dishes, a selection of toiletries, Ladybird reading-books, medication, Christmas and birthday presents for the next four years. A smaller pile in our bedroom contained what we would need during the first three months as a little family on the Orientation Course in Cameroon.

As we packed, it was sobering to recall that many of the first missionaries to the Ivory Coast had packed their possessions in coffins for shipping out. Very few survived more than a year in what used to be known as the White Man's

Graveyard, though thanks to medical advances and malaria prophylaxis, things were different now.

I spotted Heather popping in a pair of eyelash curlers at the last minute. I caught her eye, and she gave a little smile. I wondered what the customs officials would make of those?! Our upper arms were sore as we bent down into the barrels, but we were grateful for the yellow fever, tetanus and typhoid vaccinations, which gave hope for long-term survival.

These were exciting days. Our children were fast asleep upstairs, oblivious of what lay ahead of them. And in spite of our background reading, we ourselves could only guess.

Yet in the midst of our excitement about the adventure we were embarking upon, we would sometimes experience a twinge of apprehension. God was Almighty, and He held the future. We believed this with all our hearts. What we sometimes wondered was whether *we* were strong enough to see this thing through. But there was definitely no going back now. Our farewell service in Brooklands Gospel Centre was over. Plane-tickets were bought, last good-byes had been said.

Africa here we come!

STARTING OUT

28th December 1982 to 26th March 1983

Kamba Village, Cameroon

'Philip, I feel like going home.'

There were times in life that I agreed with my wife, and this was definitely one of them. The problem was, home was not just around the corner, it was three thousand miles away! Heather and I were at that moment looking at what was to be our *new* home. More precisely, our new *bedroom*.

'It's not that bad,' I offered, trying to keep the doubt from my voice.

We stood in silence and surveyed the room. It had what estate agents call 'potential', that is, changes could only improve it. We hovered on the threshold, and I found myself arguing with the Lord.

'Lord, it was you who brought us here. "His will won't take you where His grace can't keep you." Had that not been the preacher's promise to us?'

Drawing courage from the memory perhaps, and pioneer missionary that I was or hoped to be, I took the first step into the room. The surface of the mud floor crumbled into dust under my toes, crunching like a thin layer of brown snow.

'It'll soon be dark, better get cracking!' I heard myself say, with more optimism than I felt. It was true, the tropical night would fall at seven o'clock sharp, so I climbed up on a shaky chair, searched in my pocket for the nails we had brought with us, and hammered a few into the rafters. Finally, I secured the eight corners of our two mosquito nets on to the nails.

This, then, was to be our bedroom. When we had finished assembling the rickety camp beds underneath the nets, we knew that we were going to need the help of the mother of invention. 'A small but important part of married life' say the books. (At that moment, I wasn't sure it was quite so small as they made out!) Back to my mind came all that well-meaning advice about frills, colour-schemes, ambiance lighting, candles, all the little touches that are supposed, without fail, to make her respond and melt into your arms. I looked with some despair round the little room, assessing the possibilities, for it was here that we were to sleep for the next six weeks, the village phase of our Cameroon orientation. We would get to know this room intimately.

'Philip, you can see out through these walls!'

So you could. The walls were of mud-brick, held together with twigs and sticks. A reasonable view of the outside courtyard could be had at several points. I realised this could be useful for knowing who our visitors were, though I had to admit there was also a negative side: privacy would only be certain under cover of darkness.

'Claustrophobia won't be a problem then,' I laughed nervously. About eight feet up, the walls ended. On top of them were the frail rafters, which crossed our bedroom at irregular intervals, sloping gently upwards towards the middle of the house. These beams supported a roof of corrugated tin. Once again, daylight shone brightly through cracks where the tin sheets failed to overlap properly, and through nail-holes where the carpenter had obviously missed his mark.

There was a wooden 'window,' two feet square, held shut by means of a bent nail. There was no need to open it: we were already assured contact with the outside world.

No, it was not a romantic setting. The camp beds were dangerous for one, never mind two. We would lie of a night with our trimmed oil-lamp on the floor in the corner, chatting companionably over the day, playing 'Guess the Animal'. In the semi-darkness, lizards and very, very big mice motored along the tops of the walls, leaping athletically over the beams. Beam-exercises, we joked. In the morning, we would remove their offerings from the top of our nets. Cockroaches would wait until the lamp was extinguished before chewing noisily on any screwed up paper balls they could find.

We wondered how we could ever tell the folks at home about this aspect of missionary life. We mentally composed never-to-be-sent prayer-letters with headings such as: 'The missionary position' and 'Field relations'. Laughing, we tucked the nets in more carefully around our bodies, and kissed each other passionately goodnight through two layers of mosquito net.

The mother of invention was kind to us, and taught us a resourcefulness which was invaluable later on. Still, I have to say that none of our children were conceived during those six weeks of Orientation in Cameroon.

Hellos and Good-byes

But what we did have time for was... talking. Hours and hours of it, and Heather and I had the privilege of getting to know depths in each other that we never knew existed.

'Heather, I wish I could say good-bye the way you do.'

'What do you mean?'

'You seem to know instinctively what to do when you meet people or say good-bye to them. Like at our Farewell Service.'

'I don't think about it.'

'That's what I mean.'

'Good-night, my dear.'

'Sleep well.'

Long after she had dropped off to sleep, there in our darkened village house, to the accompaniment of crickets and as yet unrecognisable forest sounds, I lay and thought about hellos and goodbyes.

All part of the normal missionary life, you would guess, and you would be right. But for me, personally, it was, and would continue to be, one of the hardest parts.

I tie myself in knots. When it's time to switch continents yet again, do I try to slip away unnoticed? Or do I go round every house, every family, and end up like a wet rag? You see, I can't take the emotion of it. In a way, I envy those who look forward to these comings and goings, and tease every last drop of emotion out of them. 'Parting is such sweet sorrow' for them.

Me? I want to run a mile.

I know where my reaction comes from of course, but analysing it doesn't make it any easier to bear. It comes from those tearful, protracted partings I suffered through in my childhood, when we would hang over the railing of the ship for hours it seemed, waving down to the weeping saints on the dockside, listening to the sweet strains of the 23rd Psalm being sung from the heart as we pulled away towards the open sea and Singapore, to live for years in dangerous foreign climes.

The Lord was my Shepherd too, but as soon as possible I would slip away to the bows, to my own private excitement at the adventure of heading into the unknown.

Hellos are easier, but still... do I shake hands, do I embrace, or do I just say a casual 'Hi'? Do I shake a man's hand, hug a woman? If she's married or single, does it matter? What if her husband is not present? There's no formula, that's the problem, and if you add different nationalities, different ethnic groups, different cultural behaviours, and stir those into the mixture, then, if you are me, you are sunk.

As I say, I get tied in knots, and wish hellos and goodbyes were never invented. A world without fuss. It's only *au revoir* isn't it, so why don't we just quietly go our own way, and get on with life?

Most of the world would never let me get away with it. Perhaps counselling would help?

But just then, in Cameroon, the nearest counsellor known to me was also three thousand miles away. It struck me that we were on our own as never before. Heather and I would be thrown on each other. We would have to be each other's psychologist, each other's spiritual mentor. If we survived, we could write a book. If we failed, we were sunk.

Slowly but surely, fatigue overtook me, and I drifted off to sleep.

First Morning

We awoke together with a start, to the sound of loud but friendly laughter outside our window. It was bright, it was sunny, it felt good to be alive. My eyes moved slowly round, taking in our little bedroom: it all seemed much less fearsome now that daylight had dispelled the shadows.

'Mbembe kiri!' I jumped. The words had been shouted just a few inches from my left ear.

'Kiri mbung,' came the distant reply. Ah yes, Ewondo morning greeting. That much we had learned in the capital Yaoundé before braving the village. Languages, as I said, are my passion. I come alive when I hear a new one. So, eager to get up and about learning Ewondo, I slipped on my shorts, tee shirt and flip-flops, and ventured forth.

But first I wanted to check up on Joy. I'd left her fast asleep in her cot the night before. As I looked in on her last thing, my torch had picked out one very large fat spider on the wall above her sponge mattress. Heart pounding, I had drawn off my sandal, taken aim in the dark, and let fly. I hit the spider, and it crumpled with an amazing lack of resistance. But out of its body scurried dozens of tiny spiders! For all of five seconds I felt bad: I had just made them all orphans!

'Joy …?' I called softly, opening her bedroom door. But her little bed was empty, the mosquito net pulled back. Rising panic. Oh no, had she run off?

'Joy!' I raced out into the bright courtyard.

'Hi, daddy!' I pulled up short.

And there was my little two year old daughter, sitting on the door-step of the adjoining hut, her giant Richard Scarry book propped up on her knees, happily pointing out her favourite pictures to our host Vincent's second wife, Marie. Joy and Marie had clearly become great pals, without a word of language in common!

'Mbembe kiri!' the courtyard called out in chorus. *Now what was it …?* Half a dozen faces were turned expectantly in my direction.

'Kiri mbung!' I somehow managed to reply.

Smiles all round. I had passed my first language test.

Macho Moments

We were in at the shallow end, learning to swim in Africa.

The purpose of the Cameroon orientation course was a serious one: it was designed to break us in gently to life in

West Africa in a safe context, with staff keeping a caring eye on us in the background, giving occasional advice and encouragement before we headed for our eventual assignments. During village phase, we were involved in co-operative projects with the local villagers. The first was to provide a clean water source by building a concrete platform and pipe system around a natural spring of water. The second project was to help construct a village school.

But it was the personal, cultural lessons learned which stand out in the memory. There is one which I will never forget. It happened the very first day I spent in Kamba village, before we moved there with our families and baggage. We were about to have our first taste of village life, and I was part of an advance party invited to meet the villagers.

Our future hosts were showing us round the different dwellings we would inhabit for the next six weeks. The atmosphere was a happy one amongst the green recruits, as we walked in single-file self-consciousness alongside our new African friends. Ahead of me ambled our six foot, sixteen stone photographer, the group's most eligible bachelor, monopolised by a little old African lady who kept insisting that he needed a wife. I smiled at his attempts to put her off.

From behind me came a babble of excited voices, as our group rejoiced in new sights and discoveries.

Suddenly I felt someone's hand slip into mine. I froze. This could not be my wife: she was back in the city. With a swift glance, I ascertained that, yes, it was the nice young man who had been walking harmlessly at my side moments before.

I looked him in the eye. He smiled back, openly, with an encouraging nod. I gulped, and walked on. Just being friendly. Yes, right, I had heard of this phenomenon, I had even witnessed it on the streets of the capital between Africans, but I never expected it to actually happen to *me*! In my mind's eye, I could see the broad smiles on the faces of my golfing mates I had so recently left back home. A furtive glance over my shoulder showed colleagues too busily engrossed in their own cultural preoccupations to care. That was a relief. I decided to pretend I was enjoying myself, smile at my host, and even essay a swing to the arm as we walked on.

My mind was racing. Where I come from, men are men, we do not need to hold each other's hands to be pals. If we hold hands, it is to haul one another up severe cliff faces, to have an arm-wrestle, or possibly to engage in charismatic prayer.

I am proud to say I coped, at least on the surface, and did not offend my host. But I confess I relaxed only when, after a few companionable, lingering, fingertip moments, he eventually let go!

This was the first, but certainly not the last time that Africa brought into question my macho presuppositions. Masculine colours, men's bicycles, men's umbrellas, men don't cry... which of these were simply cultural?

I resolved not to judge a man too quickly by trivial externals. Africa was teaching me to wait until I saw what was in his heart.

Time to Go

'Au revoir, Philippe!'

I could see tears welling up in Vincent's eyes as he clasped my hand in his to say good-bye. I was surprised, and very moved.

What kindness he and his two wives had shown us! They had moved out of their main mud-house into the two smaller dwellings at the back, for the duration of the six weeks we stayed with them. Vincent, our host, would spend three nights, first with one wife, then with the other, as was the custom, in his wives' separate dwellings. It was one way, for us, of keeping track of time: we heard Vincent emerge in the morning from a different hut, and we would notch up another three days on our mental tree-trunk diary.

'Vincent, au revoir, et grand merci!'

I meant it. I was deeply grateful to him. It was Vincent who had quietly taught us how to live in an African village. Without show, without hope of gain or reward, he had patiently put up with our strange Western invasion of his courtyard.

Early on, we had discovered a common liking for (my daughters would later say 'addiction to') coffee. Making Vincent his coffee in the morning soon became part of the routine. We were glad there was a little something we could do for him in return. We would put in three teaspoonfuls of sugar and then ask him if he needed any sugar! The sweetened condensed milk, which had infiltrated every village shop in West Africa it seemed, was the principal reason for Vincent's sweet tooth. But tins of coffee were expensive to buy: ironic, when there were coffee-bushes all around us. Yes, Vincent would miss his coffee. It certainly simplified the choice of a good-bye present!

Very early on too, I had followed Vincent down through the forest, as he led me to the '*source*'. This was the spring where we would fill our buckets with water every day, provided it did not run dry during those weeks of apprenticeship, which coincided with the dusty depths of dry season.

I came to love those daily breaks from the heat, moving slowly down the narrow well-beaten path under the canopy of tall trees, with shrivelled cocoa leaves crunching underfoot. Here it was cooler, breathing was easier. These days, the thermometer was touching 100 degrees where there were no trees. Swinging my empty buckets, I savoured the sensation of being alone, away from the village buzz. It gave me a chance to reflect.

Here I was, here *we* were, middle-class and Northern Irish, a bundle of prejudices, fears and aspirations, plunged into a place where all of our presuppositions were being called into question. What was there about the old 'me' that was worth holding on to? The props were being kicked away, and at times I felt that there was precious little left worth keeping!

So a world was closing behind me, like a curtain being slowly drawn. In front of me, a new world was opening up, but I wasn't sure I wanted to move forward into it. There was too much that was new, too many hard things. I was being forced to grow, but too quickly. It was pressure-cooker growth.

Yet each day, the Lord gave just enough encouragement to continue. On the path to the *'source'*, a vivid turquoise butterfly quivered on a leaf beside me.

No rain had fallen for weeks, and thick red dust covered every surface beside the main road through the village. But one day, we were amazed and delighted to discover a bright yellow sunflower emerging from the dusty hedgerow.

To us, these spoke of God's promises. In the midst of dryness, there could be beauty. Despite barrenness, there could be fruit. Later on, we would reap the benefits of this Cameroon initiation experience, if we could only hang in there.

Vincent helped us hang in there. He and I would talk of an evening, not about the latest cars or pop-groups, for these meant nothing to him, but of catfish, palm-wine, farming and football. We shared a common humanity, and we never ran out of things to talk about under the stars.

The thought of Vincent, Marguerite and Marie kept us from sinking, for we were often very close to going under. I remember the times when our neighbours kindly brought us a bucket of squirming catfish at sundown, and we knew that, with no fridge, they would have to be gutted and cooked that night. I well remember the 'jiggers' I found in my toes and feet: I held the group record, for I discovered over forty of these burrowing fleas in their little white sacs. What they found attractive about my feet I cannot imagine. My family insists they are the least handsome part of me, and I always smile inwardly when I sing those immortal lines:

'Take my feet and let them be,
Swift and beautiful for Thee.'

I made a right hash of extracting the jiggers with a needle, pierced the little white sacs under my skin, and thus ensured further infestation. Vincent watched me without comment for a week or so, decided that the white man's intriguing method was really not very effective, then recommended that his young niece be called upon to help. The niece was brilliant, and removed them painlessly, sac and all, with a small sharpened piece of bamboo! All of which made me resolve that whenever possible, I would not deny my African friends the privilege of showing me up as the bungling amateur that I was in their environment! Maybe that way I would learn to adapt more quickly.

Visits to the latrine, situated not many yards behind the courtyard, were another tricky daily assignment. It was cordoned off with a screen of plaited reeds, brown now with age, a token gesture really when it came to ensuring privacy. We learned to visit it at night. Then at least less of our whiteness was visible, and the pit below was advantageously black. But at night, care - and a torch - were needed, as the two wooden planks which traversed the pit shook beneath your feet. However, the fear of falling in and joining the seething maggots below provided added determination somehow, with a touch of adrenaline, and one returned to base with a glowing sense of achievement.

No, it had not been easy. Looking after two young children, trying to keep them tolerably clean on that dusty floor, had been a nightmare at times. We often felt stressed out, living in a culture where folks came to visit and simply *watch* for hours, not to be entertained briefly and then leave, as we had been used to back home.

As I looked into Vincent's tear-filled eyes that final morning, I tried to read his thoughts. There was no shame, no attempt by male pride to cover up emotion. For my part, I was aware that my hardened heart had been prised open during our stay, and that perhaps now I would, with God's help, be able to start to feel in some small way as my African fellow men and women felt.

It was clear that Vincent didn't expect us to return. He did not expect to see our little family ever again. Nor could he personally anticipate living much longer, as he was already almost fifty, and forty-five was the average life expectancy. Vincent was right, we have not seen him since, but we remember him with great fondness.

Living would never be quite so basic for us again, though at times it came close. Yes, we had learned how to give each other injections, how to survive where modern conveniences were few, how to build shelters and houses using local resources, how to kill chickens and ride motorbikes, all important skills. But as we flew out from Douala airport, as the plane banked towards the purple and orange blaze of the setting sun, we were aware that significant internal changes had taken place. What our African hosts had introduced us to, taught us, brought us through, all this would remain with us, and prove invaluable later on.

Our African hosts, in the space of six very long weeks, had equipped us to walk a little more bravely into the new world of the Ivory Coast. We looked forward to this further chapter, to a new adventure. But part of our hearts remained there in Kamba village, somewhere east of Yaoundé, capital of Cameroon.

IVORY COAST

First Impressions - 28th March 1983

'Hey, where have our passports gone?'

I had set them down on the counter of the police-cubicle at Abidjan airport, and now someone was disappearing with them out of the rear door.

The khaki-uniformed official flicked a glance up in my direction, totally unconcerned. Clearly, he was used to foreigners throwing tantrums. He poked a finger twice in a direction behind my shoulder, and slowly turned his head away.

'Next!'

He reached his chubby fingers towards the next person's passport. I wanted to rush after our disappearing passports, but I checked myself. Rising within me was the by now familiar feeling of being out of control, and of total ignorance of Africa's systems, but I also recognised that I was changing. I was gradually learning to relax when such events occurred, and to pray instead. For the moment I was mystified. In time, perhaps, I would understand.

We emerged eventually, almost intact, from the airport. It was wonderful to see friendly faces behind an S.I.L. sign. But before we could reach our S.I.L. colleagues, we found ourselves being mobbed like royalty. Everyone wanted to help us. Youths fought for the privilege of carrying our cases and bags. Somehow we got to our mission truck, somehow the helpers were paid off, handsomely it seemed to me, though they left muttering and deeply downcast, the five unpaid ones arguing with the five who were.

We fell into the car seats in a perspiring, exhausted heap.

'Cheer up!' laughed our new host. 'That's the hardest part over. You can relax now!'

I watched Abidjan pass by my open window. The breeze felt good, and helped me to forget how damp and uncomfortable my shirt was. Two-year-old Joy was looking out through the side window in wide-eyed excitement, pointing out all the new sights. Baby Rachel was asleep on Heather's lap.

Every second car was an orange taxi weaving its way through the traffic on the wide boulevards. No lanes were marked or respected.

'You don't use your mirror, you just keep looking ahead.' explained our driver. As soon as traffic lights turned green, horns began to blare behind, and cars in front sped away in a black cloud of diesel fumes. *These guys are definitely Formula One material,* I thought.

Abidjan was a city of tremendous contrasts. We passed a handicapped man shuffling along the street on his bottom, in front of a glittering Mercedes car showroom. Our taxi took us across the Félix Houphouet-Boigny bridge, named after the much-revered President in power since Independence twenty years before. In front of us rose a skyline which would have graced Manhattan. Neon lights advertised Pepsi-Cola and Baygon insect spray. As we drove round the lagoon, reflected across the water through the palm-trees was the impressive Hôtel Ivoire, with its gardens and Casino. We caught our first whiff of the lagoon at low tide on our right, and took time to admire the grand football stadium and administrative towers to our left.

There were fleeting impressions of food being barbecued on outside stoves, smoke swirling round storm-lanterns and the murmur of contented conversation, but soon we were bumping along a short stretch of track, and pulling up in front of a pleasant looking building, hexagonal in shape. This was the S.I.L. centre, and this was to be our home for now, until we were assigned to a language project. Tiredness left us momentarily and we were wide-awake, keen to take in everything we could.

Up two flights of stone steps, a knock on the door of

flat 15, and there to meet us was our Irish colleague Margaret Linton, with a smile as broad as her Ballymena accent, and an unforgettable, long, cool glass of blackcurrant juice, which we gratefully consumed in the welcome breeze of a revolving fan.

We had made it. At last we were in Côte d'Ivoire, the Ivory Coast. This is where the action was really about to begin. This is where all that training had finally led us.

MEETING THE KOUYAS

There is a storm etched forever in my memory.

The first night I ever spent in Kouyaland was the night I slept at the Vavoua International School, a small anglophone community in the heart of Ivory Coast catering for the educational needs of about fifty children. It was started in the early nineteen-seventies by the W.E.C. mission (Worldwide Evangelization for Christ), on a piece of land originally cut out of virgin bush, three kilometres east of the market-town of Vavoua. Most, but not all of the children were missionary kids, and all were boarders. It was like one big extended family.

Since the Kouyas live in twelve villages, all within a radius of twenty-five miles of Vavoua, the school was a strategic place to stay while we investigated whether we would definitely undertake a linguistic and translation project among this people-group. A translator working in Bété, a related language spoken south of the Kouya area, had carried out an initial survey. This survey concluded that Kouya was significantly different from other Ivorian languages, warranting a separate translation, and it proposed Dédiafla, a Kouya village deep in the rain forest, as an ideal location for a team.

'I'll take you there' said John Maire, the Swiss director of our S.I.L. Branch. And so we had set out from Abidjan for the exploratory trip. Five hours on hardtop road, the last hour and a half on a difficult track. I admired John's skill in keeping the car on the road as he accelerated over the corrugations, avoiding the timber lorries thundering towards us. The guestroom we were shown to at the school was named Cocotier, after the tall coconut palm outside its front door. Boy, did it feel good to get under the shower, and wash off the red dust that covered us!

Next day John and I drove to Dédiafla over a very rough track. Parts of this road, we learned from Emile our

Kouya guide, would be submerged and impassable in the rainy season. So it was with relief at having made it that we finally tumbled out of the trusty Toyota estate car. Dédiafla rose gently to our left, a collection of houses built on sand-coloured earth, with an impressive backdrop of dark green rainforest. We were led towards the chief's courtyard.

The voices we heard, as we meandered through the village, were loud, and seemed aggressive. They resounded between the concrete-block walls of the houses. The place was claustrophobic, a cauldron. That day, my imagination gave unfriendly meanings to the Kouya words, because of the harshness of their tone, but I told my imagination to be quiet, as it had been wrong so many times before. Much later, I would discover the surprising gentleness that often lay behind that gruff Kouya exterior.

Soon we were sitting in a circle on wooden folding chairs, fetched from the houses and placed in the shade of an old gnarled mango. The young men who had led us here gradually grew silent, as one by one, dignified older men appeared in the courtyard and took their places, adjusting their long wrap-around garments. After the slow ritual of opening formalities, exchanging greetings, shaking many hands, and explaining who we were and where we were from, our nerves eventually settled down, and we moved on to the main reason for our visit. We had some questions for the Kouya chief and elders:

'Will the Kouya language die out?'

'No, it will not die.'

'Will it still be spoken in twenty years' time?'

'Definitely.'

'How do you know?' They looked at each other and smiled.

'We can speak all the other languages: Gouro, Bété, Nyaboa, Nyédéboa, Jula, even Dida we understand because that's where we came from long, long ago. If these people come to us we speak to them in their languages, just as we speak to you in French today. But with each other, we use

Kouya. On the way to the fields we speak to our children in Kouya. Outsiders can't speak Kouya.' (At that, my heart sank. How could *we* possibly ever learn it then?)

'Are you proud to be Kouyas?'

'Ehhnn! We are proud to be Kouyas.'

'Where is the best Kouya spoken?'

'Here, in Dema, and in Bahoulifla.'

'Philip here', said John pointing, 'and his wife who is in Abidjan, may want to come and learn your language, and work out an alphabet for it so that it can be written down. Is that a good thing?'

At that, some looked incredulous, and turned to each other, glancing at me out of the corner of their eyes. But the chief took the floor. 'Yes, it is good. Other languages have been written down. I don't know if Kouya can be, but if it is possible, then we want it.'

'It would help preserve your culture and traditions,' said John. 'Each time an old man dies, a whole library dies with him, they say.'

When this was interpreted into Kouya, there was much nodding of hoary heads. But suddenly, there was a change of mood.

'Now we want to ask *you* something!' There was feeling behind the words. We waited. 'Why is it not raining?'

We looked involuntarily at the sky. Not a cloud. Before we could reply, another chipped in:

'It's because they're chopping down the forests, that's why! The spirits don't like it! And our crops are dying of thirst!'

It was true that parts of the country were experiencing severe drought. We also remembered having driven past a sawmill on the way out from Vavoua. We had noted the piles of logs marked for export, and smelt the burning heaps of sawdust where charcoal was made. 'Just like Gehenna', we thought, as we wound up the windows to keep the thick smoke out. The sawmill provided employment, and money given for reforestation was not always correctly used: we knew there were two sides to the question, but we did not want to enter into a debate at that point. Finally, we answered:

'Yes, we see this is a real problem. You need regular rains for your crops. We promise to pray that God will send rain.'

They laughed scornfully.

'The spirits are unhappy that their forests are being cut down', they repeated. Again there was a pause, and another change of mood.

'Now we have reached agreement, you must buy us all drinks!'

John and I looked at each other. The Kouyas were certainly different! African hospitality is renowned all over the world. What was happening here? Was it their way of closing a deal? As John handed over some money, he explained that if Monsieur Philippe came to live here, he was not a great tree that could provide shelter for many, only a small branch that could give shade to a few. The old men nodded: they had understood the image. Not for the first time, I was grateful for John's experience and wisdom. The drinks arrived, Fanta, Coke, Tonic water and cheap red wine. A little was drunk by all, and the Kouyas spilt the dregs on the earth at their feet. We parted the best of buddies, it seemed.

That night, in our guestroom under the palm-tree, John and I prayed for rain, as we had promised. And, you know, whether the Lord wanted to increase my faith, or to give a sign to those disbelieving Kouyas - or both - it *did* rain that night! We heard it coming from a long way off, as you can in the forest, passing through the Vavoua International School compound, on its way to Vavoua, before wending its way down the track to Dédiafla village. This was the storm I would never forget.

I hoped the hoary heads were not too fast asleep to hear it.

Letter to Drew Craig, elder at Brooklands Gospel Centre, Dundonald, Belfast.

Abidjan, 27th April 1983

Dear Drew and all at Brooklands,

We have just got back from our exploratory trip up north, and want to tell you the news right away. During the four days, we visited four language-groups, but stayed for two days in the area of Ivory Coast where the Kouya people live (it's pronounced 'Koo-ya').

We wanted to go with an open mind, knowing that many were praying, and so we were trusting the Lord to give us peace about the decision to be made.

He has done just that, and we will be leaving in about a month's time, to begin work amongst the Kouyas. While we were there, doors opened to such an extent, that in one morning we were able to meet with the two most important local officials, and to visit a Kouya village and talk to the village chief and people! We had to have an interpreter who spoke both French and the local language. It was all very strange, but extremely moving to meet the people, and hear a language which had only been a name before.

The trip confirmed that there is a definite need for Bible Translation. About half of the Kouyas speak only their own language well, and so would not be able to understand the Scriptures in another local language. It is highly unlikely that many would want to read the Bible in Gouro, a neighbouring language, since the Kouyas are clearly a people proud of their own traditions, language and culture. Perhaps motivated by envy, they want 'a book' too.

It will not be easy. A local pastor told us that the Kouyas are 'completely pagan. They reject Christianity.'

We did however meet two Kouya Christians. There may be a handful more. One of the Christians was very discouraged, having seen fellow-believers led astray by the arrival in the district of a Christian sect. Now they had fallen away. They had no anchor to hold them fast under pressure. We believe that the Scriptures in Kouya could provide this anchor.

The plan is that we will move at the end of May to Vavoua, a small market town surrounded by Kouya villages, and stay there until we decide in which village it would be best to locate.

We know you were praying about this, and praise the Lord for answering your prayers, and also giving all concerned here peace about what has been decided.

Please remember Emile (Ay-meal). He's the young Christian we mentioned above. He works in a shop in Vavoua.

It would be great to be able to be with you all at home, but we're already excited by what is happening in the Brooklands extension in the Ivory Coast!

With love in our Lord Jesus Christ,

Philip and Heather

Bahoulifla

We decided on Bahoulifla in the end. It was the largest Kouya village, with about five thousand inhabitants. Not all were Kouyas: there were Jula, Mossi and Baoulé communities in Bahoulifla too.

Because there were no houses to rent, they offered us their village hall to live in. In it were one hundred plastic chairs, some stacks of floor tiles, and some work tools. This was to be our home for the next two years. The building had been erected right in the middle of the village, in a sizeable open area. This was great for language learning, but terrible on the nerves. The area was used every evening for football-matches by the village kids, and it quickly became a favourite pastime for locals and visitors alike to go and see how 'les blancs' ('the white people') were getting on. The building was called 'le Centre Culturel', the Cultural Centre, quite a name to live up to!

Packing all our worldly goods into a borrowed double-cabin truck, we set out for the north from Abidjan on Monday, 6th June 1983. We had the opportunity to stay for a few weeks in a W.E.C. mission house in Vavoua, which was important, as some basic renovations needed to be carried out to the Cultural Centre, before we could live there as a family. This house would be needed soon by W.E.C., so we were under some pressure to get the Cultural Centre into a habitable state.

We had no car of our own, as no suitable second-hand car had yet become available, so I travelled out daily to the village from Vavoua in a bush-taxi. Heather looked after Joy and Rachel in town while I was away during the day.

Cockroaches for Company

I vividly remember the first night I slept in the Bahoulifla village Centre. It was in one of the small storerooms at the rear of the building, which our go-between, Williams, had swept out for me. He had also kindly purchased a spray to chase out all the cockroaches. Unfortunately, he had sprayed so generously, he had also chased out all the oxygen!

Leaving the one small window ajar to let some air (and a few valiant cockroaches) back in, I decided that a walk through the village would clear the head. So off we ambled. By now I was getting to like the sedate pace at which people walked. Much more sensible in the heat, and it gave you time to see what you were about to step on. This was important in a country of snakes and scorpions, and a village full of children but with very few latrines.

Williams told me to keep my torch pointing down when I occasionally used it, as this was the time folks were bathing beside the path. He was right, I could hear the sound of water sloshing in buckets, and make out dim silhouettes, but under the stars, well to be honest, teeth were all that were visible.

We had entered a different world.

I later grew to love those walks through the village after dark, when I was no longer the white man, the centre of interest and attention, giving a performance in the Kouya language. With no street lighting, and only the occasional oil-lamp, I could be anonymous and just enjoy the sounds of a village settling down comfortably for the night. Later on, as on that first evening, we would make our way down to Williams' courtyard, where his old dad would be swinging on a hammock; the fire would be crackling under the straw roof of the open-sided kitchen, and the wives moving around sure-footed in the dark, preparing banana *foutou*, or perhaps rice, with peanut or palmnut sauce. Sometimes the smoke would swirl round in our direction and our eyes would smart, so we would move our low stools over a few inches on the hard earth.

Coldness would come slowly down from the stars in their huge sky, we had time to watch the moon plot her course, we did not need to talk to fill the silence. One night I explained how men had actually landed on the moon. It seemed incongruous and silly even as I said it: in the light of eternal things it didn't really matter, did it? They listened politely, but I'm not sure to this day that they really believed me.

That first night, though, it was time to return to the loneliness of my storeroom in the Cultural Centre. Kouyas were quietly slipping into the snug warmth of their little mud-houses, dozens it seemed in each one, wrapping their long sleeping-garments about them for warmth.

Williams came back with me. I felt tall as I walked beside him, for, like most Kouya men of the time, he would not have been more than five feet nine. Yet Williams did not possess the customary Kouya shape, which was rather squat:

his was a more angular, slim frame. His dark brown eyes, invisible to me now on that walk, were customarily watchful, intelligent. As the shape of the Cultural Centre loomed out of the blackness in front of us, he turned and said casually: 'You know, Philip, you don't have to sleep alone. Won't you be lonely in there all night?' I paused, wondering what he meant. 'Delphine, you know the girl who prepared corn for us this afternoon, she would be very happy to keep you company...'

I heard myself thanking him for his considerateness, assuring him I would be all right, but as he accompanied me inside the dark building and finally left, I found that I was inwardly shocked. That really pleasant girl, the friend of Williams who had invited us over to try some soft, bright yellow corn on the cob, it was she Williams had been talking about. I determined to learn Kouya as quickly as possible, so that I would understand everything that was going on! Later, Heather met Delphine. Even though she had had several children by different men, as a single woman in this society, she was not viewed as bad or sinful, as it is not considered wrong to sleep around. Heather and I had the same reaction to her; she was a nice person. It was clear that temptation would come in different guises, and we would have to know when to be on our guard.

The cockroaches kept me company that particular night.

The Bucket Man

We moved as a family to the Cultural Centre on 5th July 1983. Shortly afterwards, in September, Emile decided to join us in the project, leaving his secure job in the Vavoua shop. During weekdays, Emile stayed with us in the Centre, helping us with our study of Kouya.

To begin with, we had no ceilings in the Centre, and no electricity. Our water came from the village well, carried by our neighbour's daughter, so we had a roof above our heads, but that was about it! Cellophane over the windows kept out the worst of the driving rain. For the first few months we were still without a car, though I had bought a bicycle.

Some of the basic necessities of life were not yet catered for. On visits, when I had been trying to make the Centre at least liveable in, I had asked one of the neighbours, who lived in a nicely painted house which even had an air-conditioner jutting out from one of the walls, whether I might use his toilet.

He hummed and haa'd, said 'yes of course', then pointed me in the direction of a house several hundred yards away. I assumed he had some reservations about me using his facilities. Only much later did I realise he did not possess a toilet, but made use of the plentiful bush surrounding the village, like most other residents in Bahoulifla.

When we moved in with a toddler of two, and a baby of nine months, the matter became urgent! We needed a 'long-drop', and for that we needed the well diggers. These men were Moslems from the north, and only they had the proper fetish-power to do the job safely. Fetishes were objects on which animist medicine-men conferred supernatural powers, especially protective powers. However the well diggers were busy fasting that month during daylight hours! So we had to wait for several weeks for our twelve metre deep hole, which we intended to cover with a reinforced concrete slab, made on the spot, with a hole in the middle of it. This in turn, we envisaged, would be discreetly shielded by walls, and even protected by a tin roof. It would all be very private...

Meanwhile, some things could and would not wait, so we improvised. We had discovered the usefulness of covered buckets in Cameroon on our three-month Orientation Course. We had become proficient in the use of them, so that was fine. However, living as we were right in the heart of a large village, we had nowhere to dispose of the contents.

And so it was, that every so often, the 'bucket man' would make an appearance, a covered bucket delicately balanced on each side of the handlebars of his bicycle, heading for the bush, with a trowel in a plastic bag. Yours Truly was the 'bucket man.' But no matter what route or moment I chose, I would be spotted by the small boys, who would whoop and scamper after me, from biggest to smallest in a line. 'Tubaabu! Tubaabu!' 'White man! White man!' they chanted. The white man peddled furiously to keep ahead, and it became a game for the boys as to who could keep up the pace.

Reaching the edge of the village, the path had fewer people to negotiate, so the 'bucket man' could really turn on the gas. He quickly disappeared round a few corners, performed the needful, and set off home again, empty buckets swinging. He smiled at the puzzled faces of the breathless little boys he met en route. 'Ka 'yu-o pa!' he called out to them with a wave. This was an untranslatable Kouya expression of compassion. He was offering them deep sympathy in their disappointment.

However, it was a relief when our long-drop was finally completed, just a few yards from our back door. A de luxe version, it had space also for a bucket-shower on one side. There were some basic life-comforts we would never again take for granted!

Drawing the Line

Heather showed amazing restraint and patience during the two years we lived in Bahoulifla village. Bringing up two little children under the public gaze, without grandparents or close friends from her own culture to support her or to tell her what a great job she was doing, was very hard. Though based in the Centre and working from it, I would often have to be away and so could not always be around to help.

At such times, it seemed that the village kids would play up most. They loved to tease, run around the house, even jump through the windows when the shutters were open. We had tried informing the chief, talking with the parents, but all to no avail. There were hundreds of kids in the village, only a quarter of whom attended school regularly. And so they would run in through our front door, and see how far they could get into the living-room before Heather spotted them and chased them out. They were testing the limits, and one day discovered exactly where Heather's limits were drawn!

The poor wee fellow was neither the biggest nor the smallest of the group, but he was the slowest runner. As Heather ran through the front doorway into the bright sun, she was determined to catch one of them. The bigger lads were too fast, so this six-year-old became her target. He darted this way and that, with Heather in his wake. Women in the surrounding courtyards stopped their pounding to cheer her on. Finally she caught him, and marched him, quivering, back to the Cultural Centre. She would not hit him hard, but she would frighten him, and perhaps make him an example to his mates.

As she lifted him on to the veranda, his little shorts fell down to his ankles! The sight of him struggling to pull them back up almost made her lose her resolve, but she did go through with it. The little boy ran off, scared out of his wits. His mates watched from a distance, the women cheered, and Heather stood inside, heart pounding, with her back against the door, saying to herself: 'What have I done? We'll be thrown out of the village. What a testimony!' Already she could imagine the headlines: *'Christian missionary wallops native child!'*

In fact, it turned out to be the best thing that ever happened. There was no more trouble from the kids, and the adults wondered why we hadn't done this long ago.

SETTLING IN

1984

The Hammock

A hammock seemed like a great idea for siesta.
At siesta-time, the sun was directly overhead, beating down
mercilessly on our tin roof. The Centre became too hot for me,
especially as we needed to close the wooden shutters. This
was because the ladies of the Saunders household needed
some privacy, and to be truthful, it is not easy for anyone to
doze off when you have a large audience of curious village
children, and very few clothes on. Anyway, to escape the
oven, I purchased a hammock at the market.

This I then strung up just off the veranda, securing it to
two sturdy blocks of wood about four feet high, and six feet
apart. A shelter made of palm-fronds supported at regular
intervals by slim but strong stripped tree-trunks had adorned
the square in front of our house for some time now. This had
been erected for the village visit of the Daloa Préfet, and was
still in good condition.

So I had shade from the sun, my rear was six inches
above investigation by insects, and with a good book, siesta
became much more enjoyable. One leg on the ground, a little
pressure, and the gentle horizontal swing could be maintained
with a minimum of effort. I could get used to this, I thought.

One evening, I was having a gentle swing, when
Williams, who had evolved into our Kouya cultural advisor,
paid a visit to the Cultural Centre, to bring his evening
greeting.

'Filipʊ, -na gwlɛ!'
'-Aoo. Wiliamʊ, -ka yilo.'
'You have bought a hammock.' If in doubt in a Kouya
interchange, state the obvious.

'Yes, Wiliamu. I got it in the market. 3500 francs.'

His face showed great doubt and hesitancy. Had I paid too much? Oh well, too bad, that was normal. Black man's price, white man's price, American tourist's price...

'Do you feel... safe?' he asked.

'Oh yes, it's quite sturdy. Ernest helped me drive in the stakes.'

'Mm.'

It sometimes drove me mad that Williams kept so much to himself, and didn't share his thoughts. I quickly changed the subject, and thought no more about it, until one day... a hammock appeared in Williams' courtyard. The first time I saw it, his old dad was enjoying a swing in it. 'It's okay, you know,' he said. 'If you have been able to use a hammock in a Kouya village, I reckon we can too.' I was mystified. They explained.

'Many Kouyas are afraid to erect hammocks. They fear that their enemies will come while they are away at their fields, and tamper with the stakes, putting poison on them. Then when they return to use their hammock, they will be poisoned!'

Ignorance had been bliss in my case.

Was it my imagination, or did more hammocks start to sprout up around the village after that? I had never considered myself a fashion leader. Far be it from me to encourage laziness, but for the Kouyas, a cool half-hour on the net at the end of the day was hard to beat. (The World Wide Web stole my idea later on!)

Friend or Foe?

Between five and six o'clock in the evening was the time for getting out for a walk.

About six months after our arrival in Ivory Coast, I was sitting meditating on a rock in the cool of the forest late one afternoon.

I had made sure it wasn't a termite-mound: it seemed to be just a harmless rock. Rocks were rare enough in the Kouya area, and as they stored the sun's heat, their warmth made a pleasant natural seat.

Soon I was comfortably lost in my daydream, thinking back over our time so far with the Kouyas, what they thought of us, what we thought of them.

Suddenly, something moved in the corner of my eye, or rather, in my peripheral vision. My heart stopped, my vacant West African stare focused with great speed. Turning my head slowly round to the right, I could see clearly what it was. An animal I didn't know, rusty brown, bushy-tailed, the size of a small dog, was moving in my direction. It hadn't yet noticed me, it was too busy ferreting in the undergrowth.

Then it must have seen or sensed me, for it looked up. Its inquisitive face was that of a rodent, a very large rodent! The teeth were hidden under its large whiskers. Its eyes were alert, intelligent, evaluating, sizing me up.

I stared back, trying to appear unconcerned, hoping it couldn't hear my heart thumping.

'Friend or foe?' asked the eyes.

'Not sure!' mine replied.

Moments passed. For me, instinct, not rational thought took over. Finally, as if losing interest, I averted my eyes, and surveyed the tranquil forest scene. Amber evening sunlight pierced through in several places. A few seconds later, when it seemed safe, I glanced back, and saw the brown bushy tail moving slowly on through the long grass. It disappeared as quietly as it had come.

I thought to myself: in a way, the Kouyas had looked at us like that. In their society it was not rude to stare, and for months they had stared! Not with animosity, but with curiosity. I'm sure they did not like all they saw in us, but at length, it seemed they had discerned no aggression in our eyes, no need for flight or fight. And so they had moved on about their daily business, and we were left free to go about ours, and enjoy living among them, if we could.

As friends, not foes. When talking to other Africans, Kouyas were starting to call us 'our foreigners'. We felt honoured. A line of acceptance had been crossed.

On the Veranda

I get all choked up at the memory of our veranda in Bahoulifla.

In any one day we had three languages on the go, English with our children, French with non-Kouya visitors, and Kouya – as much as we could – with Kouya visitors. In French the 'veranda' was the *terrasse*, in Kouya we called it 'tɛlasɪ', a form clearly borrowed from French. We learned to identify other borrowed words, like 'viziɔ' for 'television', 'wotloo' for *voiture* (car), 'mazii' for 'machine', or 'mɛtlɪ' for 'metre' which described objects or concepts not indigenous to Kouya culture. Anyway, whether in English, French or Kouya, we were talking about the four-foot-wide covered area which surrounded three sides of the Cultural Centre in Bahoulifla.

It moves me, because so much of our early village life took place on this veranda. It was more comfortable than inside the house, as any gentle breeze going could be caught there. On it, Joy grew up from a toddler of two to a little girl of four, and Rachel from a baby to a toddler.

The girls were never short of playmates. Water games, with plastic baths, buckets, tins and a minimum of clothes, were especially popular, as they all soon got drenched and cool, and we parents knew that the heat would dry them off within the hour. Joy's friend Rosalie would tie her doll on Joy's back in African fashion, and later they would make 'tea' together in a tin heated up on a little fire in their outdoor kitchen. It was perfectly safe: no carpets or curtains to singe, no china ornaments to break, and always plenty of adults around to keep half an eye on events.

Wherever most shade could be found on the veranda as the sun moved round, Heather and I could also be found. There we would be busy welcoming the inevitable stream of visitors.

This was never wasted time. We had been told that we should spend our first two years cementing relationships, as this would form the basis of our future translation work. It made sense. The constant greeting of people was tiring for us, but it was also a wonderful way of learning the language. The Kouyas have never been accused of being shy and retiring, so we rarely had to go out looking for company or language-learning situations! Our data notebooks were always at hand.

The veranda was where we got to know folks and understand them, and where they got to know us, and understand why we were there.

Between 4.30 and 6.00 p.m., we might have twenty visitors, teenagers, adults, old men. Most women would be busy preparing the evening meal: we would see them later during our own visiting when they were freer to talk. But their men-folk were glad of a chance to sit down, rest and chat with us on their way home from a day of heavy field work.

So perhaps it might be kindly old Ernest calling on his return from his fields several miles away. We were always glad to see him. One of the very few Kouya Christians at that time, he would have an encouraging word about our language learning, delighted when we had mastered a new expression.

We knew our progress was slow, but we soaked up his flattery nonetheless.

Ernest might be followed by Gbizier and Sao Paolo (everyone had a nickname). These two young reprobates were great fun and always ready to ridicule our religious beliefs.

'You talk about God. I can't see him, where is he?!'

In spite of their talk, however, we knew that when it came to the bit, almost every African we had met *did* have a belief in God, though for many He was a distant Creator who had set the world in motion and left human beings to get on with it. And Gbizier and Sao - like the rest of this animistic Kouya group - did believe in the spirits, the *génies*, simply because they knew them! They were actively involved with them in their daily lives. The *genies*, or ancestral spirits, could be a positive force or a negative one for them, depending on how the living had treated the departed. If relationships had been harmonious during their time on earth, the departed generally left the living alone, but not if there had been problems. In this case there had to be appeasement. This explained the lavish send-offs for those who had been feared during their lives: nobody wanted to be forever plagued by a malign and dissatisfied ancestral spirit!

So Gbizier and Sao would make their family sacrifices of animals or crops at the ancient iroko tree in the forest along with the rest, just in case.

We travelled the world in those discussions. Gbizier had a rather black and white worldview at times, but his language was always colourful: 'Women?' he would say. 'Women are just like exercise books. They need correcting from time to time!'

Heather and I learned a lot about the language from these early teachers. We went as far as we could with our limited Kouya, but sometimes had to resort to French, the national language - which some could speak well - especially when the theological going got tough...

On our wall we had a poster which proclaimed: 'Not all the best theological discussions take place in Oxford.' Under the caption was a picture which showed an animated circle of African men deep in discussion. We can testify to the truth of that poster's message, for some of the best occurred on a veranda in Bahoulifla.

Little Alain

During the hours of daylight, there were always children on the veranda. Heather's mother and uncle Ronald came out from Northern Ireland to visit us in January 1984. Uncle Ronald, generous as always, produced big bags full of sweets from his suitcase, and was mobbed by two hundred children before you could say 'gobstopper'. I can see him yet, with his sweetie bag held aloft on the veranda, creating chaos out of order, his broad smiles communicating more, much more than his Ulster English. The children loved him. The Kouyas nicknamed him 'Dadi', and still ask after him twenty years later. Love never ends.

It was on the veranda, amongst the crowds of children, that we met Alain.

A little handicapped boy of six or seven, his legs wasted through polio, Alain dragged himself along in the dirt with his strong arms and upper torso. Such a cheerful spirit, and such bright eyes he had! Full of character, and an insatiable desire to communicate.

Alain was totally accepted by the other village kids, and fiercely protected by them. He would perform tricks for them on our veranda: headstands, with his little thin legs flopping uselessly over his back. The other children watched gravely, and always clapped his finale. We felt compassion, pity, and some sad joy. Yes, it was good that Alain should be growing up in a sheltered but vibrant community, where he would not be ostracised for his physical disabilities, but would be nurtured, and respected for the person he was.

His spirit was indomitable. He would come to see us from time to time as he grew older. There was nothing wrong with his brain, and he progressed well at school. He got a wheelchair, and even as a young adult, he was never lacking for a friend who would give him a break by pushing for a while.

I have one abiding memory of Alain. I last saw him speeding along the verge of the hardtop road in his wheelchair. He was propelling himself at top speed with the excited crowds as they made their way towards the village football-pitch - the 'stadium' - for a big match.

Handicapped or not, Alain was going to get all he could out of life.

Curtains

It took us several months before we understood how the Kouyas viewed the boundaries between private space and public space. Though it seemed to us that little was private, we began to learn that not everywhere was, or should be, public domain.

For example, the appropriate place for sitting down and exchanging greetings was outside the house, not inside. At the beginning, we made the mistake of inviting visitors inside, mainly because we wanted to keep away from the mosquitoes, and lower the risk of malaria. But when we did so, the visitors would stay, and stay, and stay, very often until midnight.

So we would go ahead with our evening meal, and offer around whatever we were eating, according to what we had observed as normal when we visited Kouya courtyards. The rice and peanut sauce would go down well, but our desserts usually left them cold! It was hard to see our precious chocolate Angel Delight, so lovingly packed and dispatched in parcels by churches in the homeland, treated so suspiciously and politely refused!

We began to understand that only very close intimate friends should be invited inside our home in this way: we were giving the wrong message. Moreover, if we didn't want these new friends to follow us into our bedroom, as well as picking up and examining everything that was visible on the way, then we had to make sure we had a certain indispensable barrier: a curtain. To suspend a strategically placed curtain was like erecting a 'Stop' sign!

Of course, once the slow-witted foreigners grasped this principle, they started to notice curtains everywhere in the village! The penny dropped. We saw thin pieces of cloth hanging down to protect bedrooms inside houses. Again, during the day, when folks would get washed in their 'douches' or shower-houses, open to the sky, over the doorway of these 'douches' would flap the flimsy curtain.

As we passed by the shower-house, pretending not to notice, we knew not to look too closely, but even so, we would often receive a loud greeting from a soapy head and shoulders:

'Good afternoon, Filipu! Where are you off to?'

' Hi, René! Nowhere special, just taking a walk. Saying hello to folks...'

We were learning. A piece of cloth hung up on a string, however skimpy, meant: 'Stop! Do not enter!'

Visiting

As time went by, we rarely entered Kouya houses. In the end, they rarely entered ours, except on invitation. Life was lived outdoors. Houses were for sleeping in, and for the Kouyas, to keep warm in.

Outside the front door was the culturally appropriate place for sitting down and saying hello. Whenever we arrived at a courtyard to visit, if no one was visible, we had to clap our hands twice, and call out: 'Caw! Caw!' (something like a crow) This signalled a virtual knock at the door.

Our host or another family member would then emerge. They would indicate chairs or a bench outside the house, and say:

'There is a seat.' If more chairs were needed, these would be brought out from inside the house.

'Thank you.' We would sit down.

Handshakes all round.

'Shall I come with water?'

'No, thank you. We have just drunk.'

Pause.

'Filipu, what news this evening?'

'No, there is no news this evening. It's a greeting only.'

Pause.

'And what about here? Are you all there?'

'Ah. Thank you!'

Host clasps hand of each visitor again.

'Here there is peace. There is nothing amiss. Here there is peace.'

This was the protocol. No step could or should be omitted. The routine formula over, we would settle down to watch the life of the courtyard together, making comments occasionally as they occurred to us. We were thankful for the space and leisure to compose plausible Kouya sentences.

Perhaps later, more consequential business would be discussed, but not yet. First we had to meet as persons in God's world.

Saying 'Hello'

Getting started on the language was particularly difficult. Just to say 'Hello' in Kouya was a nightmare. Our Wycliffe colleagues Eddie and Sue Arthur, when they joined us in the Kouya project in 1988, had similar problems to ourselves, which was reassuring somehow. Eddie put it well when he said:

'I can say "The three baby goats are walking round the village", but I can't yet say "Hello"!'

Our Kouya friends, with profound patience - and often with poorly concealed delight, it must be said - would repeatedly explain the basics to these remedial white people:

'For a man, you say "-na fu". That's in the morning, or if you haven't seen him for a long time. Make sure you say it on the right tone, like this "-na fu" (with exaggerated lowering and raising of pitch).

'Now for a woman - in the morning - it's "a fu", on the same pitch level. For a group of people, it's "kao sao". Got that? Good.

(Warming to their task now) 'Right, you're okay with that up until the sun reaches about there... (pointing upwards to about noon equivalent). After that, you greet with "-na gwlɛ" for a man, "a gwlɛ" for a woman, and "ka lu pa" for a group of people. You may add "oo" to any of these greetings by the way, to make your voice carry. That's important when you are in the forest.

'Of course', continued our friends, 'we've only given you the greeting when *you* start things off! There's another set for replying. If someone else says 'hello' to you, you're stuck for the moment. Just make sure you get in first. Now you also need to know whether you are coming or going. (By that stage I didn't, I was lost!) For example, if your friend is coming back to the village from his fields, you would start with the evening response greeting: "-Ka yi loo" (to a man), and he would say: "-Aoo. -Na gwlɛ." But perhaps that is enough for today? (They had learnt to recognise the glazing over of my eyes.) We'll teach you the rest tomorrow!'

Our language-learning manual had recommended we practise our greetings with about fifty people per day. It was supposed to go something like this:

'Hello, how are you? I'm fine. This is all I can say. Good-bye!'

We were failing miserably. We could not bring ourselves, somehow, to sally forth and say: 'The three baby goats are walking round the village. This is all I can say. Good-bye!' Anyway, if we had done that, we would have had fifty new friends on our doorstep the next morning, anxious to teach us those wretched greetings yet again!

Days off

To preserve our sanity, and the sanity of those trying to help us learn Kouya, we had to escape every so often. Just fifteen minutes away from us was the wood-factory. I played chess with the director.

The director of the wood-factory was not a great chess-player. But the wood he sold was good, and his swimming pool was very good. So although in other circumstances we would never have been bosom-buddies, we were thrown together, and made the best of it.

My first impression of Herr Freund (preserving anonymity) was of a very large man on a very small *mobylette*, bumping across from the sawmill to his private villa when the hooter went at noon. His impression of me was probably of a very tall linguist unfolding himself from a (borrowed) estate car, looking like a refugee from a Kouya village! But he, and subsequently his wife, were delighted to be able to talk to Heather and myself in German, and invited us to several soirées at their place. There Heather and I would revive our rusty Teutonic, make polite conversation, and contrive to make the games of chess as close as possible.

His enormous Dobermen did little to encourage visitors to the compound, but we had to brave them each time we wanted to visit the little staff swimming-pool for a day off. This shady nook became a little haven for the children and ourselves, an escape from the heat, dust and buzz of Bahoulifla.

In return, we would invite some of the factory-staff back for a village experience. We appreciated the contact with many of these expatriate Europeans, some of whom felt very lonely and isolated.

It made us realise that the privilege of living close to

Africans was what made us put up with so much adaptation that was difficult for us at the start. When we came to think of it, loneliness was a malady from which we never did suffer in the village! We missed our relatives and folks back home, sometimes very keenly, but we never lacked for a Kouya friend to talk to or to keep us company.

We would return from the little pool, cool, refreshed, and ready for whatever surprises village living had in store for us next.

The Women at the Well

'Filipu, goo-d ee-vening!'

'-Aoo. You have all come.' (*Great. Got that right...*)

'Wha-at are yoou doo-ing?' (*You don't have to speak that slowly. I'm not an absolute novice!*)

'No, nothing. I am there!'

'Is your wi-fe there too?'

'Yes (with raising of chin to denote affirmative). She is there.'

'Are your children there?'

'Yes, they are all there. Where are you going?' (*My new phrase*)

(*Delighted laughter*) 'We are go-ing to draw water!'

(*Guessing meaning, pretending to understand*)

'-Aoo. Walk well!'

'-Aoo.'

Murmurs of appreciation drifted back as the women wended their way down to the well between the mud-brick houses. Or was I deluding myself? Sometimes we wondered were they making fun of us? But that was usually when we were feeling under culture stress, and needed a break from village living. Mostly we recognised that our weak attempts at Kouya were being enjoyed. Nor could we afford to take ourselves too seriously. After all, if an African gentleman came and learned to speak English as she should be spoken, say in Ballymena, I'd have to admit I'd find it funny too!

Writing it down

'Heather, how on earth do we write down this word for "woman"?' I called out. 'It starts with a velar nasal, and ends with an ɔ,' answered Heather from the kitchen.
'Yes, but what is there in between?'
'A bi-labial, and another nasal... perhaps.'
'How about this then... ŋwnɔ!'
'Sounds good. Except... I think it's on a high tone.'
'ŋwnɔ?'
'That's it.'

Using the symbols of the International Phonetic Alphabet, many Kouya words were straightforward enough to write down. However, some vowels were so similar to each other that we found it almost impossible to differentiate between them at first. For instance, the three front close vowels i, e and ɪ, and the back set u, o and ʊ. Then we also had to mark the tone (the relative musical pitch) of each syllable, since the majority of Kouya words had counterparts whose only distinguishing feature was tone. Sú (to push), su (tree), sū (to crush) and sù (hot) were each pronounced on a different tone level, and each had a different meaning! Moreover, ɪn (pronounced like 'eh' through your nose) meant 'I', while ìn (on lower tone) meant 'you'. We regularly threw folks into confusion by getting the tone wrong, and they roared with laughter as taboo words crept in unintentionally at times!
Fortunately, our language helper Emile had an excellent ear for the tones, and we could depend on him to be accurate. As we moved from simply writing words phonetically towards a workable alphabet, his assistance with the sounds and tones was absolutely indispensable.

The Daloa Road

Daloa was our nearest large town, and there we could buy a few vegetables, like carrots, cabbage and potatoes which were not available locally. So every fortnight we would make our way down through the village to the main road to wait for a bush-taxi, for we had no car of our own to begin with. This road was the main thoroughfare linking the towns of Daloa and Vavoua. It ran due North-South, was fifty-six kilometres (thirty-five miles) long, and had about as many straight parts as a *shillelagh*. Bush-taxis - usually Renault twenty-two seaters - only left Vavoua when they were full or nearly full, so we just had to wait and hope that one would arrive soon. If one did, it was certain that we could be squeezed in.

In Africa we learned to wait.

We sat there at the roadside in a heat-induced torpor, looking around at the people and houses. We were thankful that the Cultural Centre was situated in the middle of Bahoulifla village, as homes here at the side of the track were totally covered in red dust from the passing traffic. We dreaded to think what it did for the lungs. Only the advent of the rains would wash everything clean again, but that first dry season we experienced in 1983 there was really quite a serious drought, bringing with it much hardship, sickness and death.

The Daloa road was a road that almost entered into folklore, but they tarmacadamed it just in time, in 1988. By then we had been up and down it hundreds of times, in bush-taxis, buses and in our own car, as it was the only way of getting to Daloa, then Bouaflé, Yamoussoukro, and finally Abidjan. The journey to Abidjan, the commercial capital, took a whole day.

'Were you ever on the old road to Daloa?' one would ask of another.

'No, but I've heard all about it' would come the reply, in hushed reverential tones.

It had its own beauty, and its own challenge. When you had finally mastered the beast after a seventy-five minute battle, you mentally awarded yourself and your car a sticker, which read: 'We made it to Daloa!'

The road metamorphosed according to the season. After a heavy rain, sections would change beyond recognition through mudslides, or huge trees falling across it. The trees were rarely removed: they were too heavy, and machinery was lacking. Instead, one pioneer taxi-driver would merrily blaze a trail round the tree through the thick bush. Other cavalier drivers would follow his example on the premise that 'if he made it, so can we!', and soon a new main road was created! A particularly massive rain forest giant would become a bush-taxi terminus for a while, with passengers passing over or under the trunk to continue their journey in a second taxi, parked patiently on the other side.

The Daloa road was risky to drive on, but it was also fun. You never knew which wild animals you might see, so you kept on the alert. Commonplace were the hornbills, swooping as from time immemorial like pterodactyls across your path. Or the wild frogs leaping over the bonnet of your car after rain. Bush-rats, squirrels, porcupine, deer and snakes: it was a game for many drivers to try to hit them, and take them home to the family for an unexpected supper! One fluorescent, venomous green mamba spanned almost the whole width of the road as it slithered across, but somehow managed to escape my wheels as I tried to kill it. For some reason this snake grows bigger each time I recall it ...

Adults, children, goats and sheep were a constant hazard, as they felt the road belonged to them, not to the vehicles. One evening, I saw a little old lady crossing the road a couple of hundred yards away in the twilight. Hunched over, she seemed to be taking forever to trundle across. Soon I was almost upon her, and gently beeped the horn in warning. She turned, startled, and scampered into the undergrowth! 'She' turned out to be a fully-grown chimpanzee!

Yes, the Daloa road was sometimes fun, but never with

an exhausted family on its last lap up from Abidjan, after a hot day's journey. Tired eyes had to watch out for the checkpoints, for which you had to slow down or stop and show papers. Police, customs and forest rangers would check to make sure all was in order. The checkpoints were regularly moved, and the only warning was a dusty road-sign, and by night an oil-lamp if you were fortunate.

One dark African night we were not so lucky. Perhaps the wind from a passing car had blown out the lamp, but I saw the sharp security spikes on the road just too late! Skid... scrunch!

During the next few moments I talked to myself, taking deep breaths. *Just wind down your window, and wait for the official...* Deathly hush. Crickets chirped in the undergrowth, unconcerned. *Easy does it...* Shouts approached from behind a lone torch. *Keep cool, missionary Phil.*

Our kids, exhausted after the long journey, only learner-missionaries, did not keep cool but started to cry. Big brave Missionary Phil cried too, inside. *Will have to buy new tyre. New tyres sold only in Daloa. Back on road to Daloa tomorrow for you, Missionary Phil! Groan.*

Old Daloa Road won on points that time. Checkpoints.

Flame-trees

As I said, the Daloa road had its own beauty too. Parts of it were resplendent with flame-trees. We first saw them in bloom in March 1984. The locals had a saying:

'Quand les flamboyants fleurissent, les blancs périssent.'
Roughly translated, it meant:

'When the flame-trees are in bloom, then the white man meets his doom!'

These beautiful, spreading trees, with their canopy of red flowers, blossomed towards the end of the dry season, in March and April, when earth and man cried out for rain after months without it. If the Ivorian peoples were suffering, what chance had the white man? And hence the rhyme. The presence of majestic cattle egrets signalled the dry season too, and the sight of these pure-white birds perching on the flame-trees took our breath away.

Scarlet and white. The verse from Isaiah came to our minds: 'Though your sins be as scarlet, they shall be white as snow.'

The Kouyas had never seen snow. How would we later translate such verses? Could we say: 'Though your sins be red as the flame-tree, they shall be white as the cattle-egret'? Maybe. Or we might plump for the white inside of a coconut? At that point translation still seemed a long way off - we needed to know the language much, much better before we could think of beginning - but what we saw around us impressed itself on the inner screen of our imagination, as we took our first, faltering steps towards a vibrant, relevant Kouya version of the Scriptures.

Opposition

All was not always sweetness and light in our relationships with the Kouyas. This was not surprising, since we Irish are not renowned for our even temper, and the

Kouyas' name for themselves - 'Sɔkuya' - they told us meant 'those who are to be feared'!

Although on one level we felt well accepted, and the vast majority were willing and enthusiastic to have us live with them, there was a sense, sometimes, that we were being pushed, if not in outright rejection, at least to the brink of what we could tolerate. We wondered whether we were suffering from paranoia.

The first contentious issue to arise concerned the Cultural Centre itself. The villagers had been used to having their village meetings there every Monday. We were asked could they still be held there?! Gently, we explained that we had put some basic furniture in it, would they like to come and see?

The chief and some elders came and inspected the house, and agreed that it would be hard, though not impossible, to move the hardboard screens and wooden settee and armchairs against the wall, so that the fifty or sixty Kouyas could hold their meeting inside each Monday morning.

We wondered where we would go while the meeting was in progress. I tried to explain once again that we white people are strange, that we live inside quite a lot of the time, and that it would be disruptive for us to have to move house every week. The despairing look on Heather's face, which I glimpsed from time to time, lent urgency and persuasiveness to my arguments.

In the end, goodwill won the day, and it was decided to revert to the shade of the old mango tree in the chief's courtyard, where meetings had always been held previously, before the advent of the Cultural Centre. Every Monday, then, I became the guardian of the chairs. I stood at the door of our home and personally supervised and counted the plastic chairs as they made their exit on the heads of the young men of the village. The returning chair count was made in the evening.

This arrangement worked well. But a further issue arose, which convinced us that it would be better to build our own house eventually, rather than rent or live in village property.

In lieu of rent, we had spent money on improving the Centre while we were there. At one particular village meeting, however, we were simply handing over a written record of the practical improvements we had made to the Centre, with their costs, when an unexpected problem arose. The person who had taken on the role of intermediary for that meeting, proceeded to read out each item in a haughty tone which caused the group present to take offence against us, when no offence at all was meant! We were simply intending to be accountable.

A long discussion ensued, during which we attempted to clear up the misunderstanding. A number of the older men took the floor, making emotional speeches with much waving of hands. In these meetings, everyone, or at least all the men over twenty, have their say. The women, listening just outside the circle, may also contribute.

Suddenly Heather stepped forward and I almost fell off my chair. What was she going to say? I gulped and prayed.

I had never seen her so publicly emotional before. Perhaps those long months of heat, dust, mosquitoes, small children, privacy invasion and culture-stress came to a head that day, and she just had to speak out! Hand on hip in the style of the Kouya women, she explained in passionate terms how we had been doing our best to get on well with everybody, not annoy people, do what the Kouyas thought was good and right, and what were we receiving in return? A sense that some villagers were angry with us. An impression that we weren't doing enough for the community. A feeling that even the place we had been given to live in was not ours at all, and that they wished it had never been agreed to for the two years! Heather added that she couldn't cope with having to move every time they wanted a public meeting... How did they expect us to live, work and learn Kouya in such an atmosphere of... well, it was almost rejection?!

I have to say it was a brilliant performance, though I knew it was no act: Heather was deadly serious. But I wouldn't have been surprised if the old men had given her a round of applause at the end. As it was, mouths hung open. 'A 'yu oo! A 'yu oo!' the old men repeated. This, being interpreted, meant: 'Ah, sorry, sorry, may your suffering be eased!'

There was some astonishment that a white woman could speak in that way, with a definite softening in attitude from that day on, until we left Bahoulifla, and went to live in Dema. There was genuine sorrow that we had not decided to stay on in Bahoulifla.

Not a lot happens at times in the villages, so there is an element of making up one's own soap opera. Even after such an experience, when we were feeling drained the next day, we were aware that the village had moved on to the next drama, and we were temporarily forgotten.

There was a sense now, though, that the air had been cleared, and that we had become more insiders than before. It had been hard won. It had taken two long years, but there was definitely no going back now. What we had started, if God gave us strength, we would finish.

A Church is Born

'Filipu, you can be our leader!'

My heart sank. I was supposed to be here to translate, not to lead churches. And yet the need was clear. If we wanted to see indigenous churches develop in a natural way, with Kouya as their main language of communication, then something new would have to begin, as they didn't yet exist! Otherwise, Kouyas would continue to drift into other churches in their ones and twos, and drift out again, invariably untouched. There were some good immigrant churches but Kouyas could not feel part of a foreign church.

'Let the Holy Spirit be our leader!' I heard myself say.

This was a novel thought to the men around the table that day. We discussed some more. We read 1 Corinthians 14: 26 out in French, translating it into Kouya: *'When you meet for* worship, one person may have a hymn, another a teaching, another a revelation from God, another a message in tongues, still another an explanation of what it means. Everything must be of help to the church.' The principle was that each one had his own contribution. We agreed that we would meet together, and all share in testimony, prayer, in fact in whatever way the Lord led us to participate through His Spirit.

And so began the Kouya church in Bahoulifla. In that large village of 4,500 people, there were two and a half Kouya Christians when we arrived to live there in June 1983. Old Ernest was one, totally committed and sincere, a very wise man, but illiterate. Then there was Jean-Pierre, a believer who blew hot and cold, who had three wives and twelve children. And finally there was Kalou Williams, our intermediary, the only one to start with besides ourselves who would be able to read Scripture aloud (in French).

As with so many in Africa emerging from the spirit-worship of the animist religion, Williams was faithfully following the revelation he had received, but had not yet been exposed to the whole truth. If knowledge, understanding and trust of God could be viewed as a continuum in his case, then Williams was halfway along it. He had been introduced to the Scriptures through a sect called 'Christianisme Céleste' ('Celestial Christianity'), during a stay in the large town of Bouaké several years previously. Then he had had to return to the village to look after his father.

I well remember the first time I heard Williams pray aloud in Kouya. He sounded like an Old Testament prophet! While in the sect, he had learned off by heart huge chunks of the wisdom literature of the Old Testament in French.

So this unlikely little group started to meet together regularly. Other villagers popped in to see what was going on. The little church grew, as the Christians witnessed to other family members, and one by one they were converted. David and Debbie Williams, the W.E.C. missionary couple based in Vavoua town, were a great help in these early days. David would come to preach and teach at night, straining to read his

Bible under the single oil-lamp, with rows of silent, attentive faces stretching back into the darkness of the room. What a contrast to the boisterous clamour of Kouya village life! The silence was palpable: they had never heard good news like this before.

Many came to faith in Christ, but not on impulse, and not in an emotional, highly charged atmosphere. They weighed it all up, knowing that such a step of faith could mean a measure of rejection and alienation, though never or rarely total exclusion, from their families.

'Where the Spirit of the Lord is, there is freedom!' And when He is given freedom, He gets to work. In His time, in His way, and the task is made easier if it happens in a language that the people can understand, and even more so if it is in the language of their hearts.

Baï Laurent

It was a Monday, market day in Bahoulifla. From the outlying villages and settlements, people of all ages and sizes were converging on the village to join in the weekly jamboree of buying and selling, greeting and visiting relatives, catching up with the gossip, having a great time. The village was awash with colour.

We would sit outside for a while on these days, watching the world go by slowly on foot or on bicycle. Every moveable object was piled as high as they dared with goods for sale. Bush-taxis grew to twice their usual height, bicycles became cars for the day, and men and women became mobile shops touring the courtyards. Chickens peeked unsuspectingly from baskets strapped to backs of bicycles, items of women's underwear swung merrily from travelling salesmen's arms, towers were built out of tin chests and empty barrels. The market stalls, just flimsy wooden frames for most of the week, now disappeared under a ton of merchandise for sale; the open spaces of Tuesday to Sunday were crammed with voices, smells and laughter on a Monday.

Bicycles paused on their way down to the epicentre of the market, and their riders gazed for a few moments at the Cultural Centre, where we sat. Yes, what they had heard was true: there was indeed a family of white people living there. Such pale skin, such blond hair the children had! Why have they come? What are they selling? Will they be setting up a business like the Lebanese or the Germans?

That particular Monday morning, one bicycle detached itself from the steady stream, and wended its way over towards us. It was a sturdy, green model. Its owner stopped in front of us, and slowly dismounted. He parked it against a pillar, and came over to greet us. His face, perspiring from the journey, was deeply wrinkled. It wore the broadest of smiles. As he drank a glass of cold water we fetched for him, he exuded an attractive, cheerful confidence. He was a man sure of his identity, though Kouya etiquette obliged us to wait to discover it.

'So you must be Filipu and Esther!' ('Heather' in Kouya usually came out more like 'Esther', so Heather adopted that name.) His manner was very direct. 'It is just wonderful that you have come!' We had learned not to be too quick or probing with our own unanswered questions. Still, this was a promising start. He put us out of our misery.

'I am Baï Laurent. I have come from Gouabafla village today.' Ah, the penny dropped. We had heard of Laurent, and now at last we were meeting him. Emile our language-helper often spoke of him. He had apparently been a Christian longer than any other Kouya.

'We have really been looking forward to meeting you, Laurent.'

That market day in Bahoulifla, Baï Laurent told us his story.

Life had not been easy for him. He was reared just like many a Kouya village boy; taken by his father into the tropical rain forests as early as he could hold a machete, to work on plantations carved out of the thick tangle of bush. It was the survival of the fittest, and Laurent was tough enough to survive somehow the dangerous diseases that claimed many of his little friends' lives.

His father, his uncles, and all his extended family worshipped their ancestors. As animists, they would sacrifice chickens, sheep, or oxen to placate the ever-demanding spirits and stop them wreaking havoc in their already fragile lives and courtyards. Corporately, they would follow the directions of the local fetish-priest, or a visiting diviner from a neighbouring group, in an attempt to control their precarious condition. Laurent grew up knowing no other way of life, and yet he was dissatisfied with the seeming capriciousness of the spirits, which were making his life miserable.

Then one day in the mid-1950s, Laurent's life was turned upside down. He heard the gospel preached by a Mr. Christen from Canada, a missionary with W.E.C., and he responded by turning his life over to Jesus Christ. He was not alone: others in his village responded too. What he heard took root in the heart of this young man.

However, as the days and weeks turned into months, Laurent's fellow-villagers gradually turned back to their old ancestral ways. Baï Laurent explained to us that the cares of the Kouya world choked the good seed that had been sown. He soon found himself alone.

'For many years I was alone. But the Lord gave me strength to keep on telling the Good News to everyone who would listen to me!' He visited the other eleven Kouya villages on market-days, and always drew a crowd. As Laurent preached, they would heckle and jeer, but at the same time they would listen. He became known and respected for his courage and beliefs. Laurent's skin grew thicker as he spoke out for Jesus, but he longed for a positive response. As market ended and the vendors packed up their wares, Laurent would pack his old bike up too as the sun began to set, and begin the long trek back to Gouabafla village and home.

For a long time, there were few encouragements for him. All around, the Gouros, the Nyaboas, even the Bété were responding to the gospel, but the Kouyas remained strongly opposed. A highlight for Laurent was the arrival of Gospel Recordings one day. They asked Laurent, the strongest Christian they could find among the Kouyas, to help them make a record. So Laurent preached, he sang, he exhorted, and it was all captured on an old 'seventy-eight' disc.

By 1979, Laurent was not yet fifty, but he was considered as well endowed with years, and respected for it. He was still as strong and wiry as ever. 1979 was a remarkable year, for it was then that the Gouro Bible, translated by W.E.C. missionaries, was dedicated in Vavoua town. The Kouyas liked the Gouros; they chose them as spouses. Laurent's eyes shone as he recalled that marvellous day when the Bible was dedicated. He had cycled into town to help the Gouros celebrate the arrival of the Word of God in their midst.

Another Kouya was also there that day. He was called Zébli Baï Emile. As a child, he had heard Laurent preach. Still a teenager in 1979, Baï Emile worked in a shop in Vavoua, and attended a large Evangelical Church in town. When the dedication ceremony was over, Emile asked the W.E.C. missionaries could they not send someone to translate into his own Kouya language too? Their response was to ask him to go away and pray for this. Though a little disheartened by their reply, Emile did so, and from that day on there grew within him a strong vision for his own people. The Spirit of God was starting to move in power among the Kouyas.

It was no dramatic tidal wave, more slow and sure. Old Baï Laurent carried on preaching. Young Emile kept on praying.

Laurent had heard of our arrival, and knew that his young friend Emile had now left the security of his shop job, and joined us in the Kouya translation project. He had finished his story, but before he left us that market day, he added something that we were never to forget:

'I have been praying since 1955,' he said softly, 'that the Lord would send us someone to help us put the Bible into our language. You are the answer to my prayers!'

Well, if you are the answer to someone's prayers, you

can hardly give up and go home! Many days we felt like it, but when our hearts would sink to our shoes, our spirits would rise again when we thought of old Baï Laurent, and the very thought of him would inspire us to keep on going.

SURVIVING

1984-5

Laurent came back regularly to encourage us.

'Well, is the Bible ready yet?!'

Was he joking, or serious? Surely he knew that it was always going to be a marathon, this translation, not a sprint? The Gouro Bible had taken decades, though computers were starting to take away some of the drudgery of endless re-writing. But the Kouya language still had to be written down, an alphabet had yet to be established, and Emile and our other village-friends had some task ahead to teach these Irish how to speak a tonal language fluently. With their Irish intonation, they made every sentence they spoke into a question! Would they even survive? They had clearly never used a simple oil-lamp or a machete before; Madame had never pounded *foutou (made from mashed yam or plantain banana)* nor drawn well-water by the look of her muscles. And what real work did Monsieur do, if he had no fields to till, and no wares to sell at market?

Old Laurent was a character, of that there was no doubt. Maybe it was the set to his jaw, maybe the twinkle in his eye, but it was probably a bit of both. You knew Baï Laurent could be a stubborn old man, but you knew also that a smile was never far away from his lips. Ready for a laugh, ready for a fight, he was as tough as they came.

However, it was not long before Laurent's smile was starting to get broader and broader every time we saw him. 'The Lord is at work! The Lord is at work!' he exclaimed, as he told of yet another Kouya being converted to Christ. Indeed, it seemed to be true. Kouyas, students or civil servants, were returning from their work in the cities to say they were now Christians. In the villages, the few Christians were starting to meet for worship in Kouya, their mother-tongue.

Kouyas everywhere were beginning to realise that the Lord had not passed them by or forgotten them. What old Baï Laurent had been telling them for years now had actually been the Truth. And we had the privilege of being right in the middle of it.

Anxiety

'I'm really worried about her.' Heather's voice was full of concern as we watched Rachel together. Our little daughter was playing contentedly on the mat on the concrete floor, chattering quietly to herself and to her dolls. Her arms and legs were so thin! She ate well, but food seemed to pass through her without proper absorption. Her muscle tone was weak, and she showed little desire to move or crawl about as would be normal for her age.

Regularly she would have bouts of diarrhoea, but in between do better. We took her repeatedly for tests at the local Vavoua hospital, but they revealed nothing. Then we took her to a hospital four hours away to the west. Another time we drove to the Ferké Baptist Mission hospital, seven hours away by road, but again, nothing definite could be found. The dilemma was that Rachel would seem to pick up for a time, we would see improvement, and hope that she had turned a corner. But to opt to leave the village for any journey was not easy, so we were cast upon the Lord for each decision. Everything had to be closed up and stowed away because of the termites and mice, and the subsequent long hot drive with two young children was not a prospect to relish. There was no doctor at the end of a phone from whom to ask advice. In fact there was no phone in the village at all. French medical language we could mostly understand, but we realised that when there is sickness, deep down you really want to speak your own mother-tongue!

What was happening in the Kouya church at the time was so encouraging, but anxiety over Rachel's illness gnawed constantly at the back of our minds. We really had to find out what was wrong with her.

Living by the Book

Jean-Pierre lived down near the church with his large family. His courtyard was always a hive of activity and noise. In one corner stood a building which he would rent out, and when we arrived in the village, it was occupied by two women. They were prostitutes, two of the twelve Ghanaians carrying out this trade in Bahoulifla. Just to visit Jean-Pierre, young men had a gauntlet to run, avoiding the tempting invitations as they passed by. Usually, when we visited at nightfall, next in the ladies' queue would be hanging around sheepishly outside.

For Jean-Pierre, renting was simply one way of increasing his income to support a very large family. As a Christian he had his ups and downs, but it had not been easy for Ernest and himself, the two Kouya Christians normally resident in the village, to swallow their Kouya pride, and attend the immigrant church. Services there were conducted in the Moré language, and then translated into Jula, the trade language. Jean-Pierre understood Jula, though imperfectly. Most of the Bible teaching had therefore been lost on Jean-Pierre through no fault of his own.

'Esther, Esther, are you there?' Heather recognised Jean-Pierre's quick, excited voice out on the veranda.

'I'm just coming!' she answered.

Opening the screen door, she emerged into the amber evening sunlight, where she could make out Jean-Pierre's small unmistakable silhouette.

'Ah, Jean-Pierre, you have come. Do sit down.'

Jean-Pierre's eyes darted busily, anxiously around, as they went through the necessary preliminary greetings. Finally, the 'real' news emerged.

'It's about tomorrow morning. They're all coming. The

whole family circle. It's to be a huge palaver. And I have to arbitrate!' he blurted out.

His hands moved restlessly over his knees. Heather could tell he was very worried.

'I'm scared this will all blow up. Then there will be fines to pay to injured parties, family sacrifices to make. Some of those relatives of mine... the cousins you know... they're very excitable!'

Yes, it was in the family genes, Heather thought. Well, here was an opportunity. Did we not believe the Bible could be applied to every situation? She prayed silently, and then a verse came to mind, from the Epistle of James, which we were studying at the time.

'If any of you lacks wisdom, he should ask God, who gives generously to all without finding fault, and it will be given to him.' (James 1:5)

'Hold on a minute, Jean-Pierre, I'll just fetch my Bible.' As she went to look for it, our children were still happily playing on the concrete floor, pouring water in and out of brightly coloured plastic containers. Everywhere was soaked, but no matter, it would evaporate within minutes.

Returning with her French Bible, Heather read out the James passage, with Jean-Pierre nodding his head vigorously, translating it into Kouya for himself as she spoke.

'Let's pray, and ask the Lord for wisdom, then,' he responded.

So they closed their eyes and ears to the clamour of the village, and prayed for wisdom from above for Jean-Pierre for the big meeting of the next day...

There was a happy ending. Jean-Pierre came back to us next evening, face radiant, smiling as only he can.

'It worked! The Lord helped me. God is good!' It had indeed been a peaceful meeting, and the difficult family problem had been resolved.

For Jean-Pierre, this was no small miracle. For us, it was a first small, but significant step. The Lord was helping us to understand that He wanted us to entrust our Kouya friends to Him. He would teach them to live by the Book, which was far safer, far more desirable, than for them to live according to any human voice or wisdom.

Requests

Village friends called constantly, but it was not always easy to know how to respond to their requests.

'Filipu, my prospective in-laws are arriving tonight. Can you lend me some money to pay for my wife?'

'I thought you'd paid off your wife long ago.' I smiled inwardly. *Sounded like hire purchase...*

'Oh yes. I've two of them paid off. This is the third one.'

Can't say no directly. How do I get out of this?

'Ah. Did you see that white man who just left in his truck? I had to give him a lot of money. I have very little left. Just enough for my family.'

Which was the truth. A missionary friend had been short of ready cash for a car repair, and had borrowed from us. Thank you, Lord!

'I understand. Well, see you again, Filipu!'

And he did understand. No hard feelings. He had come to me as perhaps one of his best bets, but he would be doing the rounds of all his friends that day, in the hope of collecting enough for his purposes. After all, he would help them, if he could, in *their* hour of need.

Ever since the first day we spent in the village, we had such requests, and often felt very awkward responding to them. *No training can prepare you for this*, I thought! We had come from a society of plenty, where almost every individual knows he will probably have enough to live on for the rest of his life. We had come to live in a society of 'limited good', where at times there is enough, but there is no future guarantee. So, looking at life through Kouya eyes, while there is enough you use what you can, you eat what you can, you spend what you can. If people ask of you, you share what you have, for you are not an individual primarily, you are a member of a community. This explains why money from the sale of produce or crops can be 'blown' in a matter of weeks, and not saved for a rainy day, or rather, in the case of Ivory Coast, a day of drought.

From our standpoint, we had arrived as outsiders intending to stay. We had a certain limited amount of goods and money, but needed to eke them out, and to calculate what we were likely to need in future days. This would determine what we had left over to give. We would give what we could, but if we shared with all who asked, we would soon run out of resources, and have to leave the place where we felt called to minister.

For the Kouyas, there was no shame in asking, and there should have been no guilt in saying 'no'. After all, to their way of thinking, if someone is in debt to you, it gives you - the giver - added prestige. But we did feel guilty, for ringing in our ears was the verse: *Give to everyone who asks of you.* And sometimes we did have what was being asked for. One option would have been to give and give to everyone who asked, until everything was gone. This would truly have been living as many village Kouyas did. Then when a need arose, when we needed money to buy petrol for a car journey for example, we could have gone round our village friends for a whip-round, and eventually, perhaps a few days late, made our journey. Since time did not matter too much anyway in that context, this would have been no problem.

Except that there would be emergencies. And what if the children were involved? Appendicitis, say, or dangerously high fever. Many children died there due to lack of prompt action, and we could not bring ourselves to jeopardise our children's lives like that.

So in a sense our identification with the people, I realised, would always be a compromise. We would identify where we could, and where we felt the Lord wanted us to. We would not be called rich in Western terms, but because we had more resources, and especially because we had the choice to leave both area and country, we would never be living *exactly* as the majority of the people here lived. Our situation would be more like those of the primary teachers here in the villages, who are the only ones really assured of a regular income, and therefore had more choice.

We could not pretend to be poorer than we were. We had heard that some expatriates who lived in villages bought several identical outfits, so that when one was getting washed, they wore the other, and therefore did not seem to have so many clothes. Was this being deceitful? Was it motivated by love? Perhaps they did not wish to flaunt their possessions, and accentuate the gap between those who had more and those who had less? Is it all right or is it deceitful for a nun to have ten surplices, or a monk ten habits, I wondered??

What was for certain was that in this society the requests would not stop. Even when you gave all away, you would be asked for more, though you might cease to be the first request-stop on the route.

We understood that it was considered an honour to be asked for help, for this demonstrated that one was wealthy enough to meet the need. Yet this knowledge did not help us much: the requests were a major aspect of daily living there to which we never completely adjusted.

Pillow Talk

Siesta was compulsory in the heat for poor Irish bodies, but we did not always sleep. We got into the habit in Africa of always having a book 'on the go'.

Heather had got hold of a book on personality-types on our last visit to Abidjan, and was busy categorising all and sundry. 'Got you!' she exclaimed, and the bed started to shake with her mirth. Of course, I needed to know. It was like someone chuckling over the funny parts of the Reader's

Digest, and failing to share the joke. Even if it's bad, you still have to hear it.

'You are a Monk-Crusader!' she announced triumphantly. She then proceeded to describe the type.

I lay and pondered. It's always a shock when people think they've 'got' you, perhaps more especially when you find it hard to fathom yourself.

A monk? Mm, well, the celibacy part held no attraction whatsoever, but the contemplative side did, I suppose. I did love to be on my own from time to time. A crusader? Maybe. I suppose you could say that the whole Kouya project had been a crusade, a sortie into the real world.

I did, it was true, know lots of Bible-translators who could be aptly described as 'monks with a mission'. The task demanded solitary, intense toil. Hours, days, weeks, months, years of it. That was the 'monk' bit, and most of this still lay ahead of us.

Then all this work would be in vain if it were never to be used, read, or brought out among the people who could most benefit from it. That was the 'mission' part.

I was a *Monk with a Mission*. It did have a certain ring to it. Perhaps Heather was right.

Ernest

'Ernest, that was stupid and wrong, you shouldn't have gone to him!' The tone made me wince. The Kouyas could be very direct at times: in many ways, they were the Irish of the Ivory Coast. We all awaited his reply.

'But what else could I do?' Ernest spread his hands in a helpless gesture. 'I was trying to keep the *génies* happy!'

'What did the charlatan ask for?'

'Well, first of all a chicken for the sacrifice. Then some money. And he wrote on an egg in Arabic script. I had to bury that in my fields.'

'Is it still there?'

'Yes.'

'And have the *génies* gone?'

'No. My trees still aren't producing.'

'Ah, there you are!' Ernest's circle of Christian inquisitors sat back in their wooden chairs.

There was a moment or two of quietness in the group as each pondered Ernest's dilemma, oblivious to the life of the courtyard going on around them. A few moments of discussion ensued, and finally a decision was made, which was voiced by Williams, the natural leader of the group.

'We will go and pray in Ernest's fields. On Sunday, after our morning meeting.'

And so it was, the following Sunday, that eight of us set out along the dusty road towards Vavoua. The sun had by then climbed high in a cloudless sky. I knew that the fields were about an hour's walk away. Old Ernest would walk this twice a day, every day except Sunday and market-day, to work in his fields.

A narrow track led off the main road into the thick forest, and soon we were walking along in single file beneath the towering *fromager* trees, enjoying the shade of the lower, leafy acacias. After a while, Ernest, who was leading, stooped and began to work at the ground with his machete. We all gathered round to watch in sober silence as he unearthed a yellowing egg with writing still visible on it. Turning, he nodded, and we all walked on. It always struck me how much at ease the Kouya planters were in their fields. This was their milieu, their work-place for centuries, and they always seemed to visibly relax there. But on that particular Sunday, Ernest, though at home, was not totally relaxed as he moved off down the track again.

For the uninitiated like myself, it was not always easy to see where one field stopped and the next one began. Sometimes I would spot the fetish-charms hung up to protect their fields, a snail-shell suspended from a branch perhaps, but usually I had to take the Kouyas' word for it. They knew every tree, every bump in the ground.

Soon, Ernest stopped and turned to us again. We had

clearly arrived at the place where we were to do business. I looked around me. It was darker here, just a flicker of sunlight penetrating the branches far above us. We gathered round in a circle.

As each Kouya took his turn and prayed in his own language, I strained to pick out enough words to follow the meaning. I was definitely understanding more now. But as I did so, I suddenly became aware of another noise. It came from above us. I sneaked a glance upwards. Catching Williams' eye - he was doing the same - I watched him break into a spontaneous smile and begin to nod his head slowly.

Yes, the sound we were hearing was the rustle of rain falling gently on the leafy canopy above. Unmistakable. The next Kouya in line took his turn to pray. The rain continued, unabated.

After each one had prayed, excitement broke out.

'Aya! Did you hear that? Rain! Ernest, the Lord has answered us!'

There were bright smiles all round in that dark forest, with much shouting and clapping of hands and backs. Ernest, though a little bewildered, was the happiest man alive.

Rain, the sure sign of God's blessing, had fallen on his fields. We had all heard it. But what was strange, as we walked slowly back through the forest, as we broke out on to the main road, as we eventually neared the village, was that there was no sign of dampness. The sun continued to wend its slow, scorching way across a cloudless sky. We inquired of folks in the village. Had it rained here? No! We looked at each other and nodded slowly with dawning understanding.

The Lord had given Ernest his answer, and had also given the rest of us an encouragement we would never forget.

Reaching home, I stepped into its shade out of the scorching sun. I opened the door, and Heather almost fell into my arms. She was in tears. The children had been unwell, and she had had a very discouraging morning. She was particularly distressed about Rachel. I did my best to comfort her, my elation rapidly receding. Gradually, when she began to feel better, I told her all about Ernest's fields, our praying, and the rain falling. She confirmed that it hadn't rained at all in the village. This was consolation for Heather too, after her difficult morning.

Elation and discouragement. It was a pattern we came to expect, living among the Kouyas. Would the whole venture end in elation or disappointment for us, we wondered? Would we ever finish the task? Would the Kouyas ever have a Book to live by?

FIRST FURLOUGH

'Well, where would you like to start?'

The question was put kindly and gently by the Wycliffe Member Care co-ordinator. Heather and I looked at each other. We welcomed this opportunity to talk things through, but where to begin?

Wycliffe personnel all undergo debriefing after returning from overseas. It is a very valuable exercise, for it contributes towards an understanding and interpretation of what has been experienced during the preceding field term. Sometimes it is hard to discern what has actually been achieved when you are too close to it, so a more objective appraisal by experienced workers does help.

'Perhaps we could talk about Rachel first?'

It was May 1985 by then. We had returned to begin home leave in Britain a year sooner than originally projected. We now needed time to work through our feelings about Rachel's illness, as well as to talk through the progress of the language work, and to think about our future.

We thought back to our first days in Africa. Rachel had been a baby of three and a half months when we left Ireland in December 1982. Early on she exhibited a happy, placid temperament, smiling easily at the African women who wanted to take her in their arms, and whisk her off to see their friends. These friends might in their turn stroke her blond curls or poke a finger in her mouth to feel her teeth coming through at such an unusually young age.

Emile, who came to live with us in the village hall in Bahoulifla where Rachel had her first birthday, loved to carry her off down the village for a 'wee walk'. African men, in general, love children, and are extremely good with them, showing much emotional warmth.

She enjoyed interacting with big sister Joy, peaceably for the most part! Sometimes, we would 'lose' her for a while, especially when she was older, only to discover her eventually, comfortably ensconced behind a settee, totally absorbed in a children's picture book, or in her own imaginative game.

On the one hand we were delighted with her progress and adaptation to Africa, but her physical weakness gave us great cause for concern. She would lie stretched out for long periods on the cool floor, with no desire to move about or explore her surroundings. Finding an answer to her problems became increasingly urgent, and when she began to develop painful boils, we knew we had to take her back to Britain to try to get to the root of it, and to give her a chance to regain her health in a cooler climate.

So a year before our debriefing interview, on 1st June 1984, I had left Heather, Joy and Rachel to Abidjan airport for their flight back to Ireland, and with great sadness made my way back to the S.I.L. centre. Heather and I had hoped, at that stage, that both she and the girls would be able to come back to rejoin me in Africa before too long, but none of us knew how long it would take.

Family-members and other friends were understandably dismayed when they saw how pale and limp Rachel looked on arrival at Belfast airport. Some ducked behind pillars to hide their tears. But from that day much love, prayer and concern were showered on her by family, friends, and the church fellowship at Brooklands. After extensive tests, they discovered that the chief problem was an intestinal parasite, giardia, which explained Rachel's inability to absorb her food. Giardia is apparently notoriously difficult to detect: it was ironic that we did actually keep Flagyll, the treatment for giardia, in our medicine cupboard in the village. But it is too severe to administer to children unless you are absolutely sure of the diagnosis.

Once Rachel started on Flagyll, she began immediately to show improvement. Photos taken a few weeks later showed her with rosy cheeks and the boils just a fading memory. All four grandparents took her out and about when she was well enough, to visit friends and cafés, and Grandad

Best read her endless stories and nursery rhymes! We realised again how important grandparents are, and without wishing to dwell too much on the sacrificial aspects of missionary life, this enforced separation is one of them: hard for the grandparents, depriving for the children.

After much prayer and discussion, I then left Ivory Coast and rejoined the rest of the family in Ireland in August 1984, after ten weeks of separation. We knew we would have to move from the Bahoulifla Centre when our two years' tenure expired in June 1985, the following year. We decided that I would make a trip out to Africa in November 1984, and begin to build a house in nearby Dema, our language-assistant Emile's home village. This would take me several months, but Heather would join me for a time in the New Year, 1985. The plan was that we would build this house, move our possessions from Bahoulifla, and then go on an extended furlough to allow us all to regain good physical and emotional health.

Together with Rachel, Heather and I visited a developmental physiotherapist, Isobel Thompson, who saw us several times in her Belfast home. Isobel explained the special exercises it would be essential to perform with Rachel to gradually get her walking correctly. At that point, she was more than two years old and not yet walking, but we had the joy of seeing her take her first unaided steps during those first few months after her return from Ivory Coast.

It became clear that we could not take Rachel back to Africa for some time, indeed some doubted the wisdom of ever taking her back! But where did that leave us with respect to our call to Bible Translation? There had been so many encouragements during this first term. We had witnessed the beginnings of an indigenous Kouya church. Did the Lord want us to leave at this point?

'You have had a whole succession of extremely difficult decisions to make, haven't you?' our Wycliffe colleague pointed out gently.

'Yes. We felt really torn at times. It has been draining.

We wanted to do what was best for the family, but we desperately didn't want to have to give up! Something new was happening among the Kouyas, and we wanted to be part of it! We have had to search our hearts deeply once again, and test our calling and our mission. But we keep coming back to this belief: translation work among the Kouyas is what the Lord wants us to do! In a way,' I added, 'after so much intensive self-examination, it was good to get our teeth into something concrete just before last Christmas. We had a house to build in Africa.'

Mike Whitley, an architect from Belfast, helped us to design a house which would be the complete opposite of a Northern Irish house. It would be built to keep the heat out, rather than keep it in! It was fun to think this through with Mike. Where would we place false 'chimneys' so that air could be sucked through the house? How could windows be best positioned to allow currents of wind to pass freely through? Together we decided on a 'U' shaped house, with an internal courtyard inside the arms of the 'U'. The theory was that hot air, rising from this yard, would draw air through the strategically placed windows in the body of the house. After many years of enjoying it, we can testify that the system worked, and worked well! We loved that cool house.

Then another friend, Hugh McCormick, took a month off his work as a chartered surveyor to help us with the actual building. He travelled out to Ivory Coast with Heather and Joy in January 1985, while Rachel luxuriated in the loving care of grandparents for a few months.

Having travelled out a month earlier, I was busy trying to make arrangements for the building work. Everything takes so long to organise in this part of Africa! My father and mother who, like Heather's parents, did everything in their power to support our work, also came out to help for two months, with my father setting up the plumbing and electrical systems, and my mother helping run the Bahoulifla house with Heather. Wycliffe and W.E.C. colleagues gave advice and practical help too. Hugh worked like a Trojan. Because of all this help, work progressed speedily, and by May 1985 we were able to lock up a house which, while there were no ceilings as yet and not every corner was a right angle, did look remarkably like those plans drawn up in Belfast nine months before!

We now had a home in Ivory Coast to return to. It was for us, and for our Kouya friends, a guarantee that our lives would continue to be inextricably intertwined. Much of our very selves was invested in that house. It was a sign that we always intended to come back.

'And how do you feel right now, as you begin furlough?' our colleague asked.

'We feel overwhelmingly grateful to God. His Spirit is really at work among the Kouyas. Rachel is on the mend, and our hearts are more at peace.'

And so, in May 1985, the year's home leave began. We were to spend it with the Wycliffe Centre in England as our base.

It turned out to be an excellent year, a time for healing and renewal. We lived in one place, which was a novel experience! Joy started school at Mary Towerton Primary, Rachel attended a playschool called 'Tumbletots' and grew in physical strength, and I studied for a Masters degree in Linguistics at nearby Reading University. It was a time for re-discovering our identity as a family unit, after so many months of separations and upheaval. David Meech, the Wycliffe counsellor, patiently helped us towards more inner stability and integration.

A highlight of the year was a family holiday in North Berwick, in the flat of Hamish, a Scottish colleague. It poured most of the time, but we enjoyed sloshing about the sea-front in wellington boots, with the occasional meal out at the local chippie. If only we could bottle that sea air and take it back to

Africa with us! These were simple pleasures we had looked forward to during our first term as translators.

It brought joy to our hearts and a lump to our throat to see Rachel, now nearly four, jumping and wading about in the puddles, having a splashing good time.

IN AT THE DEEP END

It was now November 1986.

Why were we going back? Were we mad? Some expressed doubts, but the vast majority of our friends and supporters recognised that it was what we had to do. Our mission remained incomplete: there was unfinished business to see to. We had in many ways come through the hardest part, that of adapting to Africa and of being accepted in a people group. We had made friends, and we had built a house, which symbolised our desire to see the project through.

We were apprehensive. We knew the dangers. Certainly we were bracing ourselves. But we were happy that it was right to go back.

The story continues through letters home to family between 1986 and 1989.

Abidjan, 30th November 1986

Dear folks,

We've been in Ivory Coast for over a week now. Events have moved quickly.

The humidity hit us as soon as we stepped off the plane. It's like a sauna, or rather a steam-room, from which there is no escape. How can people stand living, never mind working in this?!

I'm writing from Abidjan, but I've already been up to Vavoua and back! I was given the opportunity of a lift up on

Tuesday. It was a welcome escape to drier heat. An hour north of Abidjan, the steering-wheel feels less clammy, and less of your shirt sticks to your body.

I was keen to see how things were in Dema village. What state was our house in? How were our Kouya friends? What should our next step be as a family?

I left Abidjan early last Tuesday morning, arriving in Vavoua by nightfall.

Just to sit in the private courtyard of our newly-built Dema house, and enjoy the stillness of the village again after the noise of Abidjan was delightful! What changes there have been in the Kouya area. Electricity has arrived!! This is going to transform our lives. Dema village now has power, with street-lights at night! The paved road has reached almost as far as Bahoulifla, and I found it hard to recognise any of the old familiar land-marks as we travelled along this smooth, straight road from Daloa. For a few moments I felt rather sad and nostalgic, but only until we again hit the dirt track, and then I remembered what I was missing!

It really was good to see old friends again, both in the village, and at the Vavoua International School. Emile and his cousin Gilbert have looked after the house and contents well: nothing missing, and looking quite well with some rough lawn growing around it. A number of different trees have been planted: a flourishing flame tree in the front garden, several straight teaks in a row on the kitchen side, some nimes on the office side, a mango and a guava at the back, and four banana-trees which should yield fruit in February. Keith Edwards came out from V.I.S. to look at the roof. He reckons that the best and cheapest way to stop the bad leaks is to raise the whole structure in the middle. This would entail removing the tin sheets, building up from the existing frame, then replacing the tin. He calculates the cost at roughly five hundred pounds.

There is a good possibility that we could stay in David and Debbie Williams' house in Vavoua while these repairs are being carried out.

The Lord has been answering Joy's prayers for her cat, with interest! Not only has she survived the cooking-pot(!), but she is at present feeding five thin but wiry little replicas of herself. I told Joy and Rachel about these when I got back to Abidjan, and of course they can't wait to get up there to see them: Rachel was busy composing names for the kittens as she lay in bed tonight.

Emile and I travelled back down together on the overnight bus (it took seven hours), and arrived in time for breakfast here. I'll not travel at night again if I can help it: it's too dangerous with the potholes on the unlit roads. At the moment we're planning to go north as a family about the 18th of December. But we need to get a car first, and two Ivorian licences. So that is what we are working on just now. Office after office after office. Patience, patience ...

Thank you for your prayers, and much love from all of us.
Philip

3rd December 1986

We are very keen to go up to Vavoua where the temperature drops at night a fraction, and we can sleep better.

We have managed to obtain our Ivorian driving-licences this morning - after only four mornings spent in offices, about twenty taxi-rides and about thirty pounds spent! Praise the Lord, remarkably trouble-free, all achieved in a minimum of time. It means so much to us, to be able to borrow a car and make trips. Now we have to get used to driving on the right hand side of the road again.

We have only been here for two weeks, but so much (unforeseen) has happened in that time. How about this for an early Christmas surprise for you? Please sit down, take a deep breath, and wait for it... We discovered last week that Heather was pregnant - baby due in July! Thankfully, she has had two fairly trouble-free pregnancies so far, apart from fatigue during the first few months, so she can just about cope with the thought of having the baby out here, probably in one of the French-run 'cliniques'.

The other bomb-shell is that John Maire would like me to take over from him as director of the S.I.L. Branch! John and Jane are to go on an extended furlough from June 1987 onwards. It would probably be for a year and a half altogether. John would like to appoint me as acting director in his absence. Both of these pieces of news have caused quite a bit of readjustment in our thinking, as you can imagine. We are just glad that we believe in the Sovereignty of God!

When I first heard about the director possibility, I thought they were pulling my leg. We feel we have only just arrived in the Branch! It seems like the Kouya project has just begun. It is only four years since we came to Africa, and eighteen months of that have been furlough...

We soon realised they were serious. John and Jane Maire have been doing a great job, but are worn out, and need an extended break. However, we have to wait until Branch Conference in April, when members will vote, to know for sure.

Can you imagine how all of this has thrown us into a flat spin? We don't much like having our plans changed, and we were, after all, really looking forward to getting our house in Dema into order, making it feel like home, and settling into translation and language-learning for the next three years. Now there is the possibility that we may only have a single year in the Kouya area before we are due home again in 1989. Will we lose momentum? This is our fear. Pray for us.

If we do feel that it is right to take over from John, my work would be mainly with other members, making trips from time to time to visit translation teams in this country, but also in Burkina Faso, Mali and Niger, the other three countries in our Branch. So it would involve a fair amount of travelling, while Heather would mostly be at home with the children. If we lived in the S.I.L. Centre, Heather would feel safer, though neither of us particularly likes living in Abidjan at any time *because of the high humidity, even though the facilities are so good in comparison with village-living. Right now we are just longing to get out of this big city with its noise, high-rise flats, and sticky heat.*

4th December 1986

We have just had the most wonderful surprise! What, another one?? A letter arrived today from a close friend and his wife, saying 'We feel you should have an air-conditioned four-wheel-drive vehicle. Please advise what you would like, so arrangements can be made to send out a.s.a.p.' Then we received the message that they had allocated £10,000 for this! We were really bowled over by that news, and just so thankful to the Lord for such an answer to prayer. We had been looking at the possibility of buying an older vehicle to do us in the meantime, as we had no money yet for any vehicle, but could have got a loan from S.I.L. for a few thousand pounds. While I was up in Vavoua, Joy and Heather had been praying together about a car, for they were just longing to have one, instead of having to carry the shopping back every day in the heat during Heather's pregnancy! So Joy was really thrilled when this answer to prayer came so quickly. It was lovely how she felt a part of it too. Laughing, she told me: 'Daddy, Mummy's so happy about it, she just burst into tears! Isn't it great we won't need to save up for a car any more?'

The Lord is so good to have given us this huge boost early on, especially after all the possible changes in plan that were preoccupying us so much.

News from the Kouya Christians continues to encourage. Young Anatole, Old Anatole, Williams and his father, as well as an old aunt, all seem to be going on well. Emile is with us in Abidjan at the moment, translating the Ten Commandments, which he plans to preach on at the Kouya Conference. We have printed the Kouya version of the Ten Commandments out on the computer, and I am making a hundred photocopies today.

I was walking over to the S.I.L. building the other day, and a snake, a metre long, slithered out in front of me on the path, in broad day-light too. Amazing how often this happens when we embark on a new phase of this work: if it weren't so potentially serious, it would be funny. Anyway, we never go out after 6 p.m. without a torch! The girls are great these days. They are adapting well to life without school and television.

Abidjan, 15th December 1986

It is now almost the end of our first month here in Abidjan, and we are looking forward to leaving for Vavoua early on Thursday morning. Staying in David and Debbie Williams' house means that we don't need to take so much equipment with us. We will miss not having them around in person, though. David has taken regular religious education classes in the Kouya village schools, and he has really encouraged the development of the Kouya church, keeping all the different village Christians in touch with one another.

Healthwise, we are doing quite well. Heather's asthma has hardly been bothering her at all, thankfully. She noticed a big improvement as soon as she arrived in Abidjan this time, and can almost always breathe through her nose. She will continue to take Intal four times a day until we are settled, but hardly ever needs the Ventolin for the moment.

There has been some morning sickness, but generally she sleeps well at night - if our nocturnal visitor allows us, that is! What we preferred to think of as a mouse all last week has now turned out to be a large rat, which frequents the washroom part of our kitchen in this rented flat. We didn't expect it to be able to climb up to the fifth floor, but it is able to run up via the kitchens, where the metal slats and windows are always open for air. I have been setting a trap these past two nights. While we thought it was a mouse, we didn't do anything about it, such brave and hardened missionaries as we have become! But once we both saw it, we went to get a trap. African rodents don't know they are supposed to like cheese, but they do appreciate chocolate cake! The clever thing set the trap off, but escaped with the food, and then last night, the trap wasn't touched at all, so maybe the trap has scared it off? Wishful thinking. We didn't sleep much that first night, but last night we slept well, rat or no rat in the next room.

We are sleeping on our mattresses on the floor of the living room beside the open balcony doors, as that is by far the coolest place. Whatever breeze there is, we get the benefit of it. Funny to think that we didn't see a single rat in or near our village house the whole time we were there. If we keep on our cat, though, there shouldn't be any problem.

Vavoua, 23rd December 1986

Here we are in Vavoua at last
We are glad to be able to use David and Debbie's house in town, while we get our village roof repaired. We are appreciating their gas water heater, and also their waterbed, which is definitely a lot cooler than the sponge or rubber mattresses. These beds will never take off in Ireland though! Just as long as Heather doesn't forget herself and stick her sewing needles in it, as a friend did with hers! The friend woke up swimming. It has been great to be able to use all their kitchen equipment, including the Tupperware.

The house itself is fine, but it has become quite a menagerie during the months of being vacant! We all got fleas since arriving, so we spend a lot of time looking for them and killing them, though they are very good at hopping away just as we are about to swoop. A bigger problem (again!) is the mice and rats. Only the mice get into the house, but the rats live above the kitchen and our bedroom, just on top of the plywood ceilings. They clatter overhead in the night as they visit the papaya trees outside. Last night we could watch them scurrying to and fro across the living-room window. Thankfully they were on the outside of the mosquito-screens, and we were on the inside. Today we got a rat-trap, and a young kitten from the school, so he should soon be able to get rid of the mice. It takes some getting used to all of this again, so please pray that we won't get discouraged by all these little annoyances.

Rachel is colouring in at the moment, singing to herself: 'Thank you, O my Father, for giving us your Son...' a new one we have been learning from Songs of Fellowship. Joy is busy playing with our new kitten. It is mostly white, so they have decided to call it Snowy. Snow, though, it is never likely to experience! Now we have to get it house-trained.

28th December 1986

Joy and Rachel woke up to their stockings and presents here on Christmas morning, and Heather and I woke up to a large rat in the trap outside! We have since caught another smaller one. The battle continues... The girls had a great time making up some of the little craft kits that we had set aside for them. We hear the barrels have arrived safely at customs, so the girls will have a second Christmas in February. We will collect the barrels in Abidjan at the beginning of February, when I am to do a programme-planning workshop. At the moment we plan to come back up here for March and April, and try to get the Dema village house roof fixed. We hope that by then we would also have enough money to put louvre shutters on the windows, and attach strong mosquito screening to the outside frames. Anyway, we'll see. Things can *change so quickly here. One has to be ready to adapt at short notice! They call it 'keeping flexible'.*

29th December 1986

The girls enjoy feeding the monkey that the Williamses keep out in the back yard. They give it bananas several times a day, also lettuce and other scraps. The monkey is a rascal. It reached out and pulled Heather's hair yesterday. It also grabs the girls' beads and bracelets if they get too close. Rachel is still quite nervous of it. But it's certainly entertaining to watch! Who needs television?

You're wondering what we eat here at the moment? In Abidjan we can buy a mixture rather like Harvest Crunch for breakfast. It is reasonably priced, about a pound for a small packet. Then we can always buy tins of Quaker Oats. Now that it is cooler in the mornings, we usually have porridge made with dried milk, as well as fruit. Fruit is cheap and plentiful in Vavoua just now: oranges, bananas and papayas. In Abidjan we had excellent pink grapefruit, for about ten pence each. We can also find lettuce here, and slightly sour tomatoes. The tomatoes make good soup, and tomato and onion sauces of various kinds to eat with our rice. We can get the usual ox-meat, though not the best parts as in Bahoulifla.

When the new road is finished, we will probably still keep going out to Bahoulifla on Mondays for our meat. We got on well with the butcher - a Moslem trader - when we lived there, and he gave us the parts we asked for. Here in town they are very awkward, and give you fat and bones nearly every time. They go by weight. A kilo of sirloin is the same price as a kilo of fatty meat. There is always smoked mackerel, which can taste reasonable.

We eat potatoes and rice and pasta and French-style bread as staples. We can buy vanilla yoghurt at about 30p a carton, from which we make up our own batch. Then every day, water must be boiled and cooled for drinking, all fruit and raw vegetables have to be purified in Javel solution. This procedure takes so much time. It's only now that we are really getting into the swing of things again.

At the end of the week Heather hopes to start to train Gilbert, who has been looking after our Dema village house while Emile has been at Bible college. Gilbert seems to have that rare quality - initiative!! If he does well, we would consider taking him down to Abidjan as houseboy when we go there, if he can find some relatives to live with. We'll let you know how he gets on. Although it means starting again from scratch, we think it will be worth it. He can read a bit, which is a real advantage, for he will be able to follow lists, and go shopping for more than four things at a time!

Yesterday was the dedication of the Toura New Testament, a language-group about four hours' drive from here. What an exciting day for the Touras! It was a Swiss-German Wycliffe couple who helped translate it - Thomas and Ilse Bearth. They have been following our progress in the Kouya work with interest, as they had prayed for a long time for someone to be sent to the Kouyas. Sometimes we wonder if we will ever see the day of the Kouya New Testament dedication? But we keep plodding on.

30th December 1986

Since Vavoua is the main market town in the area, we get lots of folk dropping in to see us. Early on Christmas morning, even before we were washed and dressed, we had a visit from Baï Laurent and his daughter from Gouabafla. He gave us a great welcome back. He looks well, and his chuckle is as deep and hearty as ever.

Quite a few of the younger Kouya men have dropped in too. Jonas, who was at the Bible School with Emile, and Séry David, the grammar-school student from Bahoulifla. We're glad to see our Kouya doesn't seem to have deteriorated much

111

in the year and a half we have been away.

The Kouya Christian Conference is in full swing as I write. About the only thing we had to do for it this time was to type and print out the programme for all the different speakers. The Kouya church leaders organised the schedule, transport, finances and food themselves. When we attended the day before yesterday, ninety people had already paid their fee, the equivalent of two pounds for men, one pound for women and young people. (It's the women who do all the cooking.) Morale was very high, and we were encouraged to see several new Christians there, including Kalou Williams' old dad, who had resisted the gospel for so long, clapping and singing away with the best of them!

There is one young man who seems to be an excellent interpreter. His name is Kalou Ambroise. He may be able to help us with translation checking later on. The Conference is a good place to be able to spot talented individuals like this, who may later have a key role to play. They were delighted to have copies of the Ten Commandments which Emile had translated. This was the topic he spoke on. He did very well. So many do not know how the Lord wants them to live: only a select few can read French and learn this for themselves from the French Bible. Emile told them that the Ten Commandments were to show them where they had gone wrong, but that the only way to please God was to have the Lord Jesus in their hearts, and the help and power of His Spirit.

Vavoua, 10th January 1987

What a busy time we have had since I last wrote! So much has happened.

Just this morning we had a visit from an older Kouya man from Kouléyo, and his son. We had been out to this remote village a couple of years ago, and the old man's grandchild, four years old, had been ill, had never walked, and just sat doing nothing all day long. Because we had been so distressed ourselves at Rachel failing to thrive as a baby, we felt we should make a point of praying for the child, and later sending out worm medicine, for we could see his swollen tummy was probably full of worms. The child made a good recovery, and now at six years of age, can walk and run and do things normally, and was able to be at the Christian conference. Great!

The grandfather is a keen Christian, so he passed on the news from the Christians at Kouléyo, where this year's conference was held. They normally meet now on Sunday mornings in that village, and on Wednesday and Saturday evenings, so the church there seems to be growing bigger and stronger. Everywhere, there are such heartening reports. Very few people seem to have fallen away during our absence; perhaps our faith was small, but it is just so much more encouraging than we expected. It seems to be the work of God's Spirit, rather than a work depending on us. This is what we had hoped and prayed for. Did we not believe then that it would happen??

We are gradually controlling the wildlife! The presence of the kitten is discouraging the mice, the fleas have almost disappeared from the house and garden, and I have caught four rats in my trap. The last one was quite small, so maybe we are winning! We are not itching so much any more, and the noises at night are not nearly so bothersome. Everything feels more positive somehow.

Vavoua, 28th January 1987

We went out to Bahoulifla village the Sunday before last, and greeted about a thousand people in one day! We arrived at 7.30 a.m., in time for the morning meeting at church. We had not sent a message on ahead (no telephones!), so they weren't expecting us.

About thirty-five adults and teenagers were present in the meeting. Williams was presiding, and the speaker was a young man in his twenties called Alain, who was converted last March. Apart from Williams, Alain is the only adult there who can read the French Bible, apart from when the grammar and secondary school pupils are back during their vacations. Alain asks for much prayer, as he feels the weight of responsibility of the Bible teaching, and he realises that his Christian experience is very limited.

I gave a short message after Alain, and several testified to what God was doing in their lives. Williams is doing a lot of hard thinking, and trying to apply Scripture to every aspect of life. We respect him such a lot. At the moment there are many problems to sort out. For instance, what should the young people do when their parents want them to go help them in their plantations on Sunday instead of going to church?

Being involved in a new church is so refreshing. We have a good laugh at times. When it was time for the offering to be taken up, the leader solemnly produced a brand-new Tefal frying pan from a bag on a rusty nail, and it was passed around the congregation. Non-stick. Why not? Then as I was speaking, the hour struck on the plastic ornamental clock above my head, and all paused while the clock produced a rendition of 'Oh my darling, Clementine'!

The other big event of last week was the funeral of Emile's maternal grandmother. It was a real witness to the unbelievers to see how the Christians managed the funeral, with dignity and without any arguments. Usually at funerals there are lots of 'palavers', and heated exchanges. Our new Nissan truck was the hearse! Emile was responsible for paying for the coffin, one hundred and twenty pounds, almost two months' salary for him, so I gave him an advance. However, he manages his money so carefully, he should be able to pay it off in the foreseeable future. We don't know how he manages to support so many people on his income. Even though he is well paid by standards here, he is the only man supporting a lot of women and his sisters' children too. He has been wise to keep his plantations going. He works hard there at certain times of the year, so that goes a long way to provide food for the extended family, as well as some cash at harvest-time.

We continually thank the Lord for Emile: handling money well, and disciplined use of his time are two of his great strengths. We know you pray faithfully for him, and up to now he has shown an unusual ability to continue working without constant supervision. What a comfort this is, since we are forced to be apart so often.

Though the Kouya church is not massive in relation to the whole population, we see that it is going from strength to strength. Those who take a stand as Christians are not falling back into their old ways.

Vavoua, 31st January 1987

We had a big surprise since I last wrote. Sylvie came back to see us. Do you remember us telling you about Sylvie, that bright teenage girl who helped us when we first went to the village? She was such a good worker. We were really happy with her, but then her grandmother and uncle obliged her to leave and go to another village, where they married her off to some old man as one of his extra wives.

We were aware that the marriage did not work out, and that the family in Bahoulifla had taken her back (usually it's because the money for the bride-wealth is not forthcoming). We lost contact with her, apart from the time she returned for her sister's funeral. At that time she had got herself pregnant. Her 'husband' was a grammar-school student from Cameroon. The baby was duly born. Then when the man wanted to go back to Cameroon, Sylvie said she didn't want to go with him. She was scared to leave the Ivory Coast and the people she knew. She told us that now he didn't want her anymore, so she had been living with one of her sisters in Abidjan, where she earned her living by braiding hair in the street. You know those complicated plaited hairstyles, which *take all day to do, and can be left in for months?*

Well, her child died just before Christmas. She told us that it had a wound on its head. She didn't say how it got the wound. She was very upset about this, but seemed resigned somehow. Anyway, she returned to the village, but is afraid to live there now too, for she has no brothers and sisters of her own, and her parents died a few years ago. Most of her nephews and nieces have also died. We knew two of her sisters who died and some of their children who died too. They wouldn't take the children to the clinic for a diagnosis, because they said there wasn't any point, the sorcerers had already eaten them, not literally, but in a dream through sorcery.

You can probably recall that most upsetting incident of Sylvie's eight-month-old nephew - the one who had been ill with running sores and swollen glands in his neck since he was four months? It happened while she was working for us. We offered to take the baby and his mother to the clinic and to give Sylvie the day off to accompany her sister, but they wouldn't go. So the baby was too weak to suck and soon died. The family is all dying off one by one. Sylvie says that if she stays in Bahoulifla, the ancestors will come and look for her too. 'It's always like that in our family' she says, 'Nobody lives long.'

Kalou Williams thinks there was a curse put on the family, possibly by their father on his deathbed, which is now taking effect. It was great to be able to tell her that the Lord Jesus has the power to break curses like this. If she asks for forgiveness and trusts in Christ, she is then under the protection of God, and nothing will happen to her that He doesn't permit. She does not dare to believe this yet. She has had some long conversations with Kouya Christians. We do not think that the Lord has brought her into our lives for nothing. Without the Lord she has no hope in this world, but faces a life of immorality and an early death. She knows this herself. But here one cannot easily get by without a man's support, so that's why she is looking for another one. I think she must be nineteen by now. Our houseboy Gilbert told her that going from man to man was no good, and that if she became a Christian, then she could find a good Christian husband who would look after her!

The fact that there is now a church in Bahoulifla means that she now has the possibility of seeing the Christian life worked out in a Kouya community, with men being faithful to their wives (almost if not completely unheard of among the Kouyas). She is a strong-minded young lady and will not profess Christianity to please us or anyone else, which is a good thing. But if she is convinced in her own mind that it is the truth and the way ahead for her, the Lord could bring about some wonderful changes in her life.

Vavoua, 17th March 1987

By the end of April, we should know whether we will be living in Abidjan from May onwards, or returning to the village. It will depend on the vote of the other S.I.L. Branch members. We both have peace of mind about whatever decision it is, with a slight preference now for Abidjan. Heather feels it would be reassuring to have our new baby near good medical care, and much easier to deal with nappies, sterilisation, and baby food preparation in the city.

I constantly admire the way Heather is able to manage the household under such trying conditions, as well as occupy the children profitably in pre-school activities. This morning we had 'Drama', with Joy and Rachel treating us to two little plays which they had organised themselves. They are improving at this now. They were both about new babies - I wonder why?? The first was Moses, (played by Billy - or was it Sally? - one of their knitted dolls). The second was the birth of baby Jesus, which entailed the knitted doll being unceremoniously tucked into Joy's skirt. Rachel was Joseph, and they were making their way to Bethlehem, eventually finding the stable. The baby was duly born - pulled out from Joy's skirt in a dignified manner. Then the shepherds and wise men (little plastic toys) came to worship and bring their gifts, and the whole thing ended off with Joy and Rachel singing 'Away in a manger.' You would have been proud of them in terms of initiative, as well as biblical accuracy, and Joy's growing stage awareness! We enjoyed it very much, and were pleased to see them thinking through a performance like this without any prompting.

Tomorrow, I plan to go out to the sawmill, to see whether the wood for raising the roof trusses has arrived yet. If it has, we will immediately send down to Abidjan for the African roofer. We are hoping the wood arrives soon as the rainy season is beginning, and we need to get the work finished before the advent of the torrential rains.

Vavoua, 29th March 1987

The wood has arrived, and I've arranged for it to be brought to Dema village. Unfortunately, the roofer can't come until he has finished his present job. He'll be with us as soon as he can. Time is getting short, and I am getting a touch nervous!

Meanwhile, involvement in Kouya church life continues. Yesterday was quite a day. Those with responsibility for leading the church groups in the Kouya villages met in Gouabafla 'to judge affairs', as they call it. It means 'to settle disputes'. Seven of the twelve Kouya villages were represented, and about twenty-four of us crowded into a tiny room in stifling heat, and spent all day praying, reading the Word, resolving various problems, and deciding on future strategy. We stopped for an hour to eat at midday. When the meeting ended, night was closing in at 7 p.m. as it always does, so I connected a simple slide-projector to the truck battery, to show slides on the side of a village house. These showed scenes from the Kouya Conference in December, and many of the villagers gathered round to see their friends' and relatives' pictures. It was the first time I'd tried to do this. Gilbert gave an impromptu commentary in Kouya, and took the opportunity to present the Gospel too!

Such days are great for hearing and speaking Kouya, so I feel I am making some progress in the language at the same time as helping the church forward.

Vavoua, 11th April 1987

Sorry for the gap in writing. We have been hard at it!

Kaboré Jean the roofer finally turned up. We set to work. Our first job was to remove the old roof from our Dema house. Boy, did it look vulnerable when we'd finished! We removed the tin sheets carefully, as we wanted to re-use them on the new, raised roof. It is great that the really heavy rains have not started yet: you certainly wouldn't attempt this in Britain without first storing your furniture! It has only poured in twice since the roof came off, and though it was like a swimming pool afterwards, Emile and I mopped the water off the concrete floors, and the rest quickly evaporated. With such high temperatures here at the moment, things don't have time to go mouldy before they dry.

Everyone is suffering from the heat at present, including the Africans. It gets hotter and hotter as it builds up to each successive downpour. We have to conserve energy. With the roofing in full swing, we do not feel as though we have managed to do much apart from the bare necessities. Language study, and Heather's teaching of Joy have taken a back seat for now.

Kaboré Jean comes to breakfast with us in Vavoua. A substantial meal at the start of the day helps him to work better, otherwise he would probably only take bread and water. He's sleeping at the pastor's house over behind the Vavoua church. I am grateful for such good working relationships: with carpenter Jean, Emile, Art our American short-termer and myself working together every day, it has been very free of the kind of hassles we have often had with builders. I find I do not get emotionally drained the way I sometimes did during the first stage of our house building. We often start the day with prayer, and the fellowship amongst all the men is good. The carpenter is a very strong Christian, with a lively intellect. We quite often invite him for the evening meal too, as we all enjoy each other's company.

It has taken us all week to add the extra wood to the roof trusses. Jean has done an excellent, thorough job.

Vavoua, 12th April 1987

Heather accompanied us out to the village today, and was delighted to see our progress. She and I stood together in the corner of the garden and admired the new, raised roof. The metal sheets, which had been removed to raise the roof, are being replaced, and cover almost half of the new roof now. They should all be back on by Tuesday. We really look forward to living there one day, and can see ourselves feeling at home and settled. We just thank the Lord for providing such a lovely site for us, much more calm and peaceful than the other places we have lived. We shouldn't have people crowding round us all day long as in Bahoulifla - much easier on the nerves.

The trees are looking good now that they have started to grow, and Heather has been enjoying herself dreaming about getting some sort of garden going! It means such a lot to have the prospect of something beautiful to look at, for Dema is not a pretty village. The people have to work hard and long in their fields, so to give time and energy to making their homesteads attractive would be a luxury they cannot afford. The wood factory people think we're crazy for wanting to live there, but we are so sure that it is the right place. There is a real atmosphere of good-will from the villagers. Probably we're all getting used to each others' ways, and they are beginning to understand what we are here to do, and realise it should be of benefit to the whole community in the long run.

There is high motivation for literacy. Many are keen to get reading and want to see more materials in Kouya.

Whatever we manage to print out is avidly snatched up, and circulated around quite a number of people of all ages. This is a good way of checking out where there are problems with the alphabet.

There has been little formal language analysis done since work on the roof began, though I hear quite a bit of Kouya out in the village each day, and find that my understanding of the language has really deepened in recent weeks, just through being exposed to it more often.

Vavoua, 13th April 1987

We had a bit of excitement this morning when the Pastor's son saw a five-foot spitting cobra disappear into the shed beside this Vavoua house. He was really quite frightened and yelled for Gilbert. So we had a snake-hunt for over half an hour. It was too dangerous to go into the shed to look for it, as it can spit and temporarily blind you from quite a long way off. It aims for your eyes, so you need to wear glasses for protection. Local men work as a team to catch them. One man will spit to the side. The cobra then mistakes that for a person's eyes and strikes at it. The others in the group quickly attack when its spit is used up. However we didn't get treated to this particular drama today, as the cobra wouldn't come out to play! In the end we men decided to go on out to the Dema house to continue work. Joy and Rachel were warned to stay near their mum today, and to keep on the lookout!

Last Sunday, old Anatole and Lucien from Bahoulifla were baptised in Vavoua. It was great to see them taking this step. They had been in town for a three-day course of instruction for new Christians. I went over the night before the event to see them, and noticed that the outdoor baptismal pool was full of slime and little fish. I hoped that they would clean it out before the next morning, but no, old Anatole and the others were baptised in the pool with the fish and all, and didn't seem to mind a bit!

Old Anatole is a real character. Converted at 85, baptised at 86! He's a grand old age for here. A couple of people wanted to help him up the steps after he was immersed, but he would have none of it, and insisted on getting himself out! After the baptisms, he and Lucien took part in the Lord's Supper for the first time. When the bread was passed around, Old Anatole wasn't too sure whether he was to keep it or eat it, so he had a good look round to see what everybody else was doing, and then followed suit. Baï Laurent from Gouabafla was present, and so was Emile, so there was a good Kouya representation. We look forward to the day when the Kouyas will be celebrating the Lord's Supper for themselves in their own villages, now that there is a growing nucleus of baptised Christians.

Michel, our first houseboy in Bahoulifla, was very reliable, but very slow. To be fair, he was more at home with a machete than a potato-peeler. Gilbert, whom we are now training, is not used to handling money, never having earned a salary before, just working in the fields and eating whatever was produced there. Translator Emile's experience of working in the bookshop and then the little supermarket before he came to us taught him a lot about how to manage his money. Emile and I have been trying to help Gilbert to think ahead about how to budget. Planning ahead, so as not to have to ask for advances, is a completely new way of thinking for Gilbert.

Last week we gave him two days off, to go and see if he could get his wife back from another village. Her parents had summoned her. Lots of marriages are broken up by the parents. So he is trying to get that matter sorted out too. The trouble was that he didn't turn up for work for four days instead of two. This was because he had not yet been able to get the father and the mother's brother together to sort things out. Heather was going round the bend at home with the children all day, shopping, cooking, washing up and dealing with the callers. There is just so much housework with so few labour-saving machines, and being without help for four days at this stage of the pregnancy was just killing. Unfortunately, I had no choice but to be out at the village all day at the building-site, so everybody was relieved when Gilbert turned up eventually. Such is life out here at times!

Well, time to stop. I'll try to write once more before we leave Vavoua for the S.I.L. Conference in Abidjan on Wednesday 22nd April, all being well. Before that, we have to clear this house out, leave in Dema what we don't need to bring with us, and pack up what has to go to Abidjan later, should we be living there!

Vavoua, 20th April 1987

The other day I climbed to the top of the roof, just before the final row of metal sheets was put back in place. It was high! I had to gulp down a slight feeling of dizziness, as I gazed downhill, across the village to the main Daloa road, and beyond that, through the forest to the sawmill.

From up there, the sawmill factory hooter could be clearly heard at noon above the soft chatter of the village and the pounding of pestles. Below me, in our garden, I could see Emile in his yellow ASEC football tee shirt, kneeling on the grass. He was patiently moving between the last corrugated tin sheets spread out on the lawn, daubing black waterproof tar on to the nail holes. He has been busy with this for weeks, and as I watched him from the top of the roof, I must say I marvelled again at the way the Lord has called and equipped Emile for this Bible translation task. He has blessed him with a gift of perseverance, to just keep plodding on, until he has completed what he has started. He is an inspiration to us.

Since the metal sheets were put back on, it has rained almost every day! We are so thankful that the heavy rains didn't come during the month of work on the roof, for that would have made things very difficult. There is still a lot of work to do on the house before it is really habitable: another month to get ceilings in, and wooden fascia boarding, so that the dust can't blow in under the roof and into the house. We can move in without anything being painted, and maybe even without louvre windows, which would probably take another two weeks at some stage.

As yet we don't know when I will be free to come up and see to these things, but Heather will have to stay in Abidjan with the children until the ceilings are in at least. The house will not really be secure until that is done, as there's nothing to stop anyone climbing up the window bars and over the top of the wall into the house. That's why it's essential to arrange for a guard to sleep there every single night. You know, we have never had anything stolen in the village. Borrowed yes, sometimes for long periods, but always returned eventually. However, villagers have had burglaries and thefts from outsiders, and as we live on the village edge now, we are probably more vulnerable to these.

The Sunday before last we went out to Dema for the church service, and were very encouraged to see thirty adults there, as well as the usual crowd of children. There were fifteen men and fifteen women, quite a contrast to the early days when it was rare ever to see a woman showing interest in spiritual things. We took carpenter Jean with us, and he spoke of how he became a Christian. He's a Mossi from Burkina Faso. Séry Emile (not Emile who works with us) gave an evangelistic message based on the Two Roads - the narrow way which leads to Life, and the broad way leading to Destruction. I added a little about the meaning and application of the Death of Christ as we were approaching Easter time. There was plenty of singing and prayer and participation by all.

Afterwards, all the children were sent out, and those who needed prayer for family problems or physical sickness stayed behind. First they explained their problem, and then various people prayed with them: Baï Emile; Kalou Williams from Bahoulifla who had come straight after the Bahoulifla meeting that morning; Jules from Dema, who took charge of the session and was excellent; Heather and myself.) A couple of young men asked for prayer that they would be able to find Christian wives. As far as we know, there has never been a *truly Christian marriage amongst the Kouyas as yet - i.e. one man /one woman, with all prerequisites in order from the village's point of view, the bride-wealth paid, and the marriage ceremony performed in a church.*

After about three hours for the meeting, the prayer afterwards and then the sorting out of various contentious matters, we all went up to Jules' kitchen for our lunch. It was chicken in palm-nut sauce with rice, and a second bowl of dried fish in palm-nut sauce. We enjoyed the chicken, which did not have as much pimento (hot pepper) in it as usual. So we got back to Vavoua here at about half past two, and then had a long, refreshing siesta. Everybody was exhausted, but it had been so worthwhile.

Vavoua, 21st April 1987

Life here in Vavoua town goes on with its daily joys and irritations. At the moment it is the negative side which is preying on my mind.

Radios blare from our neighbours on both sides - unfortunately they have chosen conflicting channels ... The family from next door comes every evening for ice-cubes because they're feeling hot ... and daily electricity cuts mean that our fridge has had a hard enough time trying to freeze ice-cubes. Last night when we were packing for Abidjan the electricity was cut four times. Unfortunately our Aladdin lamps are in the village, so we had to keep lighting our candles. The place our neighbours' children have chosen for their toilet is right outside our gate, and they squat there throughout the day to do the needful, which sometimes finds its way inside our house on our shoes, or on the car tyres in front of the house.

These things do get us down at times. Culture stress again no doubt. We can tell it is time for a break!

Then I lie awake at night sometimes and fight off flashes of worry... What is going to become of this country if Aids ('Sida' in French) really gets a hold? Over two hundred cases medically certified so far, not to speak of countless numbers who do not even know they are infected, or who they are infecting. One person in Vavoua has died of it. He was a white man (we don't know from which country) who was in charge of building the new road. He had affairs with many of the secondary school girls, so it is frightening to think about the consequences. A lot of the young people don't take the Aids risk seriously. Almost everybody here expects to be sexually active from their early teens. Their attitude is - we've been doing this for years and it hasn't killed us yet! Unfortunately, Aids is still a subject for jokes amongst the young adults.

We heard of another white man on the staff of one of the colleges in Abidjan, who on his resignation informed the college that he had Aids, naming twenty students with whom he had had affairs. On television they apparently are warning people, and there are sometimes articles in the newspaper, but the greater percentage of the population do not have access to either of these, and therefore are not at all informed. When you consider that the village of Bahoulifla alone has twelve Ghanaian prostitutes, not to speak of hundreds of village girls and adultery cases, sometimes it doesn't bear thinking about. What is our role in all this to be? We are more informed about Aids then any of the villagers, having read about it in many

English, American and French magazines. Our role is not primarily medical, but if people are not informed, it is like letting them steal food that we know is poisoned, and not telling them they are heading for certain death. All these things sometimes weigh heavily on us. Perhaps one of the Kouya health booklets later on can treat this subject.

On the positive side, we have been preparing a short presentation for Branch Conference next month on the development of the Kouya church. It's great to stand back a bit and get a glimpse of the broader picture of what God has been doing. We look forward to hearing what he is doing in our colleagues' live too. That will be refreshing.   *(cf. Appendix B)*

First year in Abidjan (1987-88)

Abidjan, 10th May 1987

Conference is over. Two weeks of meetings, finishing up with the Lord's Supper on Friday night, and then for a few others and myself, ten hours of Executive Committee Meetings yesterday. I hope this isn't too much a taste of things to come, but so much business has to be packed in to such a short time when all the translators are together. Renewing friendships and fellowship with colleagues was the most enjoyable part. John Maire decided in the end not to stand for director, so after a talk with Africa Area director Frank Robbins, we were willing that I stand for the director's role for the two years, rather than just acting director for one year as we had originally thought. This may end up keeping us in Abidjan for two and a half years altogether! We feel strangely at peace about taking this role on, especially since it will lift the weight of responsibility off John and Jane at a time when they need to be free of it. A comforting thought is that Les Brinkerhoff will be my associate director, as he and his wife Sara are the world's best encouragers!

Abidjan, 13th May 1987

Today was fascinating. I travelled with colleagues John Maire and David Presson to an Adioukrou village on the far side of Dabou. We were to present Literacy certificates to twenty-five people who had learnt to read and write in their own language. In the south here, where Christianity has been present for over fifty years, there is now a lot of second-generation Christianity. There is a large Methodist Church in the village, which altogether seems a very prosperous one. The service lasted for four hours, from nine o'clock to one o'clock. We were sitting up at the front and had to stay awake and alert, or everyone would have noticed!

I thought several times of Dad Best and how he would have enjoyed it, with massed choirs, five or six of them, all singing familiar Methodist tunes with Adioukrou words. The best choir sang seven or eight tunes from the Messiah! A shining trophy was presented to the church, which had given the most money in the circuit, which the choir-leader held aloft like the World Cup! ('Let not your right hand know what your left hand is doing'??)

After the presentation of the diplomas, we visitors were offered a very nice meal with mixed salads, rice and foutou, fish and meat, and minerals to drink, then bananas, pineapples and mangoes afterwards. In the afternoon there was a procession through the village with the brass band and all the choirs, with a prize for the best choir.

I can see myself enjoying this aspect of my new role. Lots of new ideas to consider for the Kouya work.

Yesterday, Tuesday 12th, I wasn't feeling well, with diarrhoea and a fever. I took a malaria treatment right away, and felt much better this morning, though still weak. I'm getting to recognise the malarial symptoms now and can take preventive action. I was down in the office for a few hours this morning and this afternoon, as some people had appointments to see me, but am taking it easy. I do enjoy getting to know people better, and talking over their work and plans with them. Heather says she will have to take a photo of me sitting at my desk, so that you can see how the image has changed so quickly from village translator to smartly dressed city director. I will have to wear smarter clothes here, and can no longer go around in scruffy shorts and flip-flops!! One of our Dutch members told me rather pointedly that my flip-flops didn't match the carpet in my office, so she succeeded in convincing me where Heather had failed!

Abidjan, 1st June 1987

When I reached the ripe old age of thirty-five last November, I asked the Lord to add a little more excitement to my Christian life. A dangerous prayer. The other day I confess to backtracking a little in a follow-up prayer: 'Thank you, Lord, I am grateful, but perhaps I have received enough excitement for just now!'

I have been finding the new job demanding. I really enjoy the challenge of it, but you really do need all your wits about you. I receive an awful lot of mail, of all kinds. Gunborg, our Swedish colleague, is an excellent PA/secretary. She keeps me right, since she knows the ropes so well. To be honest, my staff make me look better than I really am! Then there are telephone calls every day to receive and to make. A lot of Africans come to visit, and if they don't get to see the 'Directeur', they go away disappointed. Today, for example, Oxfam people came to discuss literacy for market women. A grant towards this was coming from Canada, and they needed some information about literacy countrywide. These interviews are in French. There are many names and organisations to keep track of.

Another very big part of my work is to help translators plan their projects and think through personal issues, or to decide with new teams where they should begin work. It is a privilege to share at this level. I find I am getting a good overview of Côte d'Ivoire in general, and how different translation projects and churches are progressing.

I am trying to resist the lurking thought that the Kouya translation might be stalled or held back through this change of assignment. Am I making an idol out of the Kouya translation? Yet I don't want to get sidetracked, and more than ever I see that the Kouyas need God's Word. Every day I tell myself that all I am learning here should feed back into the Kouya project, later on. Without question, someone needs to do this vital job. Sometimes I wish it didn't have to be me, though!

Changes

Over the next months, our lives were full of quickfire changes, as I gradually adapted to my new role. Our third daughter Hilary Esther arrived safely on 29th July. A healthy, bouncing baby, who brought us great delight. Joy started boarding at Vavoua International School on 25th August. We had a little private weep about her leaving. Emile returned for another term of training at the W.E.C. Bible College in September.

Travelling was part of my job description, and it began with a trip to England for an Africa Area Conference in late September. There I arranged to meet up with Eddie and Sue Arthur. Eddie and Sue were a British couple with a young baby who were assigned to our S.I.L. Branch. Their home church was Above Bar Baptist in Southampton. They were considering joining us in the Kouya translation. We were delighted at the thought of working with them, but we all wanted to make sure that this was the right way ahead. British Wycliffe had asked them to be regular teachers at British S.I.L., so they would be freer to return to that on a regular basis, if they were teamed up with a couple like ourselves. We were very much in prayer that it would become clear over the coming months whether or not the Arthurs should join us, or whether they should look for another language where there was no team at all. If they were to join us, they could live in our Dema house until they had found themselves somewhere to live in another village. We would not all live together in mission-compound style. It would be better for them to make their own way, and we could all share in the responsibilities of the project. We looked forward to that.

In between trips, Abidjan was my base, but I only managed the occasional letter home to family in Ireland. Heather wrote the bulk of our letters. They show how we were trying to cope in our new administrative capacity and keep our little family happy at the same time, but also maintaining our contact with the Kouyas as best we could. Here are some extracts from Heather's letters home:

Abidjan, 5th October 1987

Dear families,

When I opened the computer-cover to type this letter to you a few minutes ago, I disturbed a little colony of ants, which had begun to make their home inside the computer. I chased most of them away, but even as I type, there must be about twenty crawling busily over it, some are even inside the screen! So I'll have to take it to the computer department downstairs, to get it all cleared out! It is very hard to keep machines in good condition here, as ants, spiders and other wildlife like to take over. Our other problem at the moment is mould. Because there has been a lot of rain, our ceiling is leaking, and the clothes are mildewing on their hangers in the cupboard! I didn't intend to begin my letter like this, but then it will give you a flavour of African life!

Sometimes it seems as if we stagger from crisis to crisis. We had another one recently. One of the missionaries in Mali was in severe pain with suspected appendicitis, and as there was nowhere there where he could safely undergo the operation, the Missionary Aviation Fellowship flew him and his wife down to the Canadian hospital here. They had to leave their three little girls (including a year-old baby) behind in Mali. He made it in time after an agonising journey, and we praise the Lord that the operation went well. The folk down here at the Centre had to make arrangements to get him into the hospital, and have a huge sum of money ready to pay for the operation. They had to organise accommodation for his wife, and then for both of them after the operation, and arrange the flight to take them back up to Mali as soon as feasible. Our work is to help and support the team members, and those of us here on the Centre regularly have such crises coming our way.

Hilary is growing fast, and weighs thirteen and a half pounds at almost ten weeks. Rachel is good at playing with her and is also doing well in her own schoolwork. She loves reading, and immerses herself in books. Joy writes a little letter to us every week from school. All the pupils probably have to, but it's still nice! We look forward so much to seeing her soon for her 'weekend off'.

The Lord is certainly helping Philip to cope with his heavy responsibilities, giving him wisdom in difficult decisions, and in his relationships with Africans, missions, non-governmental organisations, etc., as well as with our own members. He has had so much new information to take in. For example, he has just had to prepare the Branch Budget for the coming year. He is also supposed to know all about the print-shop, literacy, computers, orientation for new members, the Institute of Applied Linguistics at the University (he had recently to give an overview of our work in Côte d'Ivoire to the staff of the linguistics department - in French) and much more. He is always leaping to the phone to take international calls, some early in the morning before he has had time to waken up! Not at his best then...

Another letter from Joy today. One of the few things that Joy doesn't like about boarding school is having to get washed in cold water. Another thing she doesn't like is having to eat everything on her plate. Rachel has decided that she doesn't want to go to boarding school now. 'Why not?' I asked her. 'Because there are too many rules', she says. 'You have to eat the fat on your meat, and you can't bring many toys with you, and you have to do joined-up writing, and I don't know how to do that. As well as that you have to keep tidying up your room.' 'Well, you have to keep tidying up your room here too, don't you? Anyway, there's plenty of good fun at school, You can even see videos at the weekends.' 'Yes, that's the nice part,' she agreed!

News from Vavoua now. We need to pray for one of the church leaders, who has given in to financial temptation recently, using church funds for other purposes. I don't know all the details, or what he did with it, but in any case he has not acted honourably, and needs to find some way of repaying the money. It is not a straightforward case of theft. In these situations where they don't use banks, it is always a problem to keep a sum of money intact, in a society where belongings and property are very public. Still it is clear that he has done wrong and seriously so. As yet he does not seem to be repentant, so we need to pray that he will repent and be restored and put matters right as soon as possible. Of course all this has become public knowledge in the villages, which hasn't helped. But then depending on how the Christians handle it together, it can be a good witness.

Our Kouya houseboy, Gilbert, was able to share the gospel with his father, who has not been on good terms with him for years. Gilbert says that it is the father's wife (the 'rivale', not his own mother) who is against him. His father would be happy for him to live with them, but the second wife is opposed. She would not even allow his father to visit Gilbert while he was sick. He stayed in our house and the two 'gardiens' took care of him. His father wanted to 'give himself to God' as they say (the first step in conversion), but the wife didn't want it, and so he didn't. When I asked what made him so afraid of her, Gilbert explained that the father was afraid she might work sorcery against him, or put something harmful into his food, if he went against her. Such is their fear of evil powers. It seems that they really can make others sick, by manipulation of the spirits' power using charms, spells and so on. But it was encouraging that at least the man felt spoken to, and attracted by the gospel in some way. At some point he needs to come to believe that the Holy Spirit of God is stronger than the evil spirits people can invoke. We look forward to the day when men like Gilbert's father, whose French is painfully limited, can hear the message of freedom explained clearly in Scripture in their own language.

When we have time, Gilbert and I have been working through the gospel of Mark, discussing terms such as 'Holy Spirit', 'evil spirits' and 'sin'. It is great to be involved in this work of bringing the Bible to people. Even if we are not directly spending a lot of time working on translation at the moment, it is never far from our minds.

This has been a long letter. Not having Philip here to talk to, I guess!
Much love from us all,

Heather

Abidjan, 15th November 1987

Dear families,
It's good to have Philip back again.
We received a lovely present this week. We had decided not to send Rachel to the French school when we heard that the fees were a thousand pounds and that we would also need another five hundred for books, uniform etc. We thought that was too expensive and that I could teach her all she needed to know at home, even though it would be quite a commitment of my time. The thing that was worrying us was what we would do about her essential physical exercise. We are both tired of having her walk up and down the stairs for this, so we decided that the most important thing for Rachel would be to learn to swim, so that she would then be getting good exercise in a way that we all enjoy. Each visit for our whole family to the swimming pool costs ten pounds, so it was too much to go even once a week. Then we realised that a

yearly ticket would cost about one hundred and ninety pounds, and we would be able to go as often as we wanted. Eventually we decided to go ahead with this. When I went to our accountant to withdraw the cash for it, I learned that our S.I.L. friends here had clubbed together to pay for our ticket and that they had almost enough now to cover it. We were just so pleased and touched by their thoughtfulness.

We had three Kouyas here last night, all Christians, for an informal checking session on our very tentative draft of Mark chapter one. It took about two hours to discuss the first eight verses! We got a few surprises. There actually is a Kouya word for camel, and Kouyas know about them, as traders from the north must have travelled down on camels in times past. But there is a problem with locusts - they just have grasshoppers. Would the word for grasshoppers do? Or should we say 'insects like grasshoppers'? Passive constructions and abstract nouns are also difficult. 'John preached a baptism of repentance for the forgiveness of sins' has to be completely re-phrased, spelling out who did the baptising, the repenting and the forgiving as well as the preaching! And all in the correct chronological order!

We could write another whole epistle about last night alone! It was a very good time. We ended up with prayer together for the evangelisation of the Kouyas, and for Bible translation. Gilbert helped me to make African food, chicken in peanut sauce (plenty of pimento) with rice, which everybody enjoyed. We would like to expand the group gradually, but would prefer to finish up with a smaller number of checkers who can make incisive contributions, rather than a big crowd where there might be endless 'vain discussions about words'! We will have to look at this question more closely later: keeping the balance between involving lots of folk in the process, which is vital, and actually getting on with productive work! But our appetite is really whetted for full-time translation. One day!

Heather

Abidjan, 7th February 1988

Dear families,

I'm enjoying a few rare moments of peace and quiet. Rachel is drawing, Hilary is sleeping, Joy is at school in Vavoua, and Philip left this morning to fly to Bamako, Mali. He's so privileged to be able to visit these different countries in West Africa. He also hopes to be in Niamey, Niger, from 20th to 27th March, for a big international conference on linguistics. As it is to be his only visit to Niger during these two years, he plans on meeting up with our teams there. They jokingly refer to him as the 'King of Abidjan'! He will meet all the official people he should be keeping contact with, as well as become more informed about the linguistic situation in West Africa, not to speak of all he will learn of what is happening in the churches. Then he flies to the United States (Dallas) from 16th May until 5th June approximately, to attend Wycliffe's International Conference.

13th February now …

Sorry, I didn't get this letter finished. Hilary woke up, so the peace and quiet was short-lived!

We're looking forward to having Philip back tomorrow, and hearing about his visit to Mali. Apparently he was able to go out and visit one of the more remote teams, Dan and Lucia Brubaker with the Minyanka people, for a few days before leaving. It always helps village teams to think that someone in administration has actually been where they live. They have two little boys, aged five and one and a half, so they are a courageous couple to be living in such a remote location.

The Arthurs are in Cameroon at the moment on the Africa Orientation Course. From what we have heard from them, they are still very interested in joining us in the Kouya project. Great!

Emile is visiting us here in Abidjan again. He is now able

to go ahead and type up the various stories which he had transcribed from the tapes by hand. When we get back into language work (please, Lord!), he will now be able to do even more independent work than before.

14th February!

I really must get this letter off to you today. Philip is now back from Mali. He was made most welcome there, and returned exhilarated. We only have three language teams and one support team up there, but many more are in the pipeline. He found the drier climate much less draining than here. The first half of the week was quite demanding as he had to make several speeches to the government organisation in charge of languages and literacy, since there is no University in Mali yet. All seemed to go well though, and relationships were cordial.

Heather

Abidjan, 18th June 1988

Dear families,
The last two weeks here have been absolutely jam-packed! The main activity was that we moved house from our flat in the S.I.L. centre to Riviera 2, about two miles away. Then Philip took Rachel off for two days on the road travelling up and down to see Joy in Vavoua. Since the Arthurs have now decided to join us in the project, Sue Arthur accompanied Philip and Rachel for a preliminary look around Dema. Now it is easier for Sue to plan for their move up there: they leave in just over a week.
Philip came back from Vavoua on the Sunday evening, and went to the office on Monday morning to read the most urgent things in the three-week pile-up following his States visit. But he didn't manage to reply to any of it, because so many people were waiting to see him about different matters.

On Tuesday he had to travel to Bouaké, Ivory Coast's second city, to see the Prefect about granting land for our proposed workshop centre. We thank the Lord that it was a successful trip, and a suitable plot of land is likely to be granted.

We like our 'new' house. We are to be based here for the next year, until the move back to Dema.

One day, if ever I retire, I must write a book about houseboys, and the cross-cultural 'fun' it is as we relate together. I don't like the term 'house-boy' much, but it's the one used everywhere. Even in French, it's 'le boy'! It's really important that the expatriate wife and the 'boy' have compatible temperaments.

Not only expatriate families have houseboys, African families do too, to help with housework and child minding in this extreme heat. Many houseboys are spoken to very harshly, in a way that makes us cringe. But in a status society, if the boss speaks too kindly to someone from an 'inferior' social level, it can be misunderstood, and taken advantage of. Before long, the worker may start to consider himself too much as part of the family, help himself from the fridge, and so on. One houseboy we employed had a tendency to 'take over'. He would go round the house with his broom, and if I were in his way, would say: 'Madame, you are badly placed!' (i.e. 'Move, Madame!')

It takes a long time for some houseboys to get used to the funny things we Westerners do, or the energy-saving machines we use. Once, when I was sick, I asked for extra house-help, and Philip asked a trainee houseboy to please take out the washing at a certain time, and hang it up to dry. The machine mustn't have been working properly and didn't wash the clothes at all, but the apprentice dutifully took them out, hung them all up to dry, and then ironed and folded them neatly, having ironed the grime even further in. They looked like neatly ironed rugby clothes after a game in the mud!

Missionaries frequently sell on their cars and possessions. Dependable houseboys are happy to move to a new family too, especially within the same organisation. When

the Frank family leaves the country for good, we hope to take on their man, Marcel, who can read, cook, and generally manage things extremely well. We reckon we need someone like him, otherwise I shall never get much more done than see to the practical needs of the family. Talk about dependency relationships! I can see one fast developing there: that is, before long I will be totally dependent on Marcel!
Much love from
> *Heather*

Second Year in Abidjan (1988-89)

My first year as director was now over, and the second year followed the pattern of the previous one: I travelled a lot, while Heather stayed in Abidjan.

What impressed me, as I travelled about visiting and encouraging teams, was the way each team had adapted to widely varying circumstances. Some teams worked in villages, some in towns, some in cities. In one situation they worked with illiterate but wise men and women, in another they collaborated with university graduates. But quietly and with certainty, the job was getting done. From each situation I gleaned a wealth of ideas which I hoped would stand us in good stead when we returned to the Kouya area.

1988 was the year when the Arthur family lived in our house in Dema, then built their own home in Gouabafla, close to Baï Laurent's courtyard. Sickness struck several times, especially malaria, but they persevered through ups and downs, related well to the Kouya villagers, and made excellent progress in language learning. Gouabafla had the advantage of being closer to the more distant forest villages, so it was a strategic place to live. From there, the Arthurs were well placed to promote enthusiasm for Kouya literacy and translation in those villages.

During this year our friends and supporters John and Ruth Hamilton proceeded with their application to become long-term teachers with Wycliffe. It was exciting to see the Lord lead them to teach in Vavoua International School, from where they could witness the Kouya work at first hand! From their base at the school they provided vital support for both Kouya translation teams from the very outset. Ruth and Heather would reminisce about the year they spent together training to be teachers in Aberystwyth in 1975. Little did they realise then that one day Ruth would be teaching our children and theirs in the heart of Ivory Coast!

Rachel started Vavoua School on 6th January 1989, joining big sister Joy. As parents, we had imagined that parenting was, if not exactly a breeze, then at least straightforward, but our wee Hilary was intent on humbling us! As soon as she got moving on two legs, she led us a merry dance. Typical was the time she inserted a freezer plug into a faulty socket at a Mission station where we were guests, blowing the central fuses, and plunging the station into darkness!

November 1988 saw the four-country S.I.L. Branch divide into two, and I had to fly to Dallas to complete the formalities, which included shaking Ed Lauber's hand! Ed became director of the new Burkina Faso/Niger Branch, while my responsibilities narrowed to Côte d'Ivoire/Mali. The work-load did not lessen, and at times we were tempted to work day and night, but at a retreat for directors' wives in Togo, a group of us young leaders with young families were given some strong and helpful advice. We should strive to keep a balanced life-style, to stay reasonably fresh, joyful and clear-thinking, so that when real crises came, as they inevitably did in West Africa, we might retain some inner resources to handle them. In practice it meant having to deal with a daily feeling of guilt when we saw this, that and the other important thing left undone. We needed the peace of God which passes all understanding to keep our hearts and minds in Christ Jesus. True to His promise, that is what He generously gave us.

Good to be Back

I finished my term as director in July. It was a relief to hand the baton back to John Maire, take off those tight, shiny city shoes, and rummage in the cupboard for the old familiar sandals and flip-flops. We looked forward to a return to the low-key informality of village living, though we felt we had learned a lot through the Branch leadership experience. We had a year before furlough was due. I take up the story again through our letters home.

Dema village, 6th August 1989

Dear folks,

It's exactly five weeks since we arrived to live in the village again. It is so good to be back.

We really wanted to return, we were happy to be taking up the challenge once again of learning more of Kouya language and culture, but going back to village life has not been totally straightforward. I suppose our vision has been broadened during the time in Abidjan, so we found some inner resistance to yet another change, another narrowing of focus. Yet once again, we have felt the power of relationship. It is our Kouya friends who have eased this transition for us. They have visited, talked, encouraged and cajoled us into feeling part of them once again.

Kalou Williams is one of these faithful friends. He came over from Bahoulifla this morning. It is great to see him joining the translation team in a part-time capacity at the moment. He comes over two days a week, and what he earns enables him to hire workers to continue working his fields. Emile really enjoys having another Kouya to work with, especially as they make a good team, each complementing the other's gifts. Williams is very strong in the area of public relations, is at ease with unbelievers, and in all kinds of social situations. Right from the early days in Bahoulifla, he has guided me as to what

I should be doing and saying in various situations, something Emile isn't able to do at all, perhaps because he is younger. So it is a real strength to have them both visiting other Kouya villages together for checking sessions.

For example, the other day they went to Bonoufla, the last Kouya village before Daloa. They were looking for Prosper, the young man who leads the Christians there. He had already left for his fields, so they couldn't do the checking with him as hoped. But what happened was probably far better in the end. They went to visit the chief, and were able to explain what they had come to do. I have already met this man, who knows why we are learning Kouya. Emile read out passages from our translation of the epistle of James, which were discussed by the chief and some of the old men. They then arranged to meet again next week, so that the other village leaders could be present to hear and discuss it. We are very grateful for how this turned out, as a good reception with the chief will ensure that the other villagers will at least be open to listen and consider.

James is a very good place to start with the Kouya unbelievers, as they find themselves unable to disagree with it! The importance of taming the tongue and asking God for wisdom when you know you lack it; trials and problems leading to endurance and strength of character; these are the concepts that interest Kouyas, and solutions to the problems they run up against in everyday life. This often leads them to say, 'Yes, God's word is good', and at least we have a hearing. Later on, as they come to understand the claims of Christ and the cost involved in following Him, they will have to either accept or reject the gospel, but at least by that time we trust that they will have a fair understanding of what the gospel is about.

We are starting to feel like OWLs now (Ordinary Working Linguists), as opposed to builders or administrators! The big building push is over, the Arthurs made many improvements to our house during their stay in it, and it is gradually becoming more comfortable to live in. We are learning what Kouya we can, and enjoying the moral support and encouragement of having Eddie and Sue not too far away in Gouabafla.

Philip

Vavoua International School, 19th August 1989

Yesterday was our wedding anniversary. Our thirteenth, can you imagine! To celebrate it, we drove last night to the Chinese restaurant in Daloa, leaving our girls here at the school with Sylvia Hare, the British housemother who is a medical doctor. The school is off for the summer of course. We would never have attempted that journey by night on the old Daloa Road. Such luxury: all dressed up and somewhere to go! No longer do we have to 'save up' our events and celebrate them later on. Heather and I savoured the rare experience of being alone together for a change.

Joy has had a very high fever, feeling really ill. It was pretty clear that it was malaria, as she complained that her head was hurting badly. We started her on a chloroquine treatment, but after twenty-four hours, saw that it was having no effect. Her fever stayed up around 103 degrees, it seemed that she would need to go on quinine, and we brought her here to the school for Sylvia to examine her. We had planned to come in for a few days in any case, as the plywood ceilings are being put into our Dema house, and it would be difficult to have them going up over our heads. So we were pleased to be able to stay in the house where the Hamiltons - our Irish friends - are expected in two and a half weeks' time. Sylvia agreed that Joy needed to go on quinine: she was by then a bit delirious.

Thankfully she is much better today, though very weak. Several times a day the quinine makes her bring up the little bit of food she manages to eat. Today was her last dose of it, so she should be able to increase her food intake gradually. She had a worse case of it than Hilary did. Amazing that four of us have had malaria within six weeks, Rachel being the only one who has escaped.

It is so often the case that our return to the village is dogged by unexpected health problems. The Arthurs are finding the same. We do feel the need to resist the enemy in the area of health, because even when we feel we are taking all the necessary health precautions, these problems never seem to end.

However, there are of course natural causes. With not having ceilings in our house, apart from in the bedrooms, we have all been getting quite badly bitten at this time of year, as mosquitoes and other bugs have no trouble getting in through the big gaps between the top of the walls and the ceilings. Sylvia thinks we should now increase the amount of Paludrine Joy takes daily, to prevent a relapse. We appreciate her expert advice and care.

In spite of all the malaria, we have remained in fairly good spirits, glad to be back in the Kouya work, demanding and overwhelming though we find it. As ever, we see that our only hope of staying here long-term and persevering in learning the language and coping with the demands, is in the help and power of God Himself, for we do not have the natural resources to do so. The whole thing is totally beyond us, humanly speaking.

Tonight I have been typing up a speech in French that I hope to deliver at a big literacy event next Friday in Nyaboa country. The event is designed to boost morale, and stimulate local involvement. After fifteen years, the Nyaboa New Testament will soon be published, and there is a big push for literacy, to ensure that many will be able to read it when it appears. We are to represent S.I.L., and as guests of honour, sit in the front row along with the Sous-préfet and other notables! Looks like the old tie will make another appearance. Having a degree in French stands you in good stead on such occasions, as the people like quite a flowery rhetorical style, and a background in French literature provides an ample source of suitable phrases! It will take us about two hours to travel there, and about a thousand people are expected to be present. We're taking Emile, Williams and François with us, to give them some ideas for our own Kouya literacy work in the future!

Dema, 25th August 1989

We have not visited any other Kouya churches yet since our return. However, there is evident growth and maturity in the Dema church. They meet in the little wooden building on Sunday mornings for the main service with prayer, praise and teaching, then on Sunday afternoons for Bible Study, and Wednesday evenings for another Bible message and prayer. On Sunday mornings there are regularly thirty-five to forty adults present, equally divided between men and women.

Three other evenings a week you can hear the bell (the discarded inner metal part of a car wheel) clanging at about eight o'clock, to remind people to come to the 'evangelisations'. These take place in different courtyards. On Sundays and Wednesdays, they announce in whose compound the meetings are to be held, who is to lead the meeting and who is to give the message. We are really thrilled about this, as it is entirely their own initiative.

It is wonderful to sit around in a circle after dark, with just one or two oil lamps to light up the speaker's French Bible. They sing a lot, and give short explanations of the gospel between the different songs, accompanied by the tamtam and occasionally a hand-made traditional guitar. The unbelieving family members are usually sitting around listening. It is like having a meeting in their own living room, since the courtyard is where they eat, and then sit around at night. It is such a natural non-threatening way of introducing the gospel to the relatives, who probably would not dream of turning up at a church meeting. I think this is one of the most exciting things happening in the Dema church.

Dema, 15th September 1989

We are really pleased to get our ceilings in at last, and to have most of the gaps around the edges cemented up. This should really reduce the mosquito bites.

Speaking of insect bites, we are feeling sorry for Sue who has had a bad problem with filaria, the type which is common in Cameroon. She probably got infected in Cameroon over a year ago while on the orientation course. One day some weeks back she felt something moving in her eye. When they had a look they found a little white worm about a centimetre long, just under the cornea. It must have been very unpleasant, and very worrying for a few days until she got the correct diagnosis.

Please remember to pray for them when you pray for us. They continue to do well in language learning and relationships with the people. Eddie is great on the computer and able to get lots of material printed out clearly for us all. But it is amazing that we have so little overlap time when both families are in the Kouya area. Life is so mobile here, and workshops and Branch responsibilities mean we often miss each other. Still, it means that there is usually one or other of us present in the area to push the project forward. And later *on, when we are all involved in translating, being a double team should speed up the project no end.*

Dema, 20th October 1989

Just to recount some of today's events while they are still fresh in my mind. As soon as we wake, the village merry-go-round begins. Perhaps 'soap-opera' is more like it!

Hilary wakened us at 5.30 a.m. after which we couldn't get back to sleep. She eventually insisted on getting out of her cot at 6.30. I heated up some water and gave her an early morning bath. Germaine brought the water from the well at about six o'clock and half filled a barrel we keep outside, between our bedroom window and the kitchen door. I'm sure the water she carries in the basin on her head would be twice her own bodyweight! Normally the thud of it hitting the bottom of the barrel is a great alarm clock.

This morning, Heather was expecting Gilbert's baby to be brought back here any time after six o'clock to get the next dose of ampicillin for her pneumonia. Thank the Lord, she is starting to recover. Her fever was 103 last night and she was taking about sixty breaths a minute. She is only four months old and since they named her after Heather ('Esther'), Heather finds she has quite an emotional attachment to her. She eventually arrived at 8 o'clock.

Shortly after that, Williams cycled in from Bahoulifla on his new Kouya project bike, and gave us all the news. On the way he had just called in to see Emile next door. Emile had been quite badly ill for several days with severe head pain, bad aching all over and high fever. We were all worried because he was so ill. The morning before yesterday we were awakened by very loud voices inside Emile's house, about ten yards from our own house. I could hear that it was the Christians all praying out loud at the same time. Emile was obeying the injunction of the Epistle of James to call for the elders of the church to come and pray for him.

After that, he began to get better. We also administered malaria medicine and painkillers, and the old bothersome question raised its head again. When sickness strikes, who or what do we depend on for healing? We must not encourage these young believers to rely solely on Western medicines. They can't afford them anyway, most of the time. So then, what is the alternative to fetish healers and Western medicine, as neither of these is a satisfactory answer for the local Christian?

As we see it at the moment, herbal remedies (from indigenous plants) are fine if accompanied by prayer to God, and glory given to God after healing. Animal sacrifices should not be made by Christians, but we need to affirm what is good and available in the forest. Western medicines are also good if the people can afford them, which they usually can't, except when they have just sold their coffee or cocoa harvest. But we personally cannot cope with helping the whole village medically. There are always several serious illnesses at any one time in a village of almost three thousand people.

I think the African Christians will be able to go further in the area of faith than we can. Thankfully they aren't limited to our experience of God in this as well as other ways. Though we have seen people get better through prayer alone, this time when both Emile and Gilbert's baby were so sick, we were honestly afraid they might die, and so we paid for the medicines as well as praying. Were we not willing to rely on faith alone, or was this just being realistic?? I suppose it was because it was within our means to do something about it, and we felt a special responsibility to them. We become so aware of our limitations and inadequacies in situations such as this. Anyway, both are now much better and we are grateful and relieved. Hopefully we will have a day or two before any more health crises come our way.

Williams and I had a time of prayer and discussion of the next section in Genesis, then Williams had a go at translating it. As much of it is straightforward narrative, he was able to work fairly independently today, thankfully, as so many other things were happening at the same time. He managed to translate twenty-four verses in all, which was good going. When we tackle the Epistles in a few years' time, ten verses per day would be more realistic. We always need Emile to check the spelling and mark in the tones, but it may be some days before he is strong enough to work again. What they are producing is only a very rough draft, but good practice for later. Emile uses it regularly these days as a basis for his messages in the courtyard prayer meetings.

Heather had sent Hilary out for a walk with Marcel, and was sorting out the girls' room in preparation for their weekend off; I was spending a final hour with Williams on our word list for the dictionary, before going on to check Genesis with him, when a car drew up full of people we didn't know. There were two ladies, a man, and two young children. They turned out to be Swiss, and had apparently sent a letter to us, which never arrived. Two of them were interested in doing translation-work. They had come a long way to see us. At such times, we drop everything and concentrate on our visitors. We quickly got together a meal of rice, goat and peanut sauce for all, and spent three or four hours with them explaining the work we do.

Meanwhile, Kouya friends came and went, and it became a juggling act as we tried to keep everyone involved and happy. This could be called a 'normal' kind of day, though no two village days are ever quite the same.

Dema, 3rd November 1989

The consignment of barrels from home has arrived safely! We are very pleased indeed with the contents.

François, the Arthurs' co-worker, Emile and Williams are here in the office with me while I am writing this, and they are all delighted with their share. We are able to give each of them a woollen blanket, and some office supplies - items which are very expensive out here. I see that they have been making use of the envelopes and paper already today by writing a letter to the Kouya church in Bonoufla. The big red hard-backed notebooks are very much appreciated by everyone. We are sending one to each of the six Kouya churches. We will keep the rest here for future literacy projects.

We are keeping some of the material for ourselves, but sending most of it to the school, where they should be able to get quite a few curtains and some bedspreads out of it.

However, Heather and I both think that we shall have to declare a war on those 'Cherry lip' sweets! We were already thinking of that when we saw how they had stuck to lots of things in Joy's backpack, including the new calculator she received for her birthday. For quite a while after that we found bits of them sticking to random things. As usual, they had managed to escape from the packet. This time the plastic container had split in the barrel, and some had spilled out and got on the blankets, the red blankets fortunately. (Note to grandma from Heather: I'm sure your little granddaughters will manage to survive a cherry-lip free childhood very well from now on!!! What about polo-mints?)

Lots of folk visit us for their weekends off from the W.E.C. school. We had the Hamilton family recently, so it was great to talk 'Norn Iron'. Newly arrived S.I.L. colleagues come too, for their orientation to village life. We are glad to welcome them, and do our best to ease the transition to life here for them.

All for now. We are in good health. Hilary is having a great time with her chickens and her cat, which she adores. Then this morning we hung up our burst car tyre from the flame tree for her to climb and swing on. But Gwa, the little deaf and dumb boy who wanders round the village, had soon untied it and was wheeling it round the garden, with Hilary running after him squealing her objections. It is good to be feeling more at home now.

Christmas Day 1989

Here we are in Dema village on the day when Christians everywhere celebrate the birth of Jesus Christ our Saviour. The Kouya Christians are doing it in their own way too. We will be sharing in the Christmas meal at noon with the other village Christians. I took two of them yesterday to buy the Christmas pig in Bahoulifla. 'Christmas pig' doesn't have quite the same ring to it as 'Christmas turkey', does it?

Joy, Rachel and Hilary have a wonderful capacity for expressing pleasure and are appreciating their simple Christmas gifts. At the moment they are enjoying working at their 'Artwork from Ancient Greece' colouring books. Though Heather and I are trying to enter into the spirit of the season, to be honest we are struggling a bit. I suppose we have, all our lives, been able to have a few hours of quiet family time early on Christmas morning or at least on Christmas Eve. But even when Heather had worked hard to get a nice meal of goat meat, potatoes and ratatouille ready last night, we were just about to sit down to it when our neighbour arrived on a social call, so I went outside to sit down with him and get the news. Here, you simply cannot say you are busy and turn people away: it would be the height of rudeness. Then after the meal, we lit the candles, and were about to decorate our Christmas branch, and sing a few carols when someone else arrived to see me. All the previous day after we had arrived back from our holiday in Grand Bassam, people came to greet us, and get medical help for one thing and another, which is what we expect when we come back. But it's hard to deal with it all, when you still haven't managed to get unpacked!

By lunchtime, we had cheered up somewhat. It seems to take a day or two to recover from the day-long journey back up here. The Christians had decided that the nicest, most shady place in the village to eat Christmas dinner was under the big flame tree in our garden. So about thirty-five adults and forty or so kids all arrived sometime after midday, with mammoth pots of pork in sauce and nicely cooked village rice.

After that, there was another huge pot of fried rice, something like risotto, but with different ingredients. When the neighbours saw that there was food available, many come running up with their little bowls to get them filled up. Those serving out the food felt unable to refuse them, even though the church people had all brought so much money each to pay for the food, and the Christian women had worked so hard to get it all ready, cutting down firewood from the bush for days. With the wooden benches from the hall, and about sixteen chairs of ours, most people were comfortably seated. In the end, a good time was had by all.

It was a great encouragement to see the number of adults who now identify with the Christians in Dema, and not just when there is a meal going! On Sunday mornings there is an attendance on average of fourteen women and fourteen men, with a varying number of children. One of the young men, Jacques, has organised a Sunday school for the children. We are thankful to God that there is now a good number of women present, who also attend the mid-week prayer and Bible Study, as well as the courtyard prayer meetings. They no longer see it as exclusively a male thing. There are several men who can give quite an acceptable message, which means that when Emile is away preaching elsewhere, or when François is at Bible school as at present, then there are always others who can lead and speak at the meetings. The young Kouya church is maturing.

Last week we got word of another little group of believers beginning to meet, this time in Bouitafla near the Vavoua School, so there are now Christians meeting regularly in ten of the twelve Kouya villages. This is thrilling.

At the annual Kouya Christian Conference after Christmas, the translated Epistle of James was preached from, and the whole book read aloud. With several literacy classes springing up in the churches, there is increasing fluency in reading Kouya. Because of this desire to read the Scriptures in Kouya, Eddie and Sue Arthur have produced a preliminary reading guide, a bridge into Kouya for those who can already read French, the national language. There is much interest shown in anything produced: the 1990 calendars were sold out in a few weeks!

Both François, the Arthurs' language helper, and his wife Adèle, who had been working with Heather from time to time on language learning, have gone off for the six week introductory course at the W.E.C. Bible College in Zuénoula. They are not the only Kouyas, for there is also Williams from Bahoulifla, and Blaise, a leader of the church in Kouléyo, as well as a very nice girl Henriette from Gatifla. She is the girl that Heather secretly hopes Emile will choose as his wife! It is true that she would be very suitable. She is a really strong believer by her own conviction. Her mother is also a strong Christian whom we have known for years, and Henriette herself has been trained as a secretary. She could be invaluable in the Kouya work, and we would just love to have her as a neighbour! The fact that she is going to Bible College would give her such an insight into the many sides of Emile's ministry. The only problem is that he has yet to fall in love with her and want to marry her. So let's not get carried away! Nevertheless, I'm sure that minor detail can be overcome!

At conference we saw that Henriette is a very good singer. She often sang duets - Kouya-style of course - with Séry David from Bahoulifla, and seemed in every way perfectly suitable for the wife of a full-time Christian worker. Sorry, off I go again. We get privately rather excited about it, only if it's the Lord's will, of course!

Kouyas are much more up-front about matchmaking than we are. During conference, the session-leader might ask the group: 'Who here is unattached? Which men? Stand up! Which women? Stand up! Who wants to be married? Men? Women? On your feet!' Everybody has a good look around them, and there is much hilarity. We now have a Matchmaking committee (seriously!) in Dema church, and I really think Heather and I qualify for membership: we are just waiting for the nod. Do you think we could introduce these committees to churches in Britain??

3rd January 1990 - My First Ever Visit to Brouafla Kouya.

Dear folks,

I am indebted to my wife for the following account. I simply lay on my bed and dictated. Heather said she was a mere scribe who has learned that you have to catch me first thing after an event if you want to hear the news, as I only give it once! Even then it is often in note form. By the second time of telling I have lost interest in talking about it. All this of course is a total exaggeration... but apparently the following is what I reported.

'Brouafla Kouya is the most isolated Kouya village. Those who travelled there today were Eddie, François, Emile and myself. It lies about forty minutes by vehicle further down into the forest from Gouabafla, where the Arthurs live. The track is reasonable in height of dry season, but would be treacherous in rainy season. Fairly dense forest. Passed through at least two Baoulé settlements after Dédiafla. Turned right after second one. Cocoa and coffee buyers take their lorries down at certain times, otherwise Badjans (the valiant bush taxis!) go there two or three times a week. Today, Wednesday, was their market day. Surprised to find fairly lively and sizeable market. Jula salesmen from Bénin. No electricity of course, but two generators in village belonging to Baoulé and Beninese traders. Their shops were very well stocked. Walked through village to chief's house. Meeting in progress, but we were received very well and asked for the first news. Main, important news would come later.

'There was general astonishment at Eddie's and my ability to speak Kouya. Many did not seem to know of us before. To test my Kouya the chief asked me the Kouya name of our home village, and then if I knew my Kouya name. He smiled at my answers. I suspect I may have a Kouya nickname I am unaware of, and probably wouldn't want to know, but the

name I know is Gomi Seri Gwamine Filipu. (Gomi Seri was a well-known Kouya chief of yore, and Alain Gwamine was the goalkeeper for the Ivory Coast national team. (Philip has been known to play goalkeeper in the village, and flattery will get you everywhere, but let no one be deceived. He will not get called up! Ed.)

'Then we were asked to go and sit under the shade of an old tree, not a mango, Emile and François didn't know the name of it. It gave such fantastic shade, a bit like sitting under an umbrella, with its leafy branches curving down in a wide circle above us. We sat down and one responsible youngish man was detailed to look after us, until the chief could receive us properly. We were asked whether we were hungry. I said I was satisfied and had eaten that morning, but Eddie said he was hungry and could eat. Two long hours later our meal arrived: chicken in sauce graine, and banana foutou. By that time I was certainly hungry and was glad of Eddie's foresight. Very tasty. That's the first time that I have been offered something to eat on my first visit to a Kouya village. We sent our interpreter, Lucien, off to buy soft drinks, He came back later with the drinks but returned our money, saying that the chief would not hear of us paying for them. This again was in contrast to other villages.

'Before the meal arrived, various people came to greet us, including an old Kouya lady who sells tobacco in the village. Also the Président du Comité, a very pleasant man, and an almost drunk Beninese man, who was a bit of a nuisance. The Kouya men with us started to playfully insult the other foreigners who were passing by. "Look at how well these white men can speak Kouya! How long have you lived here and you still can't speak like that!" One trader had been there twenty-one years and still couldn't speak as well as we could, they said. Eddie protested that learning languages was our job, after all!

'Lucien, it seems, is a kind of "agent de police", a keeper of the peace. We were told later that these used to exist in all Kouya villages as the right hand men of the chief, to maintain law and order. Later, the idea was given up because it became too dangerous to be one of these people. They would be attacked at night when there was no one around. Lucien produced a whistle at one point, and blasted it to stop a squabble developing between two young men.

'Lucien was also hard on two children nearby, yelling at them to get off a tree trunk near the group. Because the chief was going to be late, still settling disputes and village affairs, we were asked: "Would you like to go and see the primary school?" They seemed very keen, so we agreed. It would be a chance to see the village. The sun was hot now, as we ambled up through the houses, searching for shade where it existed. There were lots of the traditional, circular kitchen houses with thatched roofs, with only one or two concrete block houses.

'We spotted yet another practical use for the corncob. Cut it up and it becomes a cork for a bottle! We must add this to our ever-growing list of uses in our anthropology file, alongside "spatula for frying pan", "toilet-paper", and so on.

'We noticed a middle-aged man beckoning to us enthusiastically from his little shelter. It had a green, leafy roof, and measured only about six feet by six. As we approached, we could make out the form of a much older man inside. Apparently it was the middle-aged man's father, and he insisted on greeting us. Eddie and I went in to say hello - he must have been ninety years of age. The very old man took our hands in his cupped ones, and blew on them, muttering an incantation - a blessing, no doubt.

"Have you money for palm wine?" he asked.
Drinking palm wine and providing money for palm wine seems to be the way of cementing the start of a relationship.

'Apologising that we could not linger today, perhaps next time we could sit down and chat, we continued through the village, noticing how the heavy rains had eroded the base of the mud-brick buildings. People were generally very pleased to hear us speaking Kouya. There was no feeling of hostility. One teenage girl, obviously scared, jumped up and hid as we approached: ghostly apparitions were rare in her village! Our Kouya companions laughed at her reaction. We passed a Mossi church, again a mud brick building.

'It was true, Brouafla Kouya had a remarkable school. Eddie and I agreed that it was the finest primary school we had seen anywhere in the Kouya area. Teachers' houses spaced well apart, with a clean lick of paint, and ceilings inside. The Headmaster shouted out a cheery "Bonjour!" from his porch. A Gouro, we were told. Teachers were mainly Jula, with one Gouro and one Baoulé. This tied in with the government's general policy of placing teachers from other language groups in Kouya (and other) villages, in order to promote French as the national, unifying language. It's a policy which works quite well. The village school was built in 1978. A tree-lined avenue led up to it - with red, yellow and orange Pride of China for hedging. We peeped inside the classrooms: plywood ceilings painted white, shady and very pleasant indeed.

'Then it was back through the village to continue our wait for the chief. By the way, that whole day we only saw one person smoking a cigarette: there is no money for that here. At last the chief arrived.

'We learned more about the true derivations of the Kouya village names, though it seems there are almost as many versions as there are Kouyas! The chief, tired from the day's business, just wanted a brief résumé of our mission, and suggested we fix another date to return and talk at length. We fixed it for a month later on a non-market day when he would have more time: Friday, 2nd February. We fixed it using

*the new Kouya calendar, and gave both the chief and his
Comité a copy.*

*'The 1990 calendars are selling very well. 300 were
printed, and half of them have gone already, being bought by
both Kouyas and foreigners. Good sellers are Gilbert of Dema,
fifty so far, Jacques of Dédiafla, forty so far, and Camus, who
has sold twenty in Dema and Vavoua.'*

*My scribe could tell that I was gradually running out of
steam. My voice was slowing down...*

*'There is little sign of "cadres" (educated, better-off
people) returning to live in Brouafla Kouya. Bertin was the only
cadre we met, and he was only back on a visit. No sign of
impressive buildings being constructed by rich sons of the
village, as in other places. Teachers' houses are attractive,
perhaps so that they will be encouraged to stay in such an
isolated place. Apparently they are very happy there. We
heard that Kouya cadres from the forest villages have retired
to neighbouring Bassam and Dédiafla, which are not quite so
remote.*

*'All in all, it was a very satisfying and promising day. We
noticed again how slowly things have to move at village level.
Why rush? No point in rushing. There's all the time in the
world...*

Zz Zz.'

*The scribe discerned that her source of information had
suddenly dried up!*

Dema, 16th January 1990

Let me tell you about one of our neighbours opposite.

*A young wife, Laurentine, has four young children. Her
uncle died in Vavoua, so she and the kids all went off to the
funeral. Because her husband hasn't turned up in Vavoua yet
with enough money (he works in the wood factory and won't
get paid till the end of the month), they insist on keeping the
girl with them in Vavoua. The poor husband, still only in his
twenties, had been sick for days with a bad chest infection,*

which I think was just turning to pneumonia. He had fever, a very high pulse rate, with rapid shallow breathing. We had some ampicillin which Heather gave him, and he is now making a good recovery, as well as taking a malaria treatment, for they usually develop malarial symptoms at the same time.

So with no wife to take care of him, unable to work, plus being expected to turn up with the money when there is none, he's feeling a bit sore about it. No wonder there is such a turnover of partners in all these marriage arrangements! The girl's family has more authority over her than her husband. She is often used to prise money out of the husband's family. How far from the Biblical 'leaving and cleaving' pattern!

We have puzzled over this for a long time - as to why marriage breakdown here is even worse than in the West - but it is becoming clear that often it is the parents who wreck the marriage, and not just problems between the couples themselves.

A big stress on Heather recently has been the number of sick people that come most days. While we want to show the love and compassion of Christ, it becomes very costly in terms of time, money and energy. People have not yet been paid for their cotton harvest, the world market-prices of coffee and cocoa have dropped frighteningly, so that growers are only getting one third to a half of what they got in the past. This means that money for buying medication at the chemist's in town is just not available.

Almost all of the cases that have come to us have recovered through prayer and medicine. It is great for the people concerned, but it is getting Heather a reputation that she really doesn't want! Yet what can you say when someone comes gasping for breath and with a raging fever, or a lady begs you to do something for her baby who has diarrhoea, is vomiting, and losing weight at an alarming rate?

There have been several weeks of noisy drumming in our neighbours' courtyards. Night and day, with little respite. January and February are often the most traumatic months for the local people. There have been five or six deaths in Dema village alone, and during funerals there is always a lot of mourning, wailing and frenetic beating of tamtams. Besides, there are always a great number of sick people among the mourners who subsequently come for medical help. The lack of sleep doesn't help either us or the mourners!

Perhaps eighty per cent of the illnesses that come our way are easily diagnosed and can be treated at village level. But we are looking for a long-term solution. We need to get someone trained for this work, but are not sure how to go about it. It would probably have to be a farmer, who would be available for an hour in the morning and an hour in the evening for a little clinic. We would have to work out a way to remunerate him for the time and energy he puts into it, as well as the patient's family paying at least a part of the cost of medication. There is a doctor in Vavoua, but it is costly to pay for transport, and then the medicines usually cost at least ten pounds, a whole week's wages. On most prescriptions there is a long list, and the villagers have difficulty knowing which are the vital medicines to buy. Often they just don't go, because they can't afford it, so it regularly happens that they die of something simple, the babies especially.

Furlough is coming up! We look forward to happy reunions in less than six months. I wonder how we'll adjust to living in Ireland again, in our own wee house on the Old Holywood Road for the first time in over eight years!

You would be amazed at how much Hilary has grown up, now speaking very clearly in English, making great progress during the school vacation month when Joy and Rachel were with her every day. She does miss them when they go back to school, but she makes up for it to some extent by making friends with everybody here. She is very outward going, just as Joy was at that age, quite happy to talk a mixture of mostly French and some English to our houseboy Marcel, English with us, Kouya to the children who come, and Kouya also to the pigs and chickens she chases away!

Dema, 18th February 1990

I was thinking of Psalm 103 verse 2 today: Bless the Lord O my soul, and forget not all His benefits. It helps to think back over the blessings and encouragements of recent months. Here are some of them.

I have had to be away from the village more than I would have wished on S.I.L. business, even as far as Kenya, to the Africa Area Meetings, where we assessed the progress of Bible Translation and Literacy work in the whole continent. How envious I am of Kenya's mild climate! Memories of harmonious Swahili singing and carpets of purple jacaranda blossom. I have also been fulfilling other responsibilities as Executive Committee chairman for Côte d'Ivoire and Mali. Praise the Lord for His protection on Heather and Hilary during my frequent absences. Heather says she often feels as safe in the village as she would anywhere in the world. It is true: we are surrounded by friends.

Another encouragement is that six Kouya Christians were baptised recently. As well as that, there are five Kouyas, three men and two women, presently attending the introductory course at the W.E.C. Bible College in Zuénoula. Then the Christmas Conference was a joyful time with very good ministry based on the translated Epistle of James. The women commented on how helpful the teaching had been for them this year. At the end, old Baï Laurent thanked the Lord that His Word was 'like sugar, and not bitter like Nivaquine' (malaria medicine).

Linguistic work has been progressing too. I would ask for prayer for strength to complete the write-up on Kouya phonology, which is to be published soon. The Kouya-French dictionary is growing rapidly. Eddie, Emile and I have been working together on it. Yesterday, we reached the thousand word mark. It is a more time-consuming and painstaking job than you might think! Please pray for perseverance in these tasks.

A great shock in January was the sudden death of the

chief of Gouabafla, the village where our co-workers the Arthurs live. He was widely respected. This chief had been taking great pride in learning to read Kouya, and we were touched to learn that his French Bible, the Epistle of James in Kouya, and the Reading Guide were among the prized possessions which surrounded him during the funeral.

We have now been back in the village for seven months. We have been able to get some practical jobs organised and completed in between times. We now have screen doors up inside the house; a grading machine from the wood factory has levelled the 'drive'; a temporary fence has been erected at the back which should keep the goats from eating all the flowers there; and the well-diggers have finished the well in Emile's courtyard next door. Emile's sister, Germaine, won't have so far to go to fetch our water now.

We are both very relieved that for the next two months I need to do very little travelling. It will be good to have more time to talk and plan together. We are very aware of our need for wisdom in deciding priorities in these last months before furlough, hoping to reach Northern Ireland by the 7th of August or thereabouts, Lord willing.

Lord willing. How true! We can make our plans, but the Lord determines our steps (Proverbs 16:9, New Living Translation). Our world, which had been gradually settling down into a place where we felt contented with our roles and with the progress being made in most departments, was about to be turned upside down. I gave my version of events at the outset of this book. The following is Heather's account of what happened. It was typed up from a tape recording made by Heather in hospital in Abidjan, which she sent to her brother Stephen, a doctor in N. Ireland.

It is now **Friday, 23rd March 1990.**

Stephen,

    'I'm sure you've been wondering what's been going on in the last few weeks... 'Well, I've been trying to get together some facts and figures for you. It's taken me quite a while to sort out all the medical details, but I'm just so grateful to God to be alive! And for the fact that we were in Abidjan at the time when I needed this emergency operation.

    'I had been feeling very tired all through January and February. The holiday at the beach in Grand Bassam in December had been great and set us on our feet, but I realised that anything extra happening was just putting me down again. I was struggling, just tired out all the time. We were in good spirits though, we really loved being back in the village, and Philip was happy working with Emile again.

    'We were coming up to furlough, and it's very common for translators to get extremely run down in their last year. We were doing our best to pace ourselves, and make sure we took adequate siestas, with good food and rest. It had been a strain for me to some extent with Philip travelling up and down so much to Abidjan. When I'm in the village on my own I tend not to sleep so well, for I hear all the noises, though it may be nothing more than a goat on a nocturnal ramble, or a dog going past the window. All the same, if Philip's not there I'm inclined to hear everything. I'm listening out for Hilary at the same time. So I'm always glad when he's back, although I've adapted to some degree to staying in the village by myself.

    'When he is away, I have to deal with everybody that comes. So many requests, messages to be passed on, or... well, the usual medical help people need for diarrhoea, malaria, or dysentery. Eight out of ten cases we really can help, and many children's lives are saved because of some very basic medical care. Especially when you get to know these people, and they're your friends, and they become sick, you can't turn them away. There at home you would be telling your next-door neighbour to go to the doctor, but here if you give folks that advice, they neither have money for the prescriptions nor money for the transport. And in any case, there is only one doctor for the whole region, about two hundred villages and Vavoua town. So this is something which I have got involved in. Thankfully we have tried to keep Philip out of the medical side from the very beginning. But when he's away, everyone who comes for whatever reason deals with me. When Philip's there he can take a lot of it, people coming greeting for different things.

'So we were doing our best to be sensible and not get overtired, but strange things were happening to me physically... I wasn't sure whether I was miscarrying or not. I was uncertain for over a week... I had felt very tired, but fortunately we had a super American girl called Becky Moffitt staying with us for a few days. We had met her once in Vichy, France, at the assembly there, and she came out for six months to Côte d'Ivoire. This was her second visit to us in the village, and she was a great help when Philip was away, taking care of Hilary and letting me sleep every afternoon... The problem didn't stop, so I went to see Sylvia, the doctor at Vavoua School. She thought that I had miscarried and should go down to see a gynaecologist in Abidjan as soon as possible.

'That was somewhere near the end of February. We phoned up and booked me into the same clinic where Hilary was born. But just before leaving Dema, I started to feel very ill. On Monday 26th February I couldn't eat anything. I knew there was something wrong when I couldn't eat my cheese at lunch, for I really love dairy products! For the following few days I couldn't eat anything except fruit and a piece of bread. The chills that came on Tuesday 27th and 28th made us think it must be malaria. It was ninety degrees and I had a pure wool blanket over me, along with a dressing gown and a cardigan! The obvious thing was to treat for malaria. I started to take Quinimax. Then the fever cooled off a bit and I thought maybe the treatment was working, but I still felt terrible, and could hardly do anything. When I had some energy I did a bit of packing and gathered things together for the journey. You can't rush over these things. It's like closing up your house in Northern Ireland for an indefinite period and moving down to the west coast of Ireland, a day's journey away. With all the arrangements that have to be made for the employees, and so on, it's hard to get away immediately. Sometimes if you take it all slowly you're in better shape when you reach Abidjan.

'So we travelled down on Friday 2nd March. Philip was telling me that I was actually looking surprisingly well, and I was saying that I had never felt so ill in my life! We realise now it was the beginning of my skin turning yellow. At that stage you have a glow with hepatitis, and you just look as though you have a nice tan. Marcel came down with us. I had an appointment the very next day at the GOCI clinic, and was taken in right away for a D & C, which took place on Sunday 4th. That seemed to go well. With being asthmatic, I always have to alert them to that because of the anaesthetic. I stayed in the clinic for three days altogether; I couldn't eat one single meal of the terrific food that they brought. I could eat nothing but fruit and bread. I realise now this was the very best thing for me, for you're supposed to be completely off fat with hepatitis, so at least I wasn't doing my liver any more damage. Because I had said I thought I had malaria, they put me on the drip for another three days. Well, I was starting to feel so ill and I knew it had something to do with the drip - Quiniform. I just couldn't bear it, and I had to beg them to take me off it! Meanwhile they got a negative malaria test result back, and eventually they let me stop it. I felt as though I was being poisoned, and know now with hindsight that since it wasn't malaria at all, but hepatitis, continuing the malaria treatment had been making me feel terrible.

'I got out of GOCI clinic and turned yellow the next day. It was then we realised what the illness was, and we started to piece some of these things together. On the following day I came to the Canadian clinic here to a GP, had the bilirubin tested and it was obvious that it was hepatitis. The treatment was to be total bed rest, fat-free diet, then regular weekly testing for the bilirubin.

'Feeling somewhat relieved to at least know what was wrong, Philip and I went back home to the flat on the S.I.L. centre, trying to come to terms with the hepatitis, making out lists of shopping and chores for Marcel, especially for what he should give me to eat as he uses oil in cooking most of the time. Our friends at the centre helped out with meals as they were able. It was difficult for Marcel to see to everything. He generally cooked for Philip and Hilary, while Annemarie, our Swiss hostess, kindly helped out with fat-free food for me from time to time.

'I had been trying to adjust to the fact that I would be off my feet for several weeks with hepatitis, wondering how I would put the time in, and thinking: "I'll have to do something with these weeks so that they won't just be sheer frustration." I was reading women's magazines and other bits and pieces that were lying around the centre. I hadn't the strength even to do embroidery. But I decided that I would listen to some tapes. I had been listening to David Watson, Chuck Swindoll and others, good Bible messages. I thought I might as well fill my mind with some of these things while I had to be on my back.

'I was starting to feel better, getting up a little though not for long, feeling pretty contented, and the tapes were helping. On Monday 12th during the day I felt good, very yellow, but happy enough. On the evening of Monday 12th, though I hadn't been to sleep yet, I felt as though I was going to sleep well. I went to the bathroom after midnight, but started to lose consciousness on the way. I had this terrible pain in my lower abdomen. I broke out all over in a very profuse sweat, and had to call Philip to come and get me. I was on the floor. I realised I would need to go to the hospital urgently, I didn't know what this was. Having had the D & C of course we presumed all that side of things was taken care of.

'Philip woke Jan Stoker, a nurse in the apartment next door, and called her to come and see me. He quickly made arrangements for another colleague to stay with Hilary, and the nurse's husband stayed with their children while Jan accompanied me to the hospital.

'I don't remember them carrying me down the stairs. Jan was a great comfort in the car while Philip could concentrate on driving. She was with me in the back seat with my head in her lap. She was very reassuring - nurses know all the little comforting things to do! I knew she was praying for me, and very supportive, and it was a help.

'When we arrived at casualty, the first reaction of the staff was to treat me as a hepatitis case, probably thinking of liver failure or something. I kept saying, "I have this pain in my abdomen," and tried to keep talking about that... Amazingly, I was able to understand and talk French any time I was conscious. I suppose I've dealt with so many sick Africans, my medical French is pretty fluent by now!

'It was about one o'clock in the morning by the time I was admitted, and after that there were lots of blood tests. They test you for Aids on admission, so that they know what they're dealing with, for the protection of the staff, and also to make sure that you will not sue them afterwards for contracting it there. I'm sure there must have been six or seven different staff who came and went. I was in a lot of pain, and in and out of consciousness during this time. I found them very, very pleasant. Hours must have passed. They scheduled an operation for two o'clock in the afternoon. I still didn't know what was wrong with me! This then had to be brought forward to one p.m. and it became a real emergency. I could hear them rushing about, all systems go, and running round in a hurry. My iron level went down from 11 to 4 during the twelve hours I had been in hospital in this limbo state, there was so much internal bleeding. They said that something had showed up on a scan, that there was a lot of infection and they were obliged to operate quickly. I didn't know when I went in to theatre that it was an ectopic pregnancy. There were three doctors and an anaesthetist as well as nursing staff. (I found this out later when we got the bill, and saw who had been in attendance. I obviously couldn't keep track of this at the time!)

'I actually was fighting for my life for several hours, and

I was aware of it. It was an absolutely amazing experience... to know that you could easily go one way or the other, just an amazing experience... I'll talk more about it when I get home. I would have expected that someone so ill would be unconscious and not aware, but I was tremendously lucid in my thinking, and the things that pass through one's mind...!

'Some of the words from those taped messages I had been listening to came back to me while I was in intensive care, both before and after the operation. Chuck Swindoll had spoken on "Suffering according to the will of God", from 1 Peter 4. He drew out four simple points - what you should do when you find yourself suffering (when it's not something you brought on yourself):

Point one: Don't be surprised as though something strange were happening. I was saying: How can this be? I've had one thing after another. I can't believe this is happening!
Point two: Rejoice. God is in control.
Point three: Commit yourself to your faithful Creator
Point four: Do what is right (not that I could do anything much for myself, but at least I could try to have the right attitudes.)

'Well, this came back to my mind over and over, and it was a real comfort. I had no fear for myself. I was heartbroken about how Philip would tell the girls and the family... but I had no fear for myself, which was great. I have often wondered, when it comes to the bit, will I be just as scared of the process as any unbeliever? So that was a good experience.

'Those were very tough hours for Philip, because the big Togolese gynaecologist had gone out beforehand to tell him that it would be a difficult operation. He was trying to prepare Philip in some way for the fact that it mightn't be successful. You wouldn't normally choose to operate on somebody who was, as the surgeon put it, "lying there so pale, and as yellow as an Asian." He wasn't looking forward to it. He told me this afterwards.

'I thank God for his skill, and for God's protecting hand

on me. I lost four litres of blood, so the report said. I'm sure there couldn't have been much left! I don't know what the body would normally contain. And then this had to be replaced by Aids-tested blood. They run a test on each little sachet which comes to this hospital, even though it is supposed to be tested already. I remembered you telling me to make sure of this, Stephen, if ever the need arose.

'The blood transfusions went on for several days after the operation. I was attached to all the usual things - drips in each arm and one in my neck, the heart monitor and the catheter, and something through my nose in case I had trouble breathing.

'What else was there? I can't remember. I just know I had to sleep on my back for three nights with too many lights on, and it was torture. I can't sleep on my back! The main feeling for us both was relief that the operation had been successful. I was still in a very weak state of course, still needing the transfusions. We were comforted by the thought that people at home already knew about the hepatitis, and so were praying for me, also on the prayer chain in Lurgan, even with their limited knowledge of the situation. This was a comfort for me to know.

'Philip has been great throughout the crisis. We're thinking of appointing him crisis management director in S.I.L.! (Yet another hat.) But he has become very, very exhausted and needs time to process all that we have come through. Because when we were going through it, we didn't know what was happening, we didn't know what the problem was, what the sickness was, or what it would lead to. It's just now that we're trying to get it all sorted out.

'What we do know is that this Canadian clinic is probably the only place here which could have coped with this kind of emergency, and it's the only place where there would have been enough safe blood. B+ isn't the most common type.

'They wouldn't, they couldn't give me anything to make me sleep. I was just gasping for some painkillers - which you would normally get after major abdominal surgery. But they couldn't give me anything because of my liver not being able to tolerate it. So I appreciated all the prayers that carried me through that difficult time. I was really grateful to be alive, and for the many precious thoughts that had gone through my mind during it all.

'So I've been twelve days now in this hospital, getting my strength back. Little things keep going wrong like nosebleeds, slurred speech due to an infection on the root of my tongue caused by one of the tubes, and pain under the incision. But the staff reassure me that these are minor matters that I just need to put up with, that the major crisis is over.

'At the same time I kept remembering that God was in control, God is Sovereign. Nothing would happen that would take Him by surprise, if it wasn't His time for me to die. Mostly the things that helped me were words to focus my mind on, words from the Bible. I didn't have very much imagery. I remember feeling disappointed at not "seeing" more!! (I didn't see the "pearly gates"!) I remember thinking with a slight touch of exasperation "Where are those angels?!" and then lying thinking "Ah well, maybe it's a good thing they haven't come yet, maybe they're not coming..." Another comforting thought was the image of the Lord's everlasting arms around about me. That was something that came back to me often. These thoughts could all have come in a split second. I had them probably somewhere between being operated on and coming out of the anaesthetic, because it was when I came round I remembered them. I could hear the staff talking about hypothermia, and that they couldn't get the blood pressure back up...

'I remember thinking: "It's too much work fighting on, I know now why people just want to go to be with the Lord." They must just want you to let them go. And then I would keep bringing myself back and saying, "No, now you mustn't give up, you must keep fighting, you shouldn't give up!"

'You know the way people pray: "If You bring me safely through this I'll do such and such..."? Well, I realised... that if

He brought me safely through this... I would just want to go back and do the same thing... I would just want to go back to the village... talk to the neighbours and try to learn Kouya, give them worm medicine (!), and sit for hours in church meetings. And that for me was a great thing. It showed me... that I was doing what I really wanted to do in life. That's another thing that came very clearly to me. It was so enormously reassuring.

'When I eventually came round from the anaesthetic, the staff were all so pleased and said: "You're going to be all right now, you're going to be all right now." This was before Philip was allowed back in. I was surprised they were so emotionally involved. Somehow that really helped. I said, "It's God who allowed me to be down here. You know, I'm usually up in the village." They all agreed, yes, it was God. Sounds blunt in English, but in French it's all right. "C'est Dieu." You don't come across many atheists here. Whatever their faith, animistic or Christian or whatever, they would attribute this kind of close shave to God having helped. It's amazing how aware I had been of how close I had come... to crossing over the line... and this was confirmed by everybody who came to see me afterwards.

'I told Philip some of this later, and he said, "You should get these things written down before you forget them." So that's why I'm recording so much on tape to you Stephen. I haven't the energy to write. We're both just so full of gratitude. From time to time I get very weepy. I suppose my emotions are now starting to catch up. I'm in great form most of the day, but every so often I remember just what God has graciously brought us through. I think gratitude is the overwhelming feeling at the moment.'

When Heather felt strong enough to face the journey, she flew home to Northern Ireland with Hilary. Seven weeks later, on 25th May 1990, I joined her, after packing up in the village, and collecting Joy and Rachel from Vavoua

International School. They began to attend Strandtown Primary, my old school, and we lived together on the Old Holywood Road. It took some time for the feeling of shell shock to wear off.

Africa was never far from our minds. How was Emile, we wondered? He had been through the mangle with us, though from a distance: there had not been time for Heather to say proper goodbyes. Our colleagues the Arthurs and Hamiltons kept us in touch with what was happening in the Kouya area. One September morning, the following letter came through the door. It was from John Hamilton in Vavoua School, and it encouraged us greatly to realise afresh that though we could not be there personally, the Lord worked on in the lives of Kouya Christians:

Dear Philip and Heather,

On Saturday the Christians in the nearby village of Bouitafla had the dedication of their new prayer house. This village has been resistant to Christianity for many years. The few Christians there were would walk to the evangelical church in Vavoua. However Monsieur Barthe the deputy chief of Bouitafla is an elder in Vavoua, and he has been one of the leading influences in getting the prayer house built. Also the assistant pastor in town, a young man called Konaté, comes from Bouitafla, though not a Kouya himself.

Monsieur Barthe had borrowed thirty chairs and some benches from the school for the event. Also another young man arrived, asking could he cut some flowers. We later saw them displayed in a Coke bottle on the table at the front of the new church.

We were not the only invited guests. There were elders from the Vavoua church and from some of the outlying Kouya churches. Also present were the three teachers from the village primary school and the village chief and some of his elders. None of these are Christians. All the guests and the Christians were seated inside a shelter made of branches and palm leaves which stretched out from the door of the prayer house. The door itself was open but covered by a sheet of roofing tin and across the doorway was a white strip of paper. A pair of rusty scissors hung from a convenient nail.

We sang a lot as is usual in African church meetings. Then everyone had to be introduced at length. Two pastors spoke, Jean Guéyé, the one who is just leaving Vavoua after twenty-four years, and his successor, pastor Félix. Perhaps the most moving speech of the afternoon came from an old man, Baï Laurent, the longest-standing Kouya believer. Up to then he had sat very quietly, looking rather stern. When the Bouitafla Christians were asked to stand, he was obviously moved to see so many - about thirty. He looked towards the back and said that some of the old men present were the ones who had beaten him up and thrown him out when many years ago he had come as a young man to evangelise in the village! With so many non-Christians present, it was great to see him and other speakers taking the opportunity to state the gospel.

Eventually all the speeches were over, and the opening ceremony began. Pastor John Guéyé stood facing the door, the tin now removed. As he prayed, he held the scissors aloft, and then, as we all sang and clapped, he cut the paper strip, and we all followed him in procession around the inside of the small building. The first to enter symbolically threw open the windows which up to now had remained closed.

We stayed for the meal of pork and rice. We felt it was a great privilege to have been involved in the ceremony and ask you to pray for that small group of Christians in Bouitafla, that the Lord will protect them and cause them to grow in number as they witness for Him in the village.

John

GOING UNDER

1991

After Heather's serious illness, she needed a long time in which to recover gradually from all she had been through. We spent eighteen months in the UK altogether, most of that time in Northern Ireland. Then we tried again to pick up where we had left off, and to embark on serious Bible Translation, returning to the village in November 1991. But it was beginning to seem as if each time we attempted to re-start, yet another serious obstacle would get in the way.

This time was no exception.

Things began brightly and well. We had the help of Susan Jordan a young teacher from Bangor, Northern Ireland. She was doing a great job of teaching Hilary in the mornings in the village, which freed Heather to do a great deal of literacy work. Hilary's leadership qualities were starting to emerge, and she would often arrive at her wee school-desk with her own agenda for that day. Susan had the wisdom to let her have her own way... sometimes!

We were aware that Christianity was starting to take root in Kouya culture, but the culture as a whole was very much in a state of flux. One bright, sunny morning (most were!), this struck me very forcibly as I watched some children at play.

I was sitting in our makeshift office mulling over our draft translation of James, and my eyes drifted out through the open door down towards the neighbouring courtyards, thinking how empty they seemed. Just a few women and older folk scattered here and there, sporadic pounding of pestles, the sheep, the goats, just the ordinary sounds of morning in the village.

Then I suddenly became aware of a group of perhaps nine or ten Kouya children playing on the track nearby. Their game seemed interesting. I watched them. The James translation could wait for a moment.

It became clear that they were playing church, and were totally absorbed in their game. They were pretending to worship a sacred tree. They had a leader, aged about six, who knew what he was doing, and certainly knew what he expected of his little congregation. He was the expert. 'Emile,' I whispered, 'Look over there!' Emile followed my finger, and his face broke into a quiet grin.

By now the leader was lifting up a large log, to which his little followers were paying due reverence. 'What are they doing?' I asked quietly. 'Worshipping the sacred tree,' replied Emile, still smiling. 'How does he know what to do?' 'He's seen the grown-ups do it.'

Before long, our leader had them all chanting after him in chorus, sometimes nodding their heads vigorously in unison. They sat in a semi-circle around him, but then he made them all stand up, genuflect and bow down with heads to the dirt. He tapped each on the head with his stick, and they had to repeat words after him. They looked for all the world like Moslems at prayer. They got up again. Then he had them stand and repeat 'Jesu, Jesu', cross themselves, put their hands together in prayer, and the ceremony ended with them all repeating 'Amen, Amen' after him!

It was intriguing, as it seemed to symbolise what was going on among the Kouyas at that point in their history. Their traditional animistic practices were being replaced or sometimes placed alongside Islam and Christianity, the new agents of change. Islam, embraced by ethnic groups in the north of the country, had not taken hold among the Kouyas. The children would have witnessed the practices of the immigrant communities of the village, no doubt.

The service over, off went the leader down the winding path through the courtyards, his 'iroko tree' on his head, while his congregation of three- and four-year-olds toddled in dutiful single file behind him, all repeating their chants, and clasping some sacred object to their own heads as they went.

In certain ways, Christianity was becoming an integral part of Kouya life. A very small part, in relation to the whole. But definitely, a threshold of acceptance had been crossed. We too, as a family, were feeling part of the Kouya society as never before. We were no longer a curiosity, and it was comfortable to sense that we could deepen relationships without being seen as specimens in a goldfish bowl. In short we were enjoying ourselves in the culture, and learning so much. Our friends made sure we were never lonely.

Gabriel

'Filipu!'

He used to make me jump out of my skin. I'd just be settling into a quiet evening's work, or enjoying a romantic interlude with Heather, when the call would come. It came at eight o'clock, I was going to say sharp, but that would be misleading in a village of nearly three thousand people and only three hundred watches! Anyway, around eight p.m., every night without fail that we were in the village, Gabriel would show up.

Not the angel of course, but my little Kouya friend, who like so many of my friends, had taken the initiative and adopted me. Mostly I didn't mind: Gabriel had lost his father early in life, and had taken me on as a substitute, someone to talk things over with, man-to-man.

But Gabriel was not a man yet, he was a rather awkward teenager, on whom the social graces had not yet descended. And so it was that his broken-voiced greeting would rip through the open windows and the after-dinner tranquility of our home. With a sigh and a command to my nerves to settle down, I would push back my wooden chair, and realise that I had another conversation to navigate before we could close up for the night, after the people-pressures of the day.

Yes, mostly I didn't mind, for ours was a two-way relationship. He was my little friend, I was his big friend. He spoke only Kouya, I was forced not to use any French. Once together, side-by-side on the veranda, our conversation was effortless. 'Intense' was not a word I would use to describe our interchanges. Indeed, my only effort lay in the occasional injection of some semi-stimulating comment on life to stop myself falling asleep.

'Gabriel, you have come!'
'Eh? Ah, Filipu, you have stayed!'
Pause. Our spirits quietly say hello too.
'Mm. Gabriel, what news this evening?'
'No! Nothing at all! Just an evening greeting.' Then, somewhat awkwardly, 'And what about things here?'
'No. Here there is peace. Problems there are none...'
And so we would follow the routine. No steps could be omitted. I tell him the news of my day, he tells me his. He appears to be totally astounded by anything unpredictable that has happened to disrupt my life. I for my part search around for anything different that might be interesting to him.

His turn comes. Here there is nothing new. He tells me he's been to his fields today. But he didn't do much, he felt tired: 'I... did a bit of weeding here and there... nothing to speak of. '
'It rained the day before yesterday,' I venture.
'Yes.'
'Did it fall on your fields?'
'The rain fell small small.'

Feel like saying: 'Well, that'd make it easier to hoe, wouldn't it? Not every day you get a rain like that!' But realise before starting that it is totally beyond my Kouya at that time of night, so resort to a few thoughtful 'Mm .. mms' of the type that my friend Gabriel understands very well.

I think that is what I appreciate most about Gabriel. He is most understanding, ever supportive of my feeble attempts to speak his language. I know they are feeble, he knows they are feeble, but what is infinitely more important at that moment is the enormous silvery moon rising slowly behind our teak trees. We watch it in companionable silence.

'Well Gabriel, I suppose it's late. I should be thinking about bed.'

This is naughty of me. I am breaking protocol. It should be Gabriel who says that. But, as I mentioned, the social graces were taking a while to develop fully in his life. But he catches on.

'Yes, I must go. I'm... whacked.'

We sit a moment longer. He seems to have forgotten he's going. Has he fallen asleep in the chair? Suddenly, with a creak, he sits forward. Encouragingly, I follow suit,. He rises, shuffles around in search of sandals. I stretch out a hand in the dark in his general direction. He finds it with ease.

'Gabriel, thank you. Walk well.'

'I've heard. We are there tomorrow.'

'Yes.'

And as night engulfs his silhouette at the end of the terrace, a paternal feeling creeps round my heart. I check around in my mind. Lights are out, doors are locked, mousetraps are set, Gabriel has gone.

Now we can sleep.

Emile Zola

Our Emile Zola was not the French novelist. His real name was Diko Emile, but like everyone else in Dema village he had a nickname. Diko Emile's nickname was Emile Zola.

I never did figure out whether we hired Emile Zola or whether he hired us! He 'became' our gardener, and our night-guard for the house we built in Dema. If anyone had a gift for guarding, it was Emile. He guarded the church-door during services, leaving his post only to go round and prod the congregation awake with his stick during long sermons. He would guard visitors' suitcases. He guarded the projector during film-shows. He became custodian of the Kouya literature when it began to appear. He was supposed to sell them too, but Emile was not a salesman, he was a guard. He made sure none were borrowed or stolen. And a more faithful, conscientious minder of houses, tender of gardens or custodian of books you could not hope to find anywhere in this world.

There were things we knew about Emile, there was much that was secret. We knew that he loved to come up to his (our) garden after toiling in his fields during the day. There, regular as clockwork, he would sprawl on the uncomfortable wooden chair, and somehow go to sleep. But not a deep sleep. If an undesirable person or animal approached, he would be immediately awake and alert, ready for offensive action.

We knew also that his pride and joy was the old lawn-mower that I had bought for five pounds on a Belfast pavement outside a flower-shop. I had dismantled it, and sent it out in a barrel. This became Emile Zola's piece of technology, which he would self-consciously parade up and down the lawn in front of an admiring band of village children.

Then it was obvious also that he hated change. Change would confuse him terribly, and he would require two or three attempts in order to explain a new procedure. His natural stutter did not help here. I caught myself stuttering back in Kouya one day in my efforts to get the message through.

One day, he came to us in a real fluster.

'P-P-Patron, patron, where is the book, have you seen the book?'

'What book?'

'The book in the bookcase. Over there. C-Come! C-Come and see!'

Heather and I followed him round to the other side of our house, to the room, which doubled as a study and a guard-room, where he slept when we were absent. He entered, and stopped in front of the large bookcase full of several dozen volumes.

'It was here!' he said, pointing to a fairly large gap, then turned to us with imploring eyes. 'Have you s-seen it?'

I shrugged, shook my head, but Heather said: 'Oh yes, you mean the hymnbook? I was looking at it yesterday. Hymns of Praise.'

Emile visibly relaxed.

'May I borrow it back for a few moments, Madame?'

Heather opened the door, which led into the inner courtyard of the house, and soon reappeared with the thick, blue book. She handed it over to Emile, who took it gratefully, then began to shake it vigorously. Out fluttered several banknotes! He stooped to pick them up.

We had not known, but this had been Emile's secret bank.

The problem never recurred. We fancied Emile's second choice of book had a thicker layer of dust on top of it.

But we never really found out about his family. He did not encourage them to visit him at his place of work. For a time a girl, or rather a young woman, appeared on the scene. Drawing me aside, Emile confidentially explained who she was, pointing vigorously in her direction. She looked not at all abashed. She was his 'ŋwnɔ, his 'woman' or 'wife'. Marriage for Kouyas traditionally consists in taking a girl to live with you under your roof, and paying off instalments on the bride-wealth to her family, nothing more elaborate than that.

He seemed to be asking me, as his employer, for my approval of his choice, so I nodded and smiled encouragingly, and he looked satisfied. Like admiring a friend's new car.

We never did find out quite what her status was. She disappeared off the scene, and Emile Zola reverted to his comfortable bachelor routines. He was such a creature of habit, I suspect he had never really left them.

Lament

There is a certain sadness about the Africa I know.

You see, there is no way of escape. You work hard in your fields. You grow enough food to feed your family. But if you work too hard, the climate makes you sick. And even if you do not kill yourself with work, malaria may well do the job for you.

If you work hard, if it rains at the right time and you have a productive harvest, your extended family is so large, that even a big harvest from your coffee or cocoa dwindles to a small return for each member of your family. The extended family is a black hole: you throw your money into it, and you may as well kiss it good-bye.

And yet you can not abandon them, and go your own way. If you do, your name will be blackened, jealousy will rear its head out of the jungle, and sorcery may be used to poison you. Your family is your support! Your children are your retirement provision! But your family is also the grave of your dreams.

You can ask a family-member for anything you like. His radio, her tee shirt. But if you become rich and return to the village, you will be lucky to escape in your underpants. That is what they say, and they are right.

So why work hard? What is the point of making money? Stay poor, and get on well with your brothers and sisters. A poor man is not pestered. He walks undisturbed around the village.

There is a certain sadness about the Africa I know.

Hey, the Chief's Wearing my Pyjamas!

You see, I had been sent out two pairs. One olive-green, the other light brown. Very smart they were too, with darker green and darker brown trimmings. Overly adventurous colours for me, being a departure from my customary blue or grey, but just about acceptable in the bedroom.

I had tried the green one on first. Unfortunately, whatever material the pyjamas were made from they did not 'breathe' sufficiently in the heat and humidity, so I could only wear them on the very rare cool night. The brown pair stayed in its clear plastic cover.

Until, that is, it was time to visit the chief, after a long absence from the village. What present could I bring him? I thought around and finally decided on the brown pyjamas. Our chief was growing frail now, and would appreciate the extra warmth at night. So Heather and I wended our way down the village through the courtyards, and were very cordially received by the old chief, as he sat in the shade of his veranda, clasping his carved walking stick between his knees. On this was a 'Jesus' sticker. How he had got the sticker, we have no idea!

We went through the protocol, so familiar to us now we could do it in our sleep. A gourd with practically non-alcoholic palm-wine was passed around the group: participants blew away the surface flies before taking the customary sip. It was sweet and not unpleasant to the taste. The conversation was free flowing and enjoyable. Heather and I felt pleased with how much Kouya we could speak and understand now.

Just before leaving, we gave our present. Always gracious towards us, he accepted the gift with delight on his wrinkled brown face. The pyjamas would suit him, I thought to myself.

I had imagined I would never see the pyjamas again, for obvious reasons. But I was wrong.

One day, I was driving in Vavoua town close to the Préfecture, where the Préfet, the area's principal administrator, had his offices. This was where the suits, shirts and ties congregated in the town. And who should cross the road in front of me, heading for the Préfet's office with a retinue of our Dema brothers, but the old chief. I rubbed my eyes in disbelief. He was sporting a panama hat, and one very smart pair of brown pyjamas, with an unmistakable dark brown trim!

Then it dawned on me. We had not explained what they were for. Our gift to keep him warm at night had become his Sunday-best suit!

Flirting, Kouya-style

We know how it happens in our own culture, the little side-ways glances, the feigned lack of interest, electricity, chemistry, and so on. Every culture has its own peculiar courtship techniques. But it took us a while to catch on to the Kouya way. And for good reason. It mostly happens after dark, and it is often very indirect.

There were the more obvious approaches, but it didn't look to us as if these were being very successful. Here, the boy, adolescent or man could be seen to grab the arm of a passing unmarried girl or woman, and attempt to pull her towards him. The strength of her resistance probably sent a return message to him. He might let go, and try again once they got into conversation. It was not usually clear to us whether she liked the attention or not, or whether this interchange led to anything, but it was certainly the direct method.

The indirect approach we learned was usually far more successful, and satisfactory, for both sides. A father could see a girl he would like for his son, and approach the father of the girl in question. Chemistry? Electricity? Family compatibility was more important. This arrangement often worked out fine, though it was known for young men to flee their home-villages, rather than marry a woman they did not want.

Or a man could make an approach through a third party, a friend or brother of the girl in question. If she refused, he would not then lose face. This was a very popular way.

Kouya girls do not have to be passive in the mating game. If a girl takes a fancy to a certain man, she will generally make sure she passes by his courtyard on her way to the well, preferably singing to attract his attention. Kind of taking the dog for a walk equivalent.

If there are no wells conveniently near his house, she has another option. She may offer, usually indirectly through an intermediary, to wash his clothes! She will send the message that she is doing some washing, and could include some of his if he likes. He, if he wishes to respond, will be wise to give a few of his best, cleanest clothes for washing. Dirty socks are not recommended. If all his clothes are already clean by chance, he can let her know, and well, no harm done!

Gradually, we were learning to interpret the cultural cues.

Dreaming in Church

In those days, the church services were never totally predictable. The Spirit of the Lord was at work, and while proceedings were not always neat and tidy, they were definitely orderly. We usually had an open time during the meeting in Dema where believers could give impromptu testimonies.

'Then I saw a barrel. It was blue, and it was gliding down a rope from heaven. Right down to where I was standing!' The Kouya lady continued excitedly:

'As I watched, it sped up, then hit the ground at my feet! It burst, opening up like an orange. Out spilled the most beautiful cloth you ever saw, rolls and rolls of it. It covered the ground around me. It was just amazing!'

She paused, her eyes wide, reliving her dream. We waited for an interpretation. This time the meaning came to me as I sat there, in the form of a Bible verse from the Epistle of James. I stood up, and quoted it: *'Every good and perfect gift is from above, coming down from the Father of the heavenly lights, who does not change like shifting shadows.'*

I explained that the Lord had given His gifts to His people, each for the benefit of the other, and for His glory. He had given generously, not holding back. The rolls of cloth symbolised these gifts.

James was the one New Testament book we had translated into Kouya by that stage, and here was confirmation of its message through a visual image, a dream. Where we had often previously not given much credence to dreams, this was not the Kouya way. Great significance was attached to them, and meanings were sought. To them, the world of the dream was as 'real' as the concrete world. We had to acknowledge that many times, in the early days of the Kouya church, the Lord spoke to the Christians through dreams. Often, in Kouyaland, the interpretation would be close in meaning to the Scriptures we were translating.

So that Sunday morning, we rejoiced together. There was more than enough spiritual cloth provided to go round the church body many times. Our God was a bountiful God.

1992

But as the months went on, we started to sense that Heather was not doing well physically. She was trying very hard to cope, but she was struggling. Looking back, despite the fact that we had had eighteen months of furlough, we had probably returned too soon. We had not given Heather enough time to recover fully from her trauma, physically or emotionally. I felt much to blame for that, realising that I had perhaps been pushing too hard for her to get better, even unconsciously, rather than waiting until she was definitely fully ready.

The culmination was two serious asthma attacks while in Abidjan, after which we decided together that Heather should return to Ireland for a while for a break, taking Hilary with her. They were to return after six weeks, as Heather and I had been invited to lead a Spiritual Retreat in Burkina Faso for newly arrived S.I.L. personnel. We had been planning for this together, and had both been looking forward to it.

So Heather and Hilary left together.

The day that Heather phoned me from Britain to say that she couldn't come back remains forever imprinted on my memory. My heart sank, and sank even lower when I realised the implications. Once again the pack-up, the moving of continents, telling Joy and Rachel, whom we had settled into Vavoua School, that we all had to return to Britain yet again.

We decided that it was best for me to wait and keep the Spiritual Retreat commitment, and then to take our two older girls back.

This time, in my heart of hearts, I doubted seriously whether we would ever return to Ivory Coast as a family. I had seen other families leave in similar circumstances, and for many it was a final farewell.

My spirits were at an all-time low as I spoke at that Retreat. I felt the pain of separation from Heather very keenly: we would have enjoyed leading these sessions together. But I tried to speak honestly about what might be ahead for the new folks in terms of victories and challenges, just as it was for the Children of Israel in the desert before the Promised Land was reached. I hope what I shared was of benefit. What was for sure was that these Scriptures certainly ministered to my own heavy heart.

FACING FAILURE

'Maybe you should consider Leave of Absence?'

We were speaking with our British Wycliffe director, who was taking us through the range of options open to us. He was against the fixing of any date for return to Africa as a family, however tentative.

To me, the way I felt at the time, this seemed to be abandoning hope, and so I was in no mood to discuss rationally. We decided in the end to settle in the village of Thame, near to the Wycliffe Centre, trusting that time would heal. We would again talk through issues at length with Wycliffe counsellors, Rosemary and Gordon Jones, and I (and sometimes Heather, as she felt able), would make trips out to continue work on the project, say two or three times per year, for a month at a time.

Renting a little house in Thame, we enrolled the girls in local schools, and began to attend Long Crendon Baptist Church, where pastor Jeff Steadman and his wife Hannah were very generous in their pastoral care, and contributed much to our restoration over the two years there.

Not long after settling in Thame, I experienced some panic attacks, which were new to me, and scary. At one point I was afraid to be alone, as I did not know when an attack might come. This helped me to understand Heather's feelings when asthma attacks were imminent. I grew to understand also the reason behind the panic attacks: my whole being was on red alert, producing too much adrenaline, too much adrenaline with nowhere to go!

My body was reflecting the dilemma in my mind. We were, it seemed, in a situation now from which we might never escape, and never come out of to achieve our life's dream. And there appeared to be nothing I could do about it. I had tried, we had tried, and been thwarted just one time too many.

Gordon and Rosemary did try to keep up our hopes. During sessions with them, they would say: 'When you return to Côte d'Ivoire...', not 'If you return...' They had more faith than I had at that point. I had resigned myself to making trips, and that, in a way, seemed like failure.

I could not remember failing anything of consequence in my life before, and it was a bitter pill to swallow.

Thame, 14th September 1992

Dear friends and supporters,

When we went to Africa in November 1991, Heather had been full of energy and enthusiasm for the work, and much was accomplished in the six months, but gradually the demands and pressure of living as a family out there took their toll. She feels in need of a quieter life for a time.

So we have decided to continue the work on the Kouya translation project from Britain for now, and have rented a small house not far from the Wycliffe centre. I will have an office at the centre, and plan to make regular trips out to Côte d'Ivoire. This is a change of approach for us, but we feel happy that it is the Lord's will, and the best choice in the present circumstances. We shall miss close everyday contact with the Kouya people, but our colleagues Eddie and Sue Arthur left yesterday to begin a new field-term, so there will be a continued presence in the area, one of the big advantages of double-teaming! Please pray for them, and their two boys.

We are sure you appreciate that the last three months of uncertainty have been confusing and difficult for us at times. We have been forced to face very fundamental questions about our calling, our direction, and our personal strength for this task.

However, the inner assurance remains that the Lord wants us to continue, and by whatever means, to see the Kouya Scriptures translated, in His time.

This short letter is just to let you know what is

happening, and to ask you to please keep praying. Thank you.
With love from
Philip and Heather

To this day, I am not totally sure what changed things. Outwardly, life progressed satisfactorily, the girls again did well and were happy enough in their schools, we all enjoyed the church, though I sometimes did not feel like attending and forced myself to go. Gradually, after some months, the panic attacks subsided. Heather, resilient as ever, was in better 'form' than I was. Half of me was still in Africa, wondering how the Kouya Christians were faring, wondering had Emile given up hope of us coming back. He did not often write.

At perhaps my lowest point, I attended a retreat run by 'Wholeness through Christ'. I went with a personal agenda of issues to deal with, but the Lord had His own agenda for me. It seemed He wanted to deal with a root of Fear. Fear? This was surprising news to me. I felt like Naaman being asked to dip in the river Jordan. But I went through with it, and for Heather, the change she saw in me felt like a turning point for her. Even though I could not perceive a great change within myself, I was still glad for the results! I left the retreat convinced of one thing, however. The Lord is able to heal over a period of time, and He is able, at times, through the Holy Spirit, to act like a surgeon, to remove the root cause of a problem. When the Christian awakes from the anaesthetic, so to speak, he may not know exactly how the Surgeon did it, but he can live in the good of the results. So it was for me.

As the months passed, Heather began to talk more about a return to Ivory Coast. I had now decided to leave this choice totally in her hands: I did not want there to be any element of compulsion from my side. For a long time I did not hope, for I did not dare to hope, fearing to have my hopes dashed again.

TRIPS

For me trips out to Africa were a highlight. They lasted on average five weeks at a time, with specific goals to help move on Kouya translation and literacy. Much could be accomplished in a short concentrated period, which was excellent for morale.

Often I had no car, but it was great fun to travel around Ivory Coast by public transport. On these journeys, the unexpected was included in the price of the ticket!

Taking off those City Socks

The journey between Abidjan and Daloa was one I had to make frequently. It was a five-hour bus trip, which gave me lots of chances to catch up on sleep, as well as to make a few cultural observations.

One trip stands out in my memory. As usual, all began rather formally, which was to be expected as we men were all still wearing Abidjan socks and shoes, and the women bore that indefinable aura which made them (at least temporarily) Abidjanaises. We all had images to maintain, appearances to keep up, acquired status to hang on to. As a white person, after sitting down where my ticket indicated and getting comfortable, I was ushered to a 'better' seat, near the rear door. There I was grateful for the extra legroom, but sorry there was no seat in front of me on which I could follow custom and rest my head for a doze.

We were leaving the city well behind us by now. The crowded suburbs teeming with the nation's wannabes had given way to banana plantations, rows of rubber trees, and fields of orderly pineapple-plants. Something had to happen soon to make us all relax. After all, the vegetation would soon become wild, untamed. We were on our way into the interior, back to the village, so to speak. No airs and graces there. We needed an acceptable emotional catalyst.

It was the apprentice who provided it.

These long-suffering young men are expected to race up and down the aisle at the passengers' beck and call, provide mops for sick or incontinent babies, and listen out for anguished shouts of *'Ça descend!'*- ('I get off here!') Apprentices protect their drivers from noise and requests, keep the cassette-recorder going at full blast, open and shut doors, collect fares, unload baggage. If you are an apprentice on an inter-city bus, your status is marginally higher than the chickens in cardboard boxes below the seats, but significantly lower than everybody else's is!

Our apprentice this time had obviously either had a rough night, or a bad trip last time out. From the moment we left the station, he was just that bit slow to respond, taking three full minutes to make his way from front to back of bus. This did *not* endear him to the passengers.

I feel sure that a lot of the anxiety one senses on buses these days has perfectly natural causes. In the course of a five-hour trip, there may well be only one stop, and that around the halfway point. Many of us are not equipped to last out that long. Will there be the ignominy of having to make a special request for a stop? The fear is a real one.

One male passenger clearly fell into this category on this particular day. As we made a brief stop to let someone out, off he leapt. Our apprentice, clearly disgusted at this breach of protocol, slammed the door, and yelled to the driver to move on!

This was the signal for the masks to drop. We had only been waiting for an excuse. The poor man stared after the departing bus in disbelief, and the rest of the passengers began to berate the apprentice. It was several hundred yards before we stopped again. This time half the bus climbed down and (in protest?) emulated the good fellow we had abandoned. As his running figure drew closer, the comments and insults rained on the unfortunate apprentice. 'Did he not pay his three thousand francs like everybody else?' 'Have you no pity?' One matron in particular was giving him what for, vigorously wagging her finger as she climbed back into the bus. Others urged the wounded party to 'biff him'.

Aboard the bus, the atmosphere had now totally changed. Passengers felt free to be themselves. Youths called out: 'Musique! Musique!' every time there was a lull. One ageing raconteur regaled us with stories of apprentices, bush-taxis and police-stops, and when we had heard enough, moved up the bus to tell them to a new audience. A younger woman stretched out across the aisle and promptly went to sleep. The apprentice was definitely a baddy beyond redemption, we were goodies.

And this whole process had its function. All the pent-up stresses of an Abidjan day were now being released and purged, as we agreed with each other on how unjustly the apprentice had acted towards this angel of a passenger who was only doing what was natural! Now folks felt free to lean against each other and go off to sleep like babies, until the lights and sounds of Daloa finally broke out of the night.

But it must be admitted that even apprentices have emotions. And fate smiled on this young man that night too.

As you approach Daloa, you must go through police, customs and forest-ranger checkpoints in quick succession. This often takes twenty minutes, as identity cards, and baggage may be thoroughly checked. So we all woke up, groped for our IDs, and bought snacks through the windows from the traders.

But one of our number had no identity card. And who was it but the lady of the wagging finger! As she stumbled off the bus for a long chat with the police, she was followed by distant raucous laughter from an unmistakable source, and by not a few little smiles from the rest of us.

I thought to myself: I do like the Ivorian way of releasing tension. The way folks here keep up to date seems emotionally healthy to me. When the negatives are vented, there are always plenty of referees around to make sure things don't get out of hand. It seemed I heard the Lord say in a whisper that he would like more emotional honesty from me too.

And then there was another popular way of getting around.

Taxis

Taxis went to Vavoua to die.

They began life in Abidjan, and had known the heady thrill of weaving in and out of boulevard traffic under the bright lights. Their occupants paid through the nose for the comfort of leather seats and loud reggae from radios which worked. They took a pride in their bright orange paintwork, and their drivers adorned them with trinkets, fur trimmings, football team insignia, and slick little proverbs on dashboard and windows. A miniature pair of football boots swung from the mirror.

In midlife, they sought out the quieter life of the small towns, where they could cruise the streets in more leisurely fashion. On the town streets it was the people who ruled, not the cars. A new lick of paint would be given for this stage of life: yellow for Gagnoa, green for Daloa, and white for Yamoussoukro. Life was good. Most of their parts still worked, and those that didn't could be replaced from the nearby Lebanese stores. They were comfortable, secure in themselves, and so were their passengers, especially the better upholstered ones.

And then, inevitably, old age took over, and it was time to be on the move again, and head for the more remote outposts. Taxis went no further than Vavoua. Vavoua was the end of the line. There it did not take long to familiarise themselves with the contours of the streets, which they limped and bounced along at a little above walking pace. A quick inspection of the taxi's interior revealed more sponge than leather, and a good view of the dirt road beneath at several points. Old joints now grumbled and complained when asked to get up for work.

Usually, before budging, the taxi would require a slug of petrol, poured from an old brown bottle at the petrol station beside the taxi rank. This provided a welcome pick-me-up for the journey, and it was often the prospective passenger who would foot the bill.

'*Deux Minutes*' used to take me out to Vavoua International School. This was the taxi-driver's nickname. It was plain to see why: no journey within Vavoua took less than two minutes, if he could help it! Stepping off the bus from Abidjan, I would catch his eye as he lounged on the bonnet in the shade, and we would go through the old routine.

'*Deux Minutes, ça va?*'
'*Patron, bonne arrivée!*'
'How much?'
'To the school? 1000 francs, *m'sieur.*'
'Has it gone up? It was always 400 francs!'
'It's the price of petrol, *m'sieur*. Inflation. Cost of living. The Government.'
'Ah, the Government... But I'm a regular client. I always choose you. You know that.'
'That's true. For you, 700 francs.'
'Make it 450.'
'I haven't seen you around for ages.'
'Yeah, I've been abroad... in my own village.'
'Ah, everybody's rich *there*. Rolling in it. I watch *Dallas.*'
'Mm. *Dallas et Belfast, c'est pas la même chose.* Anyway, the journey here is long, and very costly.'
'Okay, make it 600. Last price.'
'I've no change yet.'
'Have you a 500 franc note?'
'I've one of those.'
'OK. *Faut donner.*'

And off we would go. As we went, I would fish out of my travel-bag a little souvenir from home. Three bone-shaking kilometres later, we would part with much shaking of hands on the grass outside the school, wishing each other well at great length. And as I glanced back over my shoulder having taken my leave, *Deux minutes* would be rattling his way slowly back up the track in his ancient battered taxicab, the road ignored for a moment as he examined his latest little *cadeau* from his foreign friend, a broad smile on his face.

The Marriage

Vavoua, 28th November 1992

My dear Heather,

Emile got married today! The sun split the skies, and about six hundred people squeezed on to the front lawn of our house in Dema. Preliminaries began at ten o'clock this morning, and the action continued until sundown.

The local Christians had worked very hard to prepare for it. They'd erected a huge shelter of palm branches to keep us all cool, collected seats from far and wide, and organised food for the massive crowd. Emile and Juliette's relatives were all there, of course, but besides them, there were representatives from all the Kouya churches, many neighbouring Baoulé and Gouro Christians, and several missionaries. The Arthur family was present, and four teachers from Vavoua School. I felt very grateful to be able to be there to participate.

Photographer Peter (from England) had a field day. There was so much going on, he was really in his element, and he certainly contributed to the fun of the occasion.

After much singing and dancing from the different groups present, the bridal party arrived (together!) and were seated at the front, facing the guests. There were lots of presentations to make sure everyone was in no doubt as to *who was who, and finally the vows were taken. French and Kouya were the languages used. A loudspeaker system ensured that the whole of Dema village didn't miss out either!*

As the big moment approached, photographer Pete provided us with a hilarious side-show, as he balanced precariously on a stack of chairs above the happy couple, in search of the best angle for his shots! The crowd followed his every wobble. Finally, Emile and Juliette said 'Oui!' enthusiastically and at the right time, everyone cheered, and we could eat. A choice of mutton or pork, and ample for everybody. One of our blue plastic barrels, well scrubbed, came in useful for dispensing diluted fruit-juice.

What a day! I'm sorry you were not with me to enjoy it, but Peter's photos should be brilliant. It has been nerve-racking at times on this trip: I guess people in his profession often tread where angels fear to. It's been a learning experience for him, and for me!

So Emile found a great wife, all on his own, without your help. Amazing, isn't it? Well, tomorrow is another day. Night, night!

Philip

Ferkéssédougou, April 1993

Dear Heather,

Emile and I are now in Ferké to have our first book consultant-checked by Fritz Goerling. It is intensive, but going well.

Fritz is very rigorous, which I appreciate. He is also ready to note down any good ideas for translating verses that we have had, and tells us he will check them out with the Jula translation. He, Moussa and Randy Groff have that translation almost ready now. Given their busyness, it is all the kinder of Fritz to give of his time to check James for us.

We will go away from these sessions with lots to review, lots to check out with Kouyas, but satisfied that a good

job has been made of the first consultant-check. In general terms, we need to loosen up the style more, provide more linkages, make it less dense. What's for sure is that version eight of James will look vastly different from James mark one!
Look forward to seeing you all soon,
Philip

Thame, Oxfordshire

Dear Philip,

The girls and I are missing you, but we are doing well.

On Sunday, after lunch, I had to scold Hilary about something, then sat down for a break with a cup of tea. Hilary disappeared upstairs. After a while she reappeared, her face grave, and handed me this wee note:

'Dear mummy', it read.

'Pleese pray this prayer and meen it. "Dear Lord, help me to be kind to Hilary. Amen."'

I had to smile. I remembered she had been learning about Daniel and the power of prayer in Sunday school that morning! Obviously she felt I should try it.
Heather

Thame, Oxfordshire
10th May 1994

Dear friends in Brooklands,

This is Heather writing. We send you warm greetings and love from England!

I have been meaning to let you know how my three weeks in Côte d'Ivoire went. I had been looking forward to returning, though apprehensive about how I would cope back at the scene of so many of our medical emergencies. I had a few gruelling days at the start in Abidjan, where I had to work through various bad memories and fears, but I found I soon settled down, and had great peace about being there.

I spent quite a bit of time with the Arthurs. They are now well into translation work, and have drafted Matthew, Mark, 1 and 2 Thessalonians and 1 and 2 Timothy. The great news is that 25% of the Kouya New Testament has now been drafted! However, Eddie is to become Language Programmes manager in Abidjan this coming year, and will also stand in as director for the following year ('95-'96), after which they are due for furlough. So, if we return, it looks as though they are handing back the Kouya bâton to us for the next three years! They will try to keep things going from Abidjan, but it will not be easy with their ongoing administrative duties.

After those first few days, we travelled up country to Bouaké workshop centre, and were joined by Emile, and the Arthurs' co-workers, Dibert and François. Together we put together the first twenty lessons of the Kouya reading scheme. Then once I had returned to England, Eddie and Sue completed the first edition of this, and it is now being tested out in three of the Kouya villages. We trained the Kouya team to teach it, and as this work of literacy continues, it should ensure a steady flow of new readers for the Scriptures as they are translated and circulated round the villages.

It was a great encouragement to me personally to find out that I not only enjoyed the work, but that I returned home more refreshed and rested than when I left!

The Lord has confirmed to me that it is the right time to think of returning to Africa.

Thank you all so much for your support,
Heather

The day did indeed come when Heather finally announced to Rosemary Jones and myself that she was ready to go! We very slowly started to make plans. We were daring to dream again.

The next three years were to be among the best and most productive years we had spent in Africa to date.

SWIMMING

1994-1997

Zoology

We felt exhilarated to be back living in Dema village again after two and a half years' absence. Our house looked well, Emile Zola had guarded the property with his customary vigilance, the fruit-trees had grown, and the flame tree covered the front garden magnificently with a parasol of green, red and yellow foliage.

As was usual when we moved out for a while, our animal friends moved in. We spent the first few weeks persuading them that we were the real owners, and that we were back to stay! Sometimes we felt like calling it a zoo, moving to the garden and charging admittance...

Hard-working termites had tunnelled up through minute cracks in the concrete floor, and continued their journey upwards. Their reddish-brown dirt motorways wove patterns up our walls. We dismantled these at night, and by morning they were reconstructed. Paraffin, and special powders discouraged them ultimately.

The varieties of mice were particularly interesting. We were ignorant of the technical names, but besides the common or garden types, there were the 'wee clockwork mice', and the acrobatic furry-tailed variety with suckers on their feet, which had a voracious appetite for wood of any description. We would be awakened by the sound of their gnawing in the middle of the night, and the man of the house would be despatched to investigate, and if possible, exterminate.

More dangerous was the occasional centipede or scorpion, but most hated by the ladies of the house were the bats, especially when they were trapped inside the house, or whirled dizzily round their heads in the kitchen when they got up for a drink in the night. These narrowly got the unpopular vote over the salamanders, the striped lizards which wiggled their way up and down the walls when you surprised them.

But somehow, when we found out the Kouya names for all these intriguing creatures of God's world, faithfully recorded them in our notebooks, and saw our dictionary grow by leaps and bounds, so to speak, it took the sting out of the bad experiences. We all learned to coexist more or less in harmony, and we never felt lonely.

Barriers

Looking out of our living-room window, underneath the spreading branches of the flame-tree, we could see our garden gate.

It was really no more than a token gate. The two wooden gateposts stood in splendid isolation, proud and erect, linked by a single, horizontal plank. The plank slid into place between four large bent nails. I was rather proud of my inventiveness here: no need for complicated hinges.

Our faithful guard Emile Zola became expert at removing the barrier when he heard the car drive up through the village, then closing it again after me. In fact, he learned to recognise the car-engine's sound, so he could be in his own courtyard, hear the engine, race up by foot through the village, and still be in time, though rather breathless, to raise the plank.

The gate was symbolic, but effective. The village children would dart up the trail leading to it, then skid to a halt at the barrier. They would hang over the plank if they were tall enough, or little pairs of eyes would gaze longingly from underneath the plank up to the house. Mostly they were hoping for a glimpse of Hilary. Hilary would usually be playing in the shade of the house or terrace with her closer friends who were invited up, but she would sometimes make a dramatic appearance to chase after the pigs or goats with her broom held high like a charger. It was for these cameo performances that the kids would patiently wait, but we adults could also provide amusement for a time too, if we appeared.

Funny thing was, we had no fence around the property. It was forest gone wild on two sides, a Pride of China hedge at the bottom of the garden facing the house, and then the fourth side open to Emile's courtyard next door, with the gateposts in the corner.

So the kids could have walked round the gate, or crouched to enter under the plank, but they didn't. This was the point beyond which Emile Zola would not let them pass. We did not know how he threatened them when we were not present, but whatever his strategy, it was effective. On the other hand, as long as we lived in our Dema village house, adults of any age could pass freely in and out of the garden, or children accompanied by adults. It was true that at times we could be overrun, but this was the only way we could feel comfortable living in the village, where only very strange people or sorcerers cut themselves off from contact.

There were periods of quiet, for example when it had rained in the night and every able-bodied person left for the fields to work the damp soil. But there were times of great commotion too. Often we were rudely awakened by the explosive bang of a gun, then the squeals of a wounded pig, and the whoops of the youths as they chased their quarry through the flowers in our garden. Or - always it seemed at siesta-time - the village photographer would arrive with his clients and their advisors for a group photo. Our house, with its green grass, its flowers, the car, our water-barrels, these were favourite backdrops for his clients draped in their finest clothes. After much shouting, positioning and advising, the photo would be taken, and the group would disperse. From our beds we would follow their laughter across the grass, round the gateposts, down the track, until it died away in the village, and we could sleep.

Living in town was very different. We moved to Daloa later for our final two years as a family in Ivory Coast, in order to be able to work on translation without too many interruptions, and in this larger town, it was hard to be surrounded by walls, topped by cut glass and spikes. Many in town had guard-dogs, though we didn't, because we had to move around the country so often. When the bell sounded at the gate, I sometimes felt like calling out: 'Bonjour! We really are friendly, honest!' as we peeked at callers through the gap in the wrought-iron door.

But it was prudent to be cautious in town, as crime and burglary were rife at certain times. In the village on the other hand, once accepted, we felt as safe as anywhere on earth. A physical barrier was up, yes, but it was only a token one, our funny old gate. This was not meant to exclude, only to enable us to survive. Essentially all barriers were deliberately down, as our neighbours - all three thousand of them in Dema - watched how we lived, and we learned how they lived at the same time.

The colour of our skin, our odd way of doing things, these would always mean that we would be outsiders to a certain extent. We were 'outside, looking in on Kouya life and culture'. In the same way, the Kouyas were 'outside, looking in' on us, on our family life, and hopefully on our Christianity in practice.

We prayed that they would like what they saw.

Consulting the Mouse

Down through their history, the Kouyas have been very mobile. When faced with a problem or conflict with an outside group, their solution has often been to pack up and leave. Even internally, when a family or clan has been at loggerheads with another, one clan has generally opted to put space between itself and the other faction. The country has been big enough, the forest thick enough, for the twain never to meet again.

Now although proud of their own language and culture, Kouyas are not shy of adopting customs which appeal to them from other ethnic groups. So during their travels, they have picked up an eclectic mix of traditional practices.

One of these is the practice of consulting the mouse. They got the idea from the Mandé peoples: Yaouré and Gouro practise this also to this day.

What happens is this. A large calabash, or a clay pot serves as home for several captured mice. Normally they live on the ground floor of the pot, but an upper storey has been fabricated for them by means of a slim horizontal piece of wood, which divides the pot into two. On this piece of wood are arranged smaller pieces of wood and small stones. A hole in the middle allows the mice access to the upper storey.

In the morning, when it is time to consult, village or clan elders will gather round the calabash, open the lid, and drop some breakfast in for the mice on to the floor of the first storey. The mice stretch and yawn, and pop up through the hole to break their fast.

As they shuffle about, they knock against the twigs and stones, causing these to be rearranged. They finish their meal, then disappear down below.

Peering down into the gloomy interior of the pot, the elders then try to discern whether the day's omens are good or bad. If portents are bad, they may decide that no work should be attempted in the fields that day!

We felt that many Kouya customs and practices could with great profit be incorporated in the culture that we grew up in in Britain. This was not one of them. We did feel sad that so many for so long have consulted the mouse for guidance and direction, instead of the One who created the mouse in the first place! Yet was it so very different from those in our own culture who consult horoscopes, and whose lives are ruled by the stars?

Wee Boys

Heather taught me a lesson one Sunday morning.

As usual, we were in the church-service in Dema. While I sat and clapped, and stood and sang, I looked around me. Rows of happy faces. By accident and design, the building lets the air flow through, and women may be seen pounding *foutou* through the cracks. Built on a slope, the floor allows streams of water to flow towards you from little children over the cracked concrete. Services can be too long for little ones! Much is so different from the churches I grew up in. However, some things are the same everywhere.

Take the worship-leader, for example. Jules, with his gravelly voice, his sensitivity of steel, and his heart of gold, has his counterpart in many a Northern Irish congregation. Our hearts went out to him, as he exhorted us, with all the enthusiasm he could muster on an empty stomach, to 'Pray for peace in our land!', 'Fast and pray!' 'Join us after church!' 'Got any special needs? Bring them along, we're praying all afternoon!'

For it was prayer and fasting day throughout the church zone. Satisfied that he'd done his bit well, he eased his muscular frame back down on to the wooden bench, making way for the preacher of the day.

And this was where my wife came in (not as preacher, but into the story). She sat behind me. I sat in row two, behind Jules and his two little sons of six and three. The sermon went on a bit, and then a bit more, but at least there was only one language interpretation today. Jules' sons squirmed and fidgeted on the hard bench beside him. As the preacher's voice droned on, young girls fell asleep on my left, prodded into life by Emile Zola, the watchful steward. Jules' boys set up a constant moaning complaint which the preacher only just managed to drown.

I looked round in despair at my wife, knowing how much such distractions normally affect her. As I expected, she looked distressed. I tried to concentrate on the message, and in the end congratulated myself for being able to tune out the bothersome groans in front of me.

Suddenly, I jumped. There was an urgent tap on my shoulder, and a whispered: 'Keys please, dear!' As I gave Heather the bunch, I thought how well she'd done today, staying for two whole hours. Religiously, and with a certain pride, I stuck it out to the end, and did not sleep, not even during twenty minutes of announcements...

Handshakes all round, then I moved quickly up the path through the village, feeling the midday sun burn into my neck. I relaxed as I neared the friendly shade of our spreading flame-tree. Another Sunday morning successfully negotiated. Time for coffee.

As I rounded the corner to the side-door, I nearly stepped on them! Two pairs of bright eyes looked up at me from our doorstep. Two happy little boys, giving a finishing lick to our green melloware plates. Grains of rice framed their mouths, orange-peels lay at their feet.

The screen-door opened and Heather's hand came out for the plate. So *that* was why it had seemed so quiet towards the end of the church-service! She had taken the boys out, and back up home with her. While I had wanted the nuisance of their noise stopped, she had seen that their problem was an empty stomach. Jules, with the best of intentions, had forced his little boys to join him in his Sunday fast, but their little bodies just couldn't take it.

As I watched the wee boys scamper happily away round the corner in their little shorts, once upon a time red, I felt chastened. There and then, I prayed for help to discern what the real needs were around me in this African village which was our home. A Scripture passage came into my mind:

I was hungry, and you gave me meat. I was thirsty, and you gave me drink... inasmuch as you have done it unto one of the least of these my brothers, you have done it unto me. (Matthew 25: 35, 40)

The Petrified Pig

The pig eyed me doubtfully. He had been bound hand and foot, and bundled unceremoniously into the back of our estate car. I have to confess I shared his hesitancy, but I had had little choice.

Earlier that Sunday morning, I had picked up the preacher, his wife and little boy in town. Hardtop road for a few kilometres, then on to the red dusty track that led to Gatifla, a tiny Kouya village. Often we would stay in Dema, but that day we were on our way to encourage the handful of Christians in Gatifla: they had few visits from outside speakers. I drove slowly through the potholes, but had to accelerate over the rutted corrugation. A risky business. Too fast, and you were off the road: too slow, and the jolting broke your back. Over high rocky outcrops, slewing through sand, we finally broke through the bush into a neatly laid out village.

A few final bumps, and we stopped. The service was already underway, inside a house. We were offered seats at the front, facing the little congregation, where they could have a good look at us. This was not a culture for shy retiring types.

Twelve years on, it was all so familiar to me now. As I entered into the praise, and took my turn to lead in song and in prayer, I reflected on how the Spirit had been at work among this previously resistant people. Twelve years ago, this small sitting room could have held all the known Kouya Christians with room to spare. Now, it was the smallest Kouya congregation of any! God had not forgotten them after all. As one young woman sang out a line, and we all echoed it back to her, I felt the tears come. In this part of Ivory Coast, the locals say that men's emotions are in the soles of their feet, that they take a long time to reach our eyes. But something in her voice, the way she threw her whole being into the words of worship, and the accompanying mouth-organ just slightly out of tune, that's what set me off. I knew then which choir I would head for in heaven: it would have to be the Kouya one...

Ah yes, I was telling you about the pig. Well, it belonged to Henriette's granny, a nice little old lady who had been at church too, and she was very kindly sending it (with me) into the town Mission for her daughter's family. Henriette's mother that is. Henriette herself is most persuasive, and had caught me in a moment of weakness. I had just been treated to a bowl of rice and catfish after the service, and was feeling magnanimous. So off they went to fetch the pig, plus a chicken and some freshly dug yams.

The pig and I gave each other one last lingering look, and off we all set. We took away much more than we went with. We went in order to encourage, we returned laden with blessings. And two extra passengers, as it was such a waste to have two empty car seats.

It was not a very long journey, but if *you* were bound hand and foot, and lumped into a car-boot when you'd never been in a vehicle before in your life, *you* probably would have done what our pig did! Not in protest, you understand, but in abject horror at what was happening to you.

Later, as I cleared up the aftermath, I reflected on the roller-coaster highs and lows of this life we had chosen. Celestial choir one minute, petrified pig the next. But at least we had fulfilled our mission on that Sunday morning. We had gone, we had returned, and we had not got stuck in a rut. There were days when a rut seemed the most attractive place in the world to be stuck in. But that Sunday morning, in spite of the incontinent pig, it struck me afresh that I was very, very happy.

1995

The dry season that year was long and tough. Between November 1994 and March 1995 no rain fell in the Vavoua area. We longed for refreshing showers. Bush-fires devastated the region. Ernest, our friend from Bahoulifla days, lost much of his crops in a fire.

As the rivers dwindle, the fish are big and the water is low. Soon, we would see the women file out with their specially woven raffia fishing-baskets on their heads for their special days of group fishing, but Ezékiel and I had a few days of sport left yet.

Gone Fishing

'Filipu, we can get the soap in the corner shop!'
'Soap?'
'Yes, for the catfish.'
I bowed to Ezékiel's superior local knowledge. Whoever heard of using soap for bait? But stop we did at the corner shop on our way out into the forest, half closing our eyes as we moved out of the bright sunlight into the dark wooden cabin with its rows of sardines, matches, mosquito-coils, anti-cockroach spray, Coca-Cola, bags of sugar and rice, and - yes - bars of soap!

'It has to be *Panther* brand', whispered Ezékiel, almost reverently.

'Right,' I whispered back. I bought the bars at two hundred francs apiece, and off we set on our long trek.

'Where is your gear, Ezékiel?'

Smiling, he reached into the pocket of his oldest pair of trousers, and produced a few coils of the white line I had seen him plaiting the night before, rolling it on his thigh. Some large hooks hung down at intervals. He slipped the tackle back into his pocket, and marched on, unencumbered. I, on the other hand, was already beginning to struggle with my heavy tackle-bag, and especially with my rods, which it seemed every tree and bramble bush beside the forest path wanted to grab hold of.

I was glad that we had set out early, before the sun had really woken up. The ten-kilometre walk went quickly, as I followed in my fishing friend's sure-footed steps, pausing only to exchange greetings with farmers already up and about in their fields, or to leap across a battalion of soldier-ants on the march. I was pleased to note that the complicated Kouya greetings were almost second nature to me now.

We finally reached the river Dé. I could have been within a hundred yards of it, and yet not realised it was there, so thick was the foliage that hid it, so slowly and silently did it flow at that point.

Stooping carefully to avoid the itches of a wild bean bush, I finally stood on the riverbank. It was an awesome sight. Majestic. We had stepped into a cathedral. A canopy of giant trees allowed only a few rays of sun to filter through. The air was cool on my face. The call of a hornbill echoed harshly, irreverently, across the surface of the water, then died away eerily. Tree-trunks lay where they had been felled by storms long forgotten, half in, half out of the water. Nothing broke that surface, only the nimble water-spiders skated across it. As I watched, it struck me that the life of birds, fish, reptiles, and insects went on here undisturbed, day after day, a million miles from man. It might have been two thousand years BC.

But we had a job to do, and Ezékiel's voice got me down to business.

'I'll go get some more bait for us, you can start with the soap.' His eyes were twinkling in his expressive face, though, as he stood there expectantly. He wanted to see my first cast with the rod and spinning-reel, which had amused him so much when I had given a demonstration in our village-garden. Neither he nor the other curious villagers had ever seen its like, and he was intrigued as to how I could ever catch fish with such tackle. It was only now, as I searched for a tiny opening in the curtain of overhanging bushes, one wide enough to cast my line through, that I fully understood his bemusement.

After a few abortive attempts, the red and white float was safely out in open water, and after a few seconds, sat there as still as its surroundings. Ezékiel then slipped away into the forest, his initial curiosity satisfied. I sat down on my plastic bag and waited, drinking in the sensations. I would remember this place. Later on, in Ireland, as I sat by the Barmouth in Castlerock, and fished for sea trout and flatfish, my mind would return to this primeval world. Being there was what counted: the catching of fish was incidental.

I lost track of time. Some moments later, I moved to a more comfortable perch astride a great tree-trunk. Its warmth felt good beneath me. Daydreaming now, I glanced down casually at the water's edge below, and saw deep regular footprints there in the mud. Cows no doubt. No, not cows, not here. Wake up, Philip! I shuddered involuntarily, as I thought about the wild animals that might be encountered in such a place. What animal would make prints like those? I would ask Ezékiel when he got back.

I began to wish he would hurry up. My imagination was starting to turn harmless logs into dangerous predators. Insects buzzed annoyingly in my ear. So I was relieved when Ezékiel arrived, as silently as he had left.

'Filipu, everything all right?'

'Fine,' I lied.

'Got some bait.'

He opened a little cloth, and showed me. A dozen tiny frogs with enormous eyes and legs stared out at us. A tiny snake lay coiled around them.

Where did you get these?'

'Oh, over in the marsh. A place I know. A good spot!'

I'd leave that for another day. Ah yes, my question...

'Ezékiel, see those footprints?' I pointed. 'What would have made them?'

He slithered across the mud, and looked down. A smile, then he turned to me:

'Ah yes, he's come back. They're from a pigmy hippo. I thought he'd gone for good. He's an old friend.'

Ezékiel, I knew, regularly came here at night to hunt food for his family, a torch strapped to his head, like a miner. He thought nothing of killing an alligator. They were stupid, and easy to kill, apparently. Other animals were trickier. One night I must join him, I thought, perhaps when my children were married, and no longer needed me.

Suddenly, there was activity on the water: my float took off! A flutter of the heart, a firm strike, and the fish was on! My heart continued to pound in the old familiar way, but more so, for who knew what those dark mysterious depths would hold? Still, it *felt* like a fish, and a fish it proved to be! Out of those depths, into the shallows, and on to the bank slithered a splendid catfish, grunting and mewing with a high-pitched squeak. I placed my sandal with care on its dorsal spines, and extracted my square of soap from its whiskers. Yes, I thought with elation, local fishermen always knew best: this catfish had gone for the strong scent of our *Panther* soap.

Ezékiel stood watching me for several hours. It was great sport, and as we landed different types of fish, he would give me their exotic Kouya names. If he knew them, he would give me the French names as well. My favourite was the *gbaazigbli*, or African pike (*Le brochet africain,* said Ezékiel). It gave a tremendous fight for all the size of it.

But all the fish that I caught were small or medium-sized. This was a little frustrating. I could see massive carp feeding on the surface in a patch of sunlight. They turned up their noses at my offerings. What would tempt them? Ezékiel shook his head. 'Some fish you can't catch this way, Filipu,' he said.

The brilliant white of the midday sun on the upper foliage had gradually been turning to amber: evening was approaching. It became subtly cooler. I was reluctant to leave, but we had a long trek back, and darkness always came by seven o'clock. We packed up.

As we moved off down the riverbank, Ezékiel put a hand on my arm. 'I'll just check my lines. Want to have a look?' I nodded, and followed. It was news to me that he had set any.

Until Ezékiel actually lifted the branch, I couldn't see what he had done. He bent down, and then it was clear, for out of the weedy water appeared half a dozen little frogs on hooks, and one very large and discontented fish, flapping furiously as he pulled it to shore.

Ezékiel had planted two long sturdy branches, one on each side of the river, vertically, deep into the mud, and had slung his line with its hooks between them. Who knows what creatures he disturbed as he waded through those mysterious murky depths to tie his lines, but his method had landed easily the biggest fish of the day! Men and boys, I thought. What was simply a sport for me, was a livelihood for many of our Kouya friends. My spinning-reel suddenly seemed strangely irrelevant, an encumbrance, in this neck of the woods.

I watched Ezékiel pass a liana through the gills of his prize, tie a quick knot, and then we were on our way home with that warm, satisfied glow, that feeling shared by fishermen all over the globe.

Training Literacy Teachers

Ezékiel was one of the participants at our first Literacy Teacher Training week in January 1995. There were two main objectives for this week: firstly, to train teachers, and secondly, to test the first edition of the reading scheme with a larger group. The course was held in our garden at the height of dry season, when there was little field work to be done. Twelve key Kouyas attended, from six different Kouya villages. Touali Martin, an experienced literacy teacher from the neighbouring Nyaboa people-group, capably led the teaching sessions.

Ezékiel, Emile and Hippolyte all from Dema, only had a short distance to walk to classes. Others came from further afield: it took Séry Laurent most of a day to cycle in for the start of the course from the remote village of Kouléyo.

Laurent grew up in Kouléyo. When you leave the hardtop road, take a deep breath and plunge into the bush with a firm grip on your steering wheel or handlebars, drive for an hour or pedal for two, you eventually arrive at Kouléyo. The track stops there, you're at the end of the line, beyond it is nothing but deep rain forest. It is a small friendly village where everyone knows everyone else's business. A place where it is dangerous to be sick, as medical help is just too far away. He and his wife Esther had a child who died for this reason. But Kouléyo is home. Everyone knows Laurent, and Laurent knows everyone.

A faithful Christian, Laurent is the one the believers entrusted with the Kouya conference funds. They knew they could rely on him. So when Laurent became enthusiastic about teaching his people to read and write, we invited him to attend this first workshop. Martin soon had him up front teaching his first lessons in front of the group. It was not long before we knew that in Laurent we had found a gem.

The training week over, we were satisfied that the primer was a good one, and that the reading scheme, with a few minor adjustments, would work well.

Séry Laurent disappeared into the bush again, and the next we heard from him was a written request to come and test his class! He had single-handedly sought out his students, taught right through the fifty-one primer lessons, and taught them well. The youngest to receive her diploma was a girl of eight, the oldest a man in his forties. In June, Laurent won the

Kouya Literacy Cup presented in recognition of outstanding achievement by a teacher. At a special Literacy day, his colleagues lifted him on to their shoulders, and did a victory tour of the compound!

He did not rest on his laurels. The following year, he decided to start classes in two neighbouring villages, Kétro and Brouafla Kouya. The chief's wife in Brouafla, having heard about the classes, had wanted Laurent to come and teach in her village too. He began classes weekly, and one young man stood out as a sharp student. This was Marus. Laurent had the good sense and vision to train Marus to carry on the Brouafla Kouya class, as heavy rain would regularly cut this village off from the outside world.

We were regularly encouraged by Séry Laurent's enthusiasm. From being a student learning to read and write his own language, within the short span of two years, Laurent became not only a literacy teacher among the Kouya people, but a trainer of teachers. Laurent was passing on the vision, preparing hearts and minds to embrace the Kouya Scriptures when they would arrive.

The Hornbill and the Chameleon

'Give it to the white man to read. Sure you know the story by heart!'

Amused, Hippolyte passed the reading book over to me. In the dim light of the thatched roundhouse, the old men leaned forward expectantly to listen. Now they would know if their stories really *could* be written down.

Praying I would do a good job, I turned to lesson forty-two, and began to read the Kouya folk-tale.

'*The Hornbill and the Chameleon. The Hornbill and the Chameleon were having an argument. Chameleon says to Hornbill: "You know, I was born long before you were!" Hornbill replies: "Nonsense, I was born first!"*'

My audience was absolutely still. Intent. It was

unnerving. I continued:

'So they took their dispute to the village chief, and the chief sent word out to the whole village, and all the villagers arrived to listen in. That morning they all gathered at the chief's house, and the two protagonists ...'

Suddenly, there was movement. An old man slapped his thigh. 'Aya! That's enough, you can stop now! You can't possibly know this word for word. It's true! You actually are reading our Kouya language off that paper there!'

'Of course!' Hippolyte broke in. 'That's what I was telling you all along!'

My heartbeat gradually settled to its normal rate. It was wonderful to see the expressions on the old Kouya men's faces, as they turned from disbelief to astonishment to pleasure. Many never imagined that their language could be written down. For them, it immediately raised its status to that of 'important' languages like French.

'So now,' continued Hippolyte, 'your sons and daughters can write letters to you in Kouya from Abidjan. You won't need to send for the village youth to read or translate it for you from French. Now your private affairs can stay private!'

The group of old men nodded. They saw the logic and usefulness of this. 'Go on, Filipu, read the rest of the story!'

I resumed the fable. Hornbill won as always. *Good old Hippolyte*, I thought. *That's another few converts for Kouya literacy!*

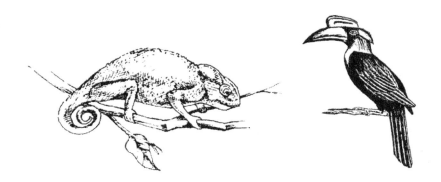

Dema, 14th February 1995

Dear families and friends,
       There has been so little rain for so long now, and the people are really suffering. Bush fires are blazing in many parts of the Kouya area, causing great devastation, and even loss of life. Many people have been burned while trying to fight the fires, because of course there is no fire brigade or other organised means of controlling them. Rivers are low, and some fields are miles away from any water source. They try to beat out the blaze with branches of trees, as well as cutting down and clearing the area ahead of the fire. But often this does not work, for the strong gusts of wind which blow several times a day, blow the sparks over a long distance, and set the forest ablaze far beyond the clearing they have worked so hard on! If coffee trees are burned, they can eventually get them going again, however for cocoa trees there is no hope, and they will have to start again, and wait for three or four years before there is any yield. It is so serious, for it is their livelihood. Our heart goes out to them.
       This evening, as we walked round the village trying to contact the literacy teachers, we came across several badly burned people, and a man with a machete wound. We helped as we could. Then Germaine's baby was sick with malaria, and taxi-driver Williams' baby has a very badly swollen neck, just under her ear. We treated Germaine's baby with nivaquine, and Williams' baby with ampicillin antibiotic. So few villagers can afford proper medical help.
       Teaching literacy, even learning to read and write, can often seem a luxury few can afford, when conditions of life are so desperate. Yet here in Dema the teachers trained last month are persevering. One class meets three times a week for those who can already read French, and the other twice a week for those who have never had any formal schooling. There is much enthusiasm, some agony as the students silently urge a classmate to get the word right, and lots of laughter. We help the teachers get set up, prepare their lessons on the

blackboard, and are busy writing out hundreds of flash-cards for the fifty-one lessons of the reading book.

It has been an encouraging start to classes. It is great to see Kouya Christians growing in maturity, and willing to take on responsibility for literacy. This reflects the way church life is developing too: over the past ten or twelve years, the young churches have become increasingly confident and self-determining. Their confidence is in God, thankfully, and not in us. Still, much of our day is spent in helping with the day-to-day needs, which arise, and we have to keep our long-term goal in mind. This is, we feel, the right time to make the move to Daloa, where we can focus on translation, though we shall miss the everyday contact with our friends here in the village. Still, we have a couple of months left here yet.

Much love from
Philip and Heather.

It was clear at that time that the Lord was at work in the hearts of individuals. Here is one example:

Call to Prayer

On the African rush mat, one of the children managed to fall asleep in spite of the commotion overhead. The others, heads bowed in varying degrees of reverence, shot furtive glances towards the fervent Christians praying in a circle above them.

They showed no fear in their bright eyes, even though the decibels would have intimidated any malevolent spirit brave enough to remain in the precincts of the school that night. Perhaps they felt safe, secure in the knowledge that it was their Headmaster father who had called this meeting. There he stood, quiet and intellectual, beside their mother, elegant in her long green robe, in the circle of adults crowded into their living room.

It was on their father's invitation that we had come. We had shaken hands and stood in the courtyard as chairs were fetched, and we had then been seated, in order of age and importance (as perceived by our hosts). The evening news was asked for.

'Nothing serious,' we replied, 'And how about you all here?'

'Nothing here either,' we were told. We all knew that the real news would come later.

So that was fine then. All was well. We let our spirits mingle for a time as others gathered for the event. I took note of the evident prosperity of the place. The house was of wood, not traditional mud-brick. The children all wore clothes, and were clearly used to the experience. From inside the home floated the sounds of a television-set.

Then it was over to Camus the drummer to start us off. Tamtam wedged securely between his ample knees, he led us into a time of singing, clapping and praising the Lord.

As we swayed to the rhythmic chants, we felt a change in the air. We were being cooled by a tropical breeze, a warning that rain was on its way. Darkness closed in rapidly around us. Then, during the opening prayer, we heard the first large drops sizzle on the paraffin lamps. It was time for evasive action. With a quick 'Amen!', we were up and into the shelter of the house. Just in time! There was a roar, as a thousand machine-gun bullets thudded on to the tin roof. A stray drop trickled down my spine. I shivered, glad of the sheltering warmth of the house and the bodies.

Our speaker had to shout his message to be heard above the storm raging outside. 'As for me and my house, we will serve the Lord!' he proclaimed. He persevered for several minutes until his voice started to give out.

And so it was that we finally arrived at the main business of the evening: prayer for the Headmaster's family. 'Here is a man of courage,' I thought to myself as I looked at his face, serious behind horn-rimmed spectacles. He had trusted the Lord some time ago, gone on well for a while, but had fallen away.

And now, at last, he was coming Home, like the Prodigal. He wanted his homecoming to be public, and to include his wife, and all the children in his extended family. He had invited the whole village church to come and to pray for his restoration.

We all prayed out loud together, each in his heart-language, and as we did so, we sensed that the Lord was pleased with this man, that He had killed the fatted calf for him. Here was honest repentance, here was a new spiritual start.

On the mat beneath us, the children lifted their heads shyly as the prayer subsided, and watched as their dad clasped the hands of each one who had come. And as they smiled up, we sensed that God was smiling down from above the wet tin roof.

In this small corner of Africa, rain is a sure sign of blessing. Without a doubt, the Lord had set His seal of approval on the night.

Masks

Many of the Kouya mask-dances are harmless fun. Masks are brought out on festive occasions, adding colour and excitement as the mask dancers giddily wheel and turn. They make beelines for the children sitting in the large circle of the public square, and the children recoil in happy horror. The dancers look weird but attractive with their grass skirts and pom-poms on ankles and wrists. Our equivalent would be Bogeymen.

But the Kouyas have a mask-dance which is not so harmless. This is performed by the Jε or 'antelope' mask, and is another custom borrowed from the Gouro people. The ordinary folk of the village were petrified when the Jε made an appearance, for, regular as clockwork, someone in the village was going to die four days after it was brought out.

'It's coming! The Jɛ is coming!'

The warning rings round the village, and soon the infamous mask will appear out of the forest where its bearer, and his attendants and singers have been holding their secret society meeting. All the women scatter and must disappear and hide behind closed doors, on pain of death should they happen to witness the Jɛ.

One night in 1980, some girls did see the Jɛ! It happened by accident. They were attending a courtyard prayer meeting at Jules' house in Dema. It was night-time, and they had not heard the signal that the mask was out. The Jɛ surprised them, and Jules hurriedly shepherded the terrified girls into his house. But it was too late. The girls had witnessed the Jɛ, and this was absolutely forbidden.

The news swept through Dema next day. Everybody knew the girls would die for sure. Jules kept them secluded in his house, and the few Christians that existed at that time prayed with all their might, imploring God to rescue them. The first day went by, and the girls lived. The second, the third, then the dangerous fourth day passed, and still the girls lived! They live to this day, and what is more, they have outlived certain members of the secret society. Nobody ever imagined the mask could be challenged in this way. Clearly, a Power was at work here, which was stronger than the strongest powers they had previously known.

Forcibly struck by this event, the chorus-leader of the Jɛ mask society in Dema gave in his notice. He became a Christian, was baptised and given a new name, and has become a lead singer in the young Kouya church, his talents being used for a very different purpose now - to praise Almighty God.

All agree that this whole incident was a significant landmark in the development of the Kouya church.

Baptisms in the Dam

Another historic event took place on May 21st 1995. These were the first baptisms carried out for Kouyas locally, close to their village area. They were held in the dam not far from Dema.

First the waters had to be tested. The brave church elders sent in a young Kouya girl, and we all watched as she looked for the best place for the candidates to stand. The sun beat down: there was certainly no need to heat the tank here!

She was a member of the choir, and had got the job because she could swim. Not many Kouyas could. The crowd watched as she thrashed around in the green slimy water in her pink and lime florescent bathing-costume. Unselfconsciously, she displayed her swimming skills to the keen Christians above, who cheered her every stroke.

The villagers knew where the fish hid out, and they knew the shadowy shape of a crocodile or a water snake when they saw one, but where was the bottom flat enough, the water deep enough, the location public enough, to do the business of the day?

Her fellow choristers looked enviously on. If they had had costumes, had they been able to swim, many surely would have joined her. As it was, they shifted from foot to foot in their uncomfortable Sunday best, for it was hot up above, well into the nineties and rising by the minute. Things could not happen just yet, because Félix, who was to conduct the ceremony, had not arrived from the church in town. But as always, the Kouyas knew how to make an occasion out of any gathering of people, so there were plenty of sideshows, and much singing practice from the choir.

The Saunders family was there in strength that day, and were explaining proceedings to Graham Lyttle, who had joined the project for ten months. While the little group of white people sought the shade, local young men zealously chopped it down to create room for the many others who were still to arrive. Children and unsuspecting adults found stinging brambles with their ankles.

Where were the twelve baptismal candidates? We looked around for them. Ah yes, there they were. For the moment, they mingled with the onlookers, but could be distinguished by brightness of their white clothes. None managed the white effect completely: a pair of dark socks protruding here, a slogan on a white tee shirt there.

By now a good spot had been discovered, and our valiant swimmer surfaced and changed reluctantly back to her sober *pagne* and headscarf. Her mates, by now sung out, decided to hunt for cool, clear drinking water in Akanzakro, the settlement up the road. They departed, and this was the cue for pastor Félix to arrive on his motorbike, with much banter and good cheer. He was immaculate in white. We wondered whether he would look so good later in slime-green … Down he came, with smiles all round.

We now had a baptiser, but no choir. Again we waited, following the decreasing shade, worrying about the level of water in our bottles, and huddling under our inappropriate black umbrellas. For the first time we noticed the group of little boys, habitués of the place, perched in a precarious row across the water on a concrete beam. They were not churchgoers. With much unholy chatter, and nonchalant swinging of legs, they jostled for position as they waited to see what happened at a Baptism.

Back came the Chorus, we all applauded, and the names of the candidates were written down for Félix on a slip of paper. There was a prayer, a message, an interpretation, another interpretation, and a final song. Then there was another final song. At last we were ready.

Baptiser and assistant baptiser were about to take the plunge. Félix remembered his non water-resistant watch, and propelled it to the crowd above. A youth caught it gracefully.

One by one the candidates waded out into the green water, and were baptised. Everything was done decently and in order. Six Kouyas, four Baoulés, and two Gouros. The character of each person shone through, and the green slime was forgotten in a joy which transcended the setting. We entered into the delight of widow Elise, whose life of drunkenness the Lord had transformed. We rejoiced also with Ezékiel, my fisherman friend, comfortable in the water and smiling radiantly as he obeyed his Lord in the appointed way.

As each one came up from the dam, tears came to our eyes. Yes, this was the first time it had ever happened, in this place, with Kouya people. In the only decent patch of water for miles around at this time of year. It was the *people* who brought dignity to the event, not robes or an organ, not even the sun or the rain forest.

We were content. It had happened. Félix slowly surfaced from the dam, bottom half green, top half white, assistant in his wake. There was much shaking of hands, and congratulations all round.

The official baptisers gone, the little boys' patience was rewarded. They leapt up, flung off holey shorts, and down they went. For a few moments, they entertained us with somersaults, splashing, whooping and abandonment as they took the watery stage!

But for one poignant moment, they stopped. One took the left arm, the other took the right, one mouthed the words, the other pinched the nose. And at six years of age, their little black brother with the shiny eyes also got baptised in the Name of the Father, the Son and the Holy Ghost, in the murky green waters of Dema dam.

Baptisms over, we all walked back to Dema village together along the main road, singing and chanting Christian songs, and in the little wooden hall beside the village market square, we joined those recently baptised in the first communion service ever held there. To commemorate the death and resurrection of our Lord Jesus together was a fitting end to a momentous day.

From time to time, the translator in me had been

listening out for how the concept of 'baptism' was being expressed by the Kouya Christians that day. I counted three ways of doing it. First, there was *wlulawlɔ*, which literally denoted the 'washing of the head'; then they sometimes used *nyu fa*, which meant to 'plant in water'; and finally there was *batise*, like the French verb *'baptiser'* a transliteration from the Greek.

For the moment, we filed away the three alternatives in our minds. A decision would have to be made on it later.

Daloa (*1995-1997*)

Translation work really began in earnest now, and time was short, as we knew that we would have to leave the Ivory Coast as a family in July 1997, for Joy to start her 'A' level courses in Britain. For this reason we moved to Daloa town, thirty-five miles away. There we hoped to be able to sustain concentrated work without the many distractions of village living. The Arthurs were translating the Gospel of John and the Book of Revelation at this point, and we were well underway in Luke and Acts.

We had great help from the two young Northern Irish folk who lived with us for a number of months: first Graham Lyttle, and later Clare Tughan. Graham, a Cambridge graduate in Computer Science, helped us produce a Kouya Lexicon, along with the final version of the Primer – brilliant!; Clare, a Modern Languages graduate, typed up reams of French back-translations from both Kouya and Bété, and helped in countless other ways. Our daughters quizzed her on life, fashion and gossip from the homeland - essential preparation for their return! We felt we had gained another daughter.

Village living had become familiar over the years. We had also experienced life in the big city during our time in Abidjan. Town life in Daloa proved to be quite different again.

At the Bank

In Britain we have 'holes in the wall'. One morning, as I checked my socks for holes, picked out my matching shirt and trousers and adjusted hair and glasses, I reflected that there is a world of difference between the way we make cash withdrawals over there, and here.

In Britain, I go to the bank on automatic. I do not even say: 'Hello, wall ', never mind 'How are you? Did it rain in on you today? Has devaluation affected you much?' No, I avoid personal comments. My sole concern is that the suspicious-looking housewife behind me will not get a glimpse of my pin-number. And that, if she happens to be innocent, I will not keep her waiting longer than the requisite forty-eight seconds.

As I stood and waited in my African bank that day, I had plenty of time to reflect. I amused myself by trying to calculate how many times forty-eight seconds went into fifty-five minutes. And my bankbook and passport were still languishing about three back from the lady bank-clerk sweltering in her fish bowl.

I had entered hopeful, and foolishly optimistic. After all, it was the middle of the month, mid-morning, bank seeming emptyish as I made my entry. I had donned my most confident demeanour, chest was suitably expanded, best shoes gleaming, stomach 'on hold'. I had made every possible mistake in this bank before, both cultural and procedural, so there was no fear left in my heart.

An hour's wait was the average. Yet it is astonishing how swiftly time goes by when everybody else is enjoying themselves. Why did *I* never seem to meet old friends in banks as they did? Why did clerks not smile broadly at *me*, pass the time of day, and take *my* book first? What had gone wrong since that memorable day when I had opened up my account with this bank...?

Thirteen years ago it was. I had dutifully joined the queue, somewhat nervously, all too aware of the poverty of my French banking vocabulary. I need not have worried. After an hour, and a few minutes of making my intentions clear to the clerk, he took down a few essential facts, then set up his 'Position closed' sign, and whisked me off to have a celebratory Coke in the café opposite. What amazed me most was the absolute acceptance of this by those behind me, who sidled off to an adjoining queue, without so much as a glare in my direction!

That was my auspicious introduction, and, to be frank, things have gone downhill ever since. Maybe, I mused, I have been so successful in my cross-cultural adjustment that I am no longer being given special treatment? Fond hope. More like, I have taken few pains to foster relationships as I should have done. There has been little effort on my part to add my strand to the complicated web of relationships that bank staff have with their clients. All *I* wanted was to extract my money: all *they* wanted were return Cokes... and perhaps a few other trivialities later on.

In some way I had failed, and was now paying the price month after month.

But there are compensations, I told myself. Is it not such fun seeing whether I will beat the one-hour barrier? Or whether the wee woman will eventually get her 10,000 franc note changed after the supermarket across the street refused it? How absorbing to listen to the two men beside me discuss in detail the budget for the funeral of their recently deceased older brother! I have time, as I wait, to admire the power of the uniform, as policemen, customs officers, forest-rangers and supermarket security-men jump the queues ahead of me. I have time to notice again how important it is to strut, march, or waddle into the arena to let all and sundry appreciate your exalted status, and the high opinion you have of yourself.

After thirteen years, there are still things I do not understand about the bank. The unsolved mysteries. Why do the clerks leave their little cubicles every so often? And why lock the door behind them every time, as though we customers could ever jump through the bulletproof glass! Is it some physical deformity on my part which does not allow me to speak through that little hole, unless I take a pace back, bend my knees, and break my back? (I did try the head sideways method, but it was rather degrading, as my French came out funny, and after the clerk's fifth *'Pardon, monsieur?'* I gave up.) Then last month, why did I have to go up to visit the new bank-manager, before they'd give me my money?

Yes, there is much I have still to learn. I have learned, however, the value of literacy. Now I write lots of little notes, and pass them through the glass. 'Fifty thousand, please.' Or, 'Would you please see if our transfer has come through?' Or, 'How's your grandfather doing after his operation?' I tried a new one today: 'Have you time for a quick Coke across the road?'

The French Club

We missed regular daily contact with our Kouya friends in the village, apart from those on the translation team who would regularly come down to stay with us in Daloa. But there were definite compensations. For a start, we could take regular exercise at the French Club.

We often had the small pool to ourselves on those hot, hazy days. The water was cool and pleasant. Never again would we be able to brave the Irish Sea, whatever the weather!

The half-days we spent there were a break from the intensive routine of translation, but in a way they became a routine in themselves. It was hard, at that stage, to pull ourselves away from the desks that we loved, from making such tangible progress on the translation which had seemed an impossible dream. But our bodies needed it, so off we went!

For these final years in Daloa, we owned an old white battered Toyota Corolla. It would pull faithfully up over the roots of the ancient nime tree, and lie panting in its shade, while we slowly unpacked our towels and swimsuits, water bottles and biscuits. We would pick our way across to the deeper shade of the thatched roundhouse with its open, pillared sides, and would just sit for a moment looking out at the brightness of the blue pool. Our eyes would take in the deep pink of the bougainvillaea cascading over the white boundary-walls, the restful greens of the manicured fig trees. Such a haven from the restless green taxis outside, constantly seeking out clients. Here at the poolside, the hum of the Daloa traffic was distant and irrelevant.

There was time, time to enjoy the beauty of the luxuriant flowers and bushes, time to watch the endless variety of colourful vibrant birds. A Senegal coucal hopped unobtrusively in the undergrowth beside the wall, treating us to a rendering of its six-note descending scale, before swooping low across to a fresh patch behind the ornamental travellers' palm. A sleek white front, with a clean, sharp coat and tails in brown. Handsome, and he knew it!

Our hearts grew quiet, in tune with the scene. A few moments later, and we would be slipping into the water. But first, there was a step which could not be missed out. Our friend Lazare, the waiter, knew this, and was hovering discreetly. *'Deux Oranginas, m'sieur?'* *'Oui, comme toujours,'* I smiled back. Some things were better not changed. Who wants to think in this heat?

But it was a different matter in the comfort of the water. As I moved down the pool in a gentle breaststroke, my body was happily occupied, but my mind began to busy itself too, contented with the rhythmic physical motion perhaps.

'Let's see. Seven thousand, six hundred and fifty-nine verses in the New Testament. What is ten per cent of that? Seven hundred and sixty-six, give or take. Now James is 108 verses.' I reach the end of the pool. Turn. Push off again. 'Luke is 1151, Acts is 1007. So what is that all told? Two thousand two hundred and sixty-six verses. Divide by seven hundred and sixty-six. The hard bit. Mm.' Reach the end, turn and push. 'Almost thirty per cent! And Arthurs have thirty-five per cent already. That makes sixty-five per cent now. We're two thirds of the way there!'

Rolling over on to my back, I half expected to see the crowds jumping up and down cheering at the side of the pool. But no, the only movement was a gentle breeze rippling through the fig trees. Heather stirred on her sun-lounger, and the landmark was acknowledged between God and myself, with thanksgiving.

Up the pool. Turn. Down the pool. Turn. Translate a verse. Turn. Translate another. Turn. Slowly but surely we were inching towards our goal. The waters were calm. There was a certain loneliness, true, but we had God, each other, and quiet comforters like Lazare, who knew, and seemed to intuitively understand our need for routine in these days. Lazare had his own little routine too: between the drinks, he would carry on a side business in repairing motorcycles behind the far hedge. Drinks, repairs, drinks. A most sensible use of his time!

We were moving. We were swimming. We were enjoying it. Our heads were above water.

Visiting the Bakwé

Still, translation was such intensive work that we needed to take longer breaks away from Daloa too.

Some were built in, as I had to travel in my role as Executive Committee chairman of the Branch. With the three girls all at Vavoua School now, Heather was able to accompany me, and we enjoyed a week together in Abidjan, Bouaké, and Bamako in Mali.

Another promise I had made was to work with an American colleague, Csaba Leidenfrost, on a preliminary survey of a Kru language related to Kouya, called Kwadia. Kwadia was also related to Bakwé, the language group in which Csaba and Lisa were working. Away back in 1982, Dr. John Bendor-Samuel had mentioned the Bakwé to us as an unreached people group where translation would be needed, and in 1988, the Leidenfrosts began a ministry there. So it was fun to do this survey together.

On the journey across the wide Sassandra river in a heavily laden canoe, Csaba told me stories of hippos which delighted in capsizing these fragile vessels. A heavy sack of rice, brought as a present for the Kwadia chief, weighed us down, so that the sides of the boat were no more than two inches above the surface of the water. But our boatman manoeuvred us skilfully through the strong currents to the other side.

The day was spent meeting the Kwadia people, listening to them, finding out what they thought of their language, which other Kru language groups they could understand, and which they felt close to. Did they want books in their own language?

Later in the day, we played them a tape of Kouya, Bété and Bakwé stories, to see how much they could understand. Then we took recordings of the Kwadia language, with word-lists for comparison and analysis.

Before nightfall, we crossed back over the river, and then back through the forest to Touadji 2, where the Leidenfrosts lived. The next few days were spent analysing the Kwadias' linguistic and sociolinguistic situation. Our conclusion was that they could understand Godié - a neighbouring Kru language and a group with whom they enjoyed good relationships - sufficiently well to use much of the literature and literacy books which would be printed in that language. But some materials, for example a primer and Scripture portions, could usefully be produced in Kwadia. This would make God's Word accessible to them.

But they had pleaded with us for a church to be set up in their village. They had been very disappointed in a sect, the Deima, which had come and gone, the leader having misbehaved morally. Yet they knew there was a true Way. Could we send someone who would preach the truth? We promised we would let the local believers know of their desire when we got back.

On the Sunday which I spent at the Leidenfrosts, Csaba took me to the village Harris church. I knew of the prophet Harris, a John the Baptist figure who had walked along the coast from Liberia in the early 1900s, fearlessly preaching a gospel of repentance, being baptised and turning to God. Many had responded, burning their fetish-idols, and setting up small churches. Often, huge English family Bibles would sit at the front of these churches, open but not understood. Prophet Harris exhorted the Ivorian peoples to 'wait for the white man, the white man who will bring you the Bible. If a man comes, and he don't give you the Bible, he's a lying man. Wait for the man with the Bible!'

Three Candles and a Clock

As we passed through the village, heading for the Harris church, Csaba and I saw a large group milling round a pick-up truck. The driver was honking his horn impatiently.

Laughing, some girls jumped on the back of the vehicle in their black, figure-hugging dresses, and in a cloud of red dust they were off! Off for a good time at the funeral in the next-door Bakwé village. Off for a laugh in a place of grief, looking for life in a place of death. Because of the funeral, the Harris church would be almost empty that Sunday morning. Empty and sad, where there could have been fullness, and joy.

We were by now outside the church. We stooped instinctively as we entered the long, low building with its whitewashed walls, and made our way towards a bench near the front.

To begin the service, a choir of six swayed slowly up the central aisle. Over and over again, they sang a hauntingly beautiful melody. Its harmonies reached out and put a hand over our hearts, taking away the walls we put up to stop tears trickling down. Emotional or spiritual I do not know, but it mingled fittingly with the nostalgic atmosphere of that place, that Sunday morning. Perhaps the tears were flowing for what was missing, for what might have been...

It struck me that somehow, somewhere, these Harrist Bakwés had missed the point. That they had not understood even the little that had been revealed to them, almost a century ago. That they had got stuck in time, and their religious needle had worn them so far down into the same groove, that they could no longer see over the edges.

The steward woke me from my reverie, as he quietly walked the empty rows, offering his enamel plate to invisible worshippers. Going through the motions, as if those vacant seats were full. *Why?* I wondered. Even the spirits of the absentees could put nothing on his plate. A question for my friend Csaba later. It heightened the sense of unreality in the place.

A bell tinkled at the front, and the Harris priest called us to order. Dignified and impressive he looked in his flowing white robe, with its black bands criss-crossing his front. Recalling the ancient images of the founding prophet, William Wade Harris, I realised that nothing had changed here either. In front of the priest stood a simple wooden table. Three candles burned slowly down towards the table. Why three? Father, Son and Holy Spirit? I had so many questions. On the table, on the priest's right, stood an old alarm clock. I strained to see in the dim light, fully expecting a picture of a farmyard rooster on it. That I could find out later too.

As the service wore on, the priest would consult the clock, obsessively almost, every few minutes, to see if it was time. Time for what? No one knew, not even the priest. It was a service which, appropriately, did not have a closing prayer...

Sing a hymn
Consult the clock
Say a prayer
Consult the clock
Meditate
Consult the clock
Time has moved slowly on
For the Bakwé

William Wade is no more
But is not yet gone
They have done what he asked
Now they wait for more
Time has moved slowly on
For the Bakwé

Time has moved slowly on
For the Bakwé
But the clock
The clock
We fear that the tick
Of the clock has
Stopped

That Sunday morning, the Bakwé girls looked for life in a place of death, and we found death in a place of life. One day, I prayed, they would find life by the Book.

Caveat Vendor

In Daloa I owned a nice mountain-bike. Our houseboy liked it too, and would ask to use it, sometimes for personal reasons, sometimes to go to market to buy our meat. Since he ended up using it most of the time anyway, I decided to offer him the chance to buy it. We agreed on 60,000 cfa, which he would pay off in monthly instalments of 5,000 cfa from his wages. We shook hands on the deal, and the bike was his.

Or so I thought. One fine day, he got a puncture.

'*Patron*, the bike has a puncture.' I looked at him, and he looked at me. Yes, said my inner man, so the owner should repair it. I think his inner man said the same. My outer man, responding to the expectancy on his face, fished out 300 francs and gave it to him. Several months passed, and I forgot the incident.

One fine day, he came to me and dolefully announced:

'*Patron*, the gear-lever is broken.'

'Isn't it great,' I said, 'that there are lots of these bikes around now, and you can easily find spare parts?'

'Yes, there are lots of these bikes about now.'

'How much might a gear-lever cost?'

'2,000 francs.'

'Let's see, you've been paying the bike off for six months now. Whose bike would it be?'

'Yours, *patron*.'

'Ah, I thought perhaps the front wheel would be mine, and the back wheel yours.'

He looked at me, wondering whether this was another of my little jokes, and should he perhaps laugh?

Our houseboy was Dagari, from southern Burkina Faso. In his mind, because he sometimes used the bike for work-purposes, it was not yet fully his. Indeed it seemed to be fully mine. So I should be the one to foot any repair bills. From my viewpoint, the bike was his, he was paying it off, and only if he were using it purely for work would I have seen any obligation to help with repairs.

So I guessed I had another six months of repairs to go before the hire purchase was complete. One of those little cultural adjustments that were hard to get used to. (Or was I being conned?)

Come to think of it, our houseboy was also in the process of paying off his bride-wealth. I began to wonder how much of his wife he actually owned...?

Caveat emptor. Let the buyer beware. *Caveat vendor* too, I suppose.

A Linguistic Discovery

Filipu, I have a problem.'

I glanced over at Emile. He was busy transcribing a Kouya story. Or at least he had been a moment before. Right now he was chewing the end of his pencil. Never one for flamboyant exhibitionism, Emile often registered his deepest emotions with the slightest raising of an eyebrow, or the gentlest quiver of a lip. I scanned his face, discerned his perplexity, and I suddenly became totally alert.

'What's wrong?'

'I can't write this word down!' He looked up from his page at me, incredulous. Emile had been writing Kouya words down for years now.

'What do you mean?' I crossed the room for a closer look at his work.

'We've no letters for it!'

This could not be. Emile had been introduced to phonetic symbols way back in Bahoulifla days, and had learned to write his language using phonetic transcription. For over ten years since then, more recently along with the Arthurs, we had toiled together to establish a workable, economical alphabet for Kouya. We had tested it out, defending our decisions with a technical analysis of the Kouya sound-system. It had been approved by the national university before we began to translate in earnest. Over the years, we had found excellent 'minimal pairs' of words, which clearly demonstrated why certain sounds required their own symbols in our alphabet. We had ended up with twenty-eight letters. The Kouyas had been happy with it, and able to write all their words down ... until now that is!

'Are you sure?' I asked Emile.

'Well, how do you write *this* word?' He then slowly pronounced a word which had sounds in it I had never heard in Kouya before. It came out like 'glagle', but the 'g' sounds were different. I was intrigued.

'What does it mean?'

'It's a kind of tree you find in the forest.'

'Does this sound exist in other words?'

Emile pondered. After a few moments, he nodded his head slowly, and finally replied: 'I can think of one. 'Glegle'. It's an adjective. It describes water which is unusually clear. Where you can see the bottom of the river.'

Meanwhile, I was getting quietly excited. Could this be our 'missing' phoneme? The consonant which completed the paradigm? As Emile repeated these two words, the 'g' sounds were not hard or strong. There was an audible friction in the velar region as the lung air passed through the mouth. There it was: a velar fricative in all its glory.

'Wow!' This was quite a discovery. 'Can you think of any more, Emile?' I was getting greedy: moments like these are rare pleasures for a linguist.

But in spite of his best efforts, he could not think of other words, which included the new sound. 'I'll ask the others when I get back to the village,' he promised.

And so it was that twelve years after we began to analyse Kouya, we had to add another sound to our list. In our dictionary, there are only four examples to date, but we keep on the lookout for others. We write the sound as 'gh', both of which letters were already in use in our alphabet, so fortunately no new symbol was required. The four words mean: 1) 'clear, limpid'; 2) 'great whooshing noise (as of tree falling)'; 3) 'type of tree' and 4) '(locally produced) whisky'.

None of the four managed to make it into the Kouya New Testament!

Spiritual Battle

Heather and I did not see ourselves as the kind of Christians who suspected demons behind every coffee-cup. But there were times, while working and living amongst the Kouyas, when we felt the heat of spiritual battle more intensely, when we were convinced that evil principalities and powers were hard at work. There were occasions when we were forced to see certain events not as mere coincidences but as obstacles thrown up by a desperate Enemy in opposition to God's intentions. This Enemy did not want the Scriptures translated, that was certain.

One week we felt the heat of spiritual battle at close

quarters.

Four Kouya men had travelled down from the village to Daloa town to be with us for a checking-session with our German translation-consultant, Dr. Fritz Goerling. He himself flew from Mali to finish the second half of Luke, and the second half of Acts. Time was short: work would be intensive. Heather and I needed the last few days before the session started to finalise our own check.

However, there was a series of minor hassles, the sort we regularly face out here. Our toilet-system got blocked, and the plumber we usually call on couldn't fix it. I needed to beg and borrow suction-plungers from our good friends in town, and Heather and I rolled up our sleeves, and managed, with luck and a sense of timing learned over twenty-one years of marriage, to simultaneously create enough suction to unblock the offending pipe. Relief all round, as with all the extra visitors, it would not have been easy.

And then our phone was cut off. At first I thought it was due to one of the electric storms, but when it persisted for two days, I took time out and went down to the head office to inquire.

'Your number, *monsieur*?'
'78-01-86' He consulted a list in front of him.
'Ah, yes. Line suspended!'
'Why?'
'Bill not paid.'
'But we haven't received our bill yet.'
'What? Let me see... what was your number again?'
'78-01-86'
The agent flicked through a pile of bills stacked on his desk, and drew one out.

'Here it is!', he announced triumphantly. I tried to stay cool.

'It's hard to pay our bill, when we didn't receive it.' Sort of obvious, I know, but...

'What area did you say you lived in?'

237

'*Evêché* quarter.'

'That explains it. Our man who normally takes the bills to Evêché is sick.'

'Ah. I suppose there won't be a charge for re-connecting us?' I asked in a small voice, anticipating a further need to plead our case.

'Oh no! Your line will be restored at 6 p.m.' he reassured me. And so it was. Just another one of the routine hassles, eating up yet more valuable time.

What was not so routine was the five-foot spitting cobra the Kouya men killed outside our front door on the path. Nor the second snake, a deadly viper, I killed in the same spot that very night. Nor the fact that between these two episodes, Clare had taken a sharp pain in her right side, and was now spending the night in hospital, with Heather at her side.

And all this just happened to happen the day before we were due to check Luke 22-24, *the death and glorious resurrection of our Lord Jesus Christ.*

Coincidences? No. Scare tactics? We believe yes. Because the Enemy was scared himself, scared of the power of the Word of God, and what it would do for the Kouya people, he tried to scare us. What did we do? We paused for a day until things settled down, and Clare was over the worst. Then with hearts more at peace we worked in God's strength from early morning until after dark, right until we had heard and checked the story - in Kouya - of how death was swallowed up in victory, the victory secured at the Cross.

Blocked pipes, telephones disconnected. It happens. Occasionally, every month or two, we get a snake in our garden somewhere. But two in the same day? Outside the front door? I am glad I didn't know that the little viper I killed was the most deadly snake our Kouya men know. '*Serpent-minute*' they call it: you have about a minute to live, should it bite you!

And then there was Clare's illness. Not all sickness can be *directly* linked to spiritual causes, we know. It *is* a result of the Fall, and in that sense comes - indirectly - from the Evil One. But this was Clare's first ever night sick in a hospital, anywhere! What impressed us most about all these incidents was that they all happened around the same time, and the worst ones on that very same day. The second thing that struck us was the underlying sense of peace we were all given to cope with the onslaught, and just keep going.

And all this at a time when the consultant was about to approve the Kouya version of the most dramatic, earth-shattering event of all time. Men saw what happened on the surface at Calvary. God knew what was really going on underneath. And we know He knew what was happening under the surface in our case too, and He had it under control.

For we wrestle not against flesh and blood, but against principalities, against powers, against the rulers of the darkness of this world, against spiritual wickedness in high places. (Ephesians 6:12)

By the end of that eventful week, the telephone worked, the toilets flushed, the snakes were no more, Clare was well on the road to recovery, and the verse-by-verse check of the Gospel of Luke was complete, praise God.

Village Trips

Even a consultant-check is not the final stage for a translated book. Changes had been made, and these changes needed to be checked out for accuracy in the Kouya villages. So the three principal translators on the Saunders team - Emile, Hippolyte and Ezékiel - would return to Dema from Daloa, and sit down for long sessions with other villagers, Christian and non-Christian, to fine-tune the translation. Then Heather and I would travel up by car, pick up the team, and make a tour of other villages, to check out specific passages or problems.

Sometimes we would come across slight dialectal

differences, but nothing too significant: Kouya is not spoken over a wide geographical area. We discovered there were 'purists' who wanted to purge the language of all foreign influences or loan words, for instance from Gouro. On the other hand, some objected that there would be no Kouya language left if all the loan words were eradicated! But we felt that the purpose of the Scriptures was to be relevant, meaningful and to communicate, and not simply to be a repository for obscure words. So if there was a choice between two equally valid words, we opted for the word that the under-thirties would readily understand, rather than one which was dying out and would need to be resurrected! However, these visits were invariably good fun, and had the added bonus of including many in the process, and of spreading the news of how the translation was progressing.

Challenges in Acts

Get yourself ready and go south to the road that goes from Jerusalem to Gaza. (Acts 8:26)
       As usual we had read it aloud in several different French versions, we had read the Gouro, and consulted the Jula. I had looked at my English translations, and checked the Greek. The translation table before us lay piled high with commentaries, dictionaries, and translators' helps. But still the three Kouya translators' faces were thoughtful. Hippolyte, usually so quick to suggest a version, was clearly hesitating. Ezékiel looked pensive. Emile was gazing out of the window for inspiration.

       'What's wrong?' I asked eventually.
       'It's that word "south" that is the problem,' answered Hippolyte.
       'Why?'
       'We can say it, but it's a mouthful.' Ezékiel sounded very dubious.

'On the eat-eat-hand of the rising of the sun,'
explained Emile. 'When you're looking towards the sunrise,
the south is on your right hand side, on the hand that
you eat with!'

'So you'd have to include all that in your translation of
"south" in this verse?'

'Yes, if you wanted to be really accurate,' said Emile.

'But it wouldn't sound very natural.' This came from
Hippolyte.

'It would be very cumbersome,' Ezékiel agreed.

'Some versions leave it out,' I offered. There was a
stunned silence. Hippolyte broke it.

'I suppose they might know the direction anyway from
the context?' We looked back at our versions.

'Perhaps we could leave it out for now, with a note to
ask the consultant?' suggested Emile.

'Yes, and meanwhile we can think it over, and see if
there is any alternative.'

This was typical of our discussions as we translated
together. Emile, Hippolyte and Ezékiel - Mr Care, Mr Flair and
Mr Style we called them! The nicknames reflected their gifts;
Emile with his attention to detail, Hippolyte the clear
communicator, and Ezékiel the man who loved words, and
could often find us just the one we were looking for.

They were riveted by the story of the Acts of the
Apostles. They loved the movement, the drama, the unfolding
account of how God guided the early Church. Much of the
action was fairly straightforward narrative to translate into
Kouya, and though it is a long book, we made rapid progress.
However, we began to be aware that we had to be very
careful to be consistent. The story of Paul's conversion was
told three times; Peter and Cornelius twice; the same names
occurred over and over again, and had to be written in the
same way each time, despite variations in the way Kouyas
pronounced them at times. There were speeches, there were
speeches within speeches, Old Testament quotations with

embedded quotations: we had to decide how we were going to write these down, and stick with it. If we were at least consistent for now, later we could more easily change them all to another form.

'Kings', 'rulers', 'governors', 'centurions', 'emperors'. All had to be differentiated in our Acts translation, but Kouya society was not a hierarchical one, with the result that there were few words to denote levels of government. So we had to make use of adjectives like ''kadʋ' meaning 'big', along with some descriptive phrases. Thus 'dʋdʋʋ 'wlulapɩlɩnyɔ 'kadʋ', meaning 'the great ruler of the territory', was our way of saying 'The Emperor'. A 'centurion' we called the 'chief of one hundred Roman soldiers'.

Acts chapter 27 was a challenge! It describes Paul's sea voyage to Italy, and finally Rome. There is a storm at sea and a shipwreck on Malta, and the chapter includes much detailed nautical vocabulary. How do you translate this for a landlocked people group, most of whom have never seen the ocean? All they know are small rivers and dugout canoes.

We knew that we could later insert some illustrations during the final paging process which would help the Kouya readers to picture what was happening, but meanwhile we struggled to find or invent meaningful terms. The 'ship' was a 'big canoe' and the 'passengers' were 'the people in the big canoe'; the 'crew' were the 'workers in the big canoe'; the 'pilot' was the 'driver of the big canoe'; the 'big canoe stopping place' was the 'harbour', and the 'big canoe stopping metal' was the 'anchor'! Later, we decided that the borrowed French word 'batoo' (*'bateau'*) was sufficiently well known to replace 'glu' meaning 'canoe' and was preferable because it would convey the idea of a bigger vessel.

Old Anatole

Village visits were essential for checking, but gave us an opportunity to renew old friendships too. Returning to Bahoulifla was always a bit special, and one courtyard we always tried to include was Old Anatole's.

Old Anatole was born in the same year as Elizabeth the Queen Mother - in 1900. When we visited him from Daloa, he was in his 96th year, but as alert as ever, though his physical frame had become painfully frail. He was the oldest Kouya along the Daloa-Vavoua line.

Old Anatole came to know the Lord when he was eighty-five. He made a clear statement by walking across the public square in an evangelistic meeting and taking his seat with the Christians. Life is not over when you are eighty-five, that was clear, for Anatole had a very powerful impact on his community after that! In the society we came from, some think that if you are over seventy you are past being influential - not so!! Old Anatole was baptised at eighty-six years of age.

'Would you like to see the new Millennium, Anatole?' we inquired of him that day. 'We'll have to organise a great feast for you!'

'Ha! I don't know if I will have the strength, for I am old and tired now, and I would like to go to God's Village. But see here, when I die, don't you go killing all those sheep and oxen and running into debt on my account! That would be a waste of money. Just clap your hands and praise God, for I will be in His Village!'

To see an old man so looking forward to being with the Lord was wonderful. A few months later he did pass away, and though we miss him terribly, he also remains an inspiration to us. Active in God's work, and of great use in God's service even in his declining years, Old Anatole lives on not only in God's eternal Village, but also in the memories of those he left behind in Kouyaland.

Eugénie

We always enjoyed visiting Barthe and Eugénie in Bouitafla village, close to the Vavoua School. Barthe was the vigorous leader of the new church in Bouitafla. We had met him years before, for he had come to stay with us in the early days in Bahoulifla, specifically to fast and pray, so that God might find him a good wife! Just a few days later, into his life the Lord had graciously sent ... Eugénie.

Tapé Tie Eugénie was the first woman to teach literacy among the Kouya people. She graduated from the second teacher-training course, held in January 1996. After the second course, there were a total of twenty male teachers ... and Eugénie.

Eugénie *was* different. She had a dignified, regal bearing, and a distinctive presence when teaching a class to read and write Kouya. Perhaps it came from the fact that her late father was chief over the whole of the Vavoua district, where the Kouyas live. And her husband, Barthe, was deputy-chief of Bouitafla at the time. So she was a very well connected lady!

Eugénie had not been a Christian for long: she was converted after her husband, Barthe. But both have sought, for many years now, to sustain a Christian witness in a village where fetish-worship is strong. Indeed, people come from all over Ivory Coast to Bouitafla for certain cures. There is a danger that the Kouya language may one day die out in this village, due to its geographical location on the fringe of the Gouro area, for the Gouros are a large, dominant people-group.

But not if Eugénie can help it!

She drank in everything she was taught during the training week. At her feet, the whole time, sat her little toddler, playing quietly and contentedly, with just a word of correction now and then from her mother. When Eugénie's turn came to practise teaching class, up went the child on to her back, tied on securely with a cloth, and there she bobbed and danced until Eugénie had finished her lesson.

When we visited, it was great to see that Eugénie had started her literacy class back in Bouitafla, holding it under a shady mango-tree in her yard. She was playing her part to secure a future for the Kouya language in her village of

Bouitafla. Barthe helped her get set up, carrying out the blackboard from his tin-roofed house. Eugénie is a fluent reader of Kouya, and when the children were bathed and the family fed, it was moving to see her settle beside Barthe with the baby in her arms, and quietly and confidently read out the newly translated Scriptures in her own mother-tongue.

Family Farewell

On Sunday, 6th July 1997, a week before we left Ivory Coast as a family, all five of us travelled out to Dema to say goodbye.

I remember very little about the content of that morning service, but I do remember the emotion of it. We were seated at right angles to the little congregation, facing the different speakers who came up to participate. It was as hot as ever, the seats were as hard as ever, the service as long as ever, but it was a time for thinking back with gratitude. I sat beside Emile and Williams in front of Heather, Joy, Rachel and Hilary.

It seemed unlikely that we would ever return together as a family. After all, we were shortly returning to live in Northern Ireland, and the girls would soon be pursuing their own schooling and careers.

After the main service was over, Williams stood up and began to give a tribute to us. We had not expected this. Then when Williams had sat down, Emile stood up, and recalled many of the experiences we had had together. Hadn't the Lord been good to bring us through them in the end? I looked round, and saw that Heather was crying, though valiantly trying to will her tears to evaporate before they dropped. I glanced around further, and out of the corner of my eye could see that all three daughters were in similar mode!

Turning back again, I found my mind suddenly flooding with memories, in no particular order. Yes, I would miss so much. Crowds of happy people. In church yes, but also lining the touchline at football matches, singing and celebrating. Games where all were winners, never mind the score. I would miss the rhythm of the drum, as Kouya youths and maidens would show off their dancing prowess and agility, an appreciative audience roaring them on in the orange glow of the public-square by night. I would miss the fellowship of the courtyard prayer meetings around the open fire. I would miss Gabriel, Zola, Ezékiel and all the others ... yes, we would miss all our Kouya friends.

It was fitting that Williams, the very first Kouya I had met when I came to Bahoulifla in 1983, hanging out of the window of his mud house, should have been present at our family farewell that day. It was also fitting that Emile, our long-term low-key companion in the work, should have the last word.

Later, in Emile's house, we joined Juliette and their wee family for chicken, rice and peanut sauce. Emile sent for Cokes and Fantas in that wee corner shop, where you can buy Panther soap for fishing. The meal was harmonious, and our hearts were full.

Can you be happy and sad all at once? We were.

FINISHING OFF

1997-2002

When I returned as a boy from Singapore to Northern Ireland in 1963, my family had three weeks to get used to all the changes, for we sailed by boat. In many ways I still prefer boat travel to the plane. If you travel by plane, you arrive physically, but the rest of you seems to sail in three weeks later!

July 13th 1997 was the first time we ever returned from Africa according to schedule! We had known that we would need to leave by that summer, as Joy would be beginning her A-level course, which she could only do in Britain. In August 1995, Heather had been back for a short visit to see her father who was to have a heart bypass operation, and while there, she had put the older girls' names down for Strathearn school, and Hilary's for Strandtown Primary, both close to home in Belfast.

We were looking forward to living in our Belmont Park house, which had been rented out during our years abroad. A general amnesty of Saunders' possessions in family attics around the province was declared. I could continue the Kouya translation through trips, and work on the manuscript in Belfast in between. Heather would help me as she was free to, but would have her hands full with family and other responsibilities.

A setback to our hopes came with Eddie Arthur having to resume directorial responsibilities in Côte d'Ivoire earlier than anticipated, but Sue, freer now that their boys were older, took over where Eddie had to leave off.

Tra Didier worked alongside her. It was exciting to see how the Lord led him to join the translation project. His father had been the chief of Gouabafla village, and his uncle was none other than Baï Laurent, the evangelist who had seen us as an answer to his prayers! Studying English at university in Abidjan, Didier helped the Arthurs' team part-time at first, but grew more and more interested. While translating the Gospel of John with Sue, the Kouya version spoke to him in a new way. He felt the force of its truth in his mother-tongue, responded by committing himself to Christ in June 1998, and then returned to Gouabafla to make a clear public confession in his own village. Didier completed his degree, enrolled for a Masters degree, and was to remain with the Kouya translation project until the very end.

We all worked with a greater sense of purpose and optimism now, knowing that with three-quarters of the New Testament now drafted, the finishing line was in sight, though very dim and distant as yet.

Translating in the Attic

It was a strange experience, checking the translation in our attic in Belmont Park, Belfast. My body was in Britain; the rest of me was in Ivory Coast much of the time, as my wife was often to remark! But it was reassuring to know each day that several thousand miles away the work was advancing too. Emile, Hippolyte and Ezékiel were keeping each other at it as they met in our living room in Dema village, and Sue and Didier were making steady progress in Abidjan.

I had cleared out this roofspace while Heather made a visit to Ivory Coast in April 1998. Several decades of grime and dust were removed, then the experts came in, installed a ladder, flooring, walls and a window, and soon after Heather came back, it had become an office! During her trip, a consultant checked the rest of Kouya Acts, and the draft of Galatians was improved at a workshop.

During the next five years, I was to make a total of six trips out, each lasting four to five weeks. Working in the attic was solitary. My moods would fluctuate without colleagues to temper them, so I looked forward eagerly to the trips. These were very productive, and I always returned home feeling encouraged. But in between, my mood would sometimes plummet.

Doubts

Will we ever make it? Back come the old doubts. Nag, nag, nag. 'You'll never make it!' We are so near. Yet we are so far.

It is not for others, for Heather, for the Arthurs, for Emile or for Didier that I doubt, at times like these. It is for myself.

I wonder, today, if I will have the physical strength. Will my body hold out? It seems to register stress so readily. Those adrenaline surges were scary. Heather rang the doctor in the night, but when he explained what was happening, the terror in it subsided. I remembered then the times they had come uninvited in Thame, eight years ago now, when we thought that Africa had become a closed door.

But why now? When we are nearly there in the translation, and I am not unhappy? Perhaps because I am imagining that bringing this translation to a conclusion depends totally on little me, and for little me the strain of this responsibility is too heavy.

Will I survive spiritually? What forces are ranged against us in this fight? I fall so often, I disappoint myself, never mind You, Lord.

And yet, behind and beneath and within it all, You keep the hope there. My body does keep going, somehow. There are little spiritual victories, just tiny ones as far as eternity is concerned, but they encourage me.

If only it weren't so SLOW! Verse by verse by verse, and not even Belmont Park knows to applaud those little milestones reached here in the attic. But when they clap a good shot in the Bowling Green adjacent to our house, I sometimes rise and take a modest bow of acknowledgement.

Don't tell anybody.

Fitting in Back Home

You have to be careful, when you have just returned from Ivory Coast!

'Think left, think left!' I tell myself as I pull out of our driveway on the wrong side of the road. I manage fine for a few minutes, then find myself grabbing the armrest instead of the gear lever! I park at the supermarket, and stroll towards the entrance, so as not to get too overheated. Except that all around me people are scurrying about, as if it were a race to get in there first! Of course, no heat. Move quickly, Philip, got to keep warm.

Once inside, I stand and stare at the cereal shelves for a while, until a few curious looks force me to move on, even before I have decided: I will come back later. Perhaps the yoghurt will be easier? Low-fat, high-fat, medium-fat, set, Greek, fruit fools, petit filou - ah, that's a brand I recognise - I pop them in the basket. Except ... what's that? Special offer! Twelve pots for ten, two extra. How much is that for one? Let's see. And what's the pot-weight? My mental arithmetic can't cope with the calculation, so I stick to the French brand I know.

I move along. AIR MILES! yells the sign. Now that's interesting. For chocolate mousses? Great. We all like those. Never mind the price, think of all those lovely free trips. Maybe if I only come here looking for air mile offers, this could be quite fun! I take a mental note.

Taking my place in the queue at the checkout, I slip a cream egg into my basket. That's for later, for my nerves. My turn comes. I have followed the others, like a good missionary participant-observer, in loading up my purchases behind the wee sign which separates your yoghurt from my yoghurt. I have taken care not to pile too high, because of the jerky conveyer-belt. Now comes the tricky bit.

'Hello, how are you?' Credit card. Shop card. Pack the food in quick! All those people behind me, and they're all in a race. Sign here please. No pen? Here you are. Very pleasant lady. Shall I ask her how her family is? Better not.

'Cashback or vouchers?'

'Ah... mm...'

'Air miles?' she adds helpfully.

'Yes, please.' I reply with relief. She hands me back cards, receipts and vouchers. Oops, my right hand is occupied, carrying my bags. Left hand is impolite. Turn aside to set bags down carefully, and take cards with right hand. Girl looks at me questioningly. Ah yes, left hand is okay here. Must remember that. Take another mental note, search for cream egg, and join crowd in the hundred-metre dash for the cars.

So much has been written about this: culture-shock, reverse culture-shock when you return to what you thought was 'home', and reverse reverse culture-shock, when you had become a little comfortable again in the home-land, it was time to leave again, and you find yourself reacting to the adopted country the second time round.

After many years of this coming and going, I sometimes wonder who I am and where 'home' is for me now. Books talk soothingly of becoming 'international people', of being able to take on multiple personae according to where you find yourself. However true and even desirable this may be, you do lose something of yourself along the way. In many ways I feel Irish, and love my Irish identity, but am often struck by how unlike the Irish around me I feel. Sitting in a group of Ivorians now I can sometimes feel more at ease, because I know what to do and what is expected of me.

British society changes so much more quickly than Ivorian society. Technological advances, work patterns, leisure, topics of conversation: when you have been absent even for three years, the changes are staggering.

The first time it was video-machines. I never did work out how to set the timer to regularly tape a programme. The second time it was compact disks. Our daughters, more enterprising and ready to embrace what is new, were soon owners of CD players. We guessed we would probably buy one when we are retiring (by which time they would be obsolete).

We remained at the blunt edge of progress. Wherever low-tech was, that's where we were. The last time we returned to the country of our passport, half of the people we met on the street did not respond to our 'hello', for they had just recently bought a mobile phone, and were busy being very cheerful to someone far away.

I found I could have a surprisingly strong internal reaction to these changes. I could experience hatred for a VCR, covetousness for an expensive CD player or music-centre, and resentment of a mobile phone of whatever colour, especially when it went off behind you on the first tee when you were addressing a golf-ball. I maintained that only little round white chaps with dimples should be addressed on the tee. But perhaps that just showed that I had been in Africa too long.

At such times of cultural adjustment, I coaxed into my mind visions of cool walks along the coast (ah yes, even 'cool' was no longer the 'cool' it used to be). I would think of cinnamon loaves from the local home bakery, and an Ulster Fry when nobody was looking. I would think of cosy gatherings of relatives, of Match of the Day, of friendships which have lasted the years, of the doctor just a phone-call away, and then I would start to fit back in just a little bit.

Ireland had changed, I had changed. There was no going back, but there was lots of potential for us both, together, in the future. This was what I told myself anyway.

Birthday

Hilary is ten years old already. What a lot of living there has been since that night in Abidjan when she was born.

29th July 1997

Dear Hilary,
You were born strong. Ten years ago today, you clenched the doctor's thumbs in your tiny palms, and pulled yourself up as high as you could off the cool clinical shelf. 'All

252

those French vitamins during pregnancy', we joked.

You grew up strong. You walked earlier, talked earlier, fought earlier. You were the supermarket trolley with a mind of its own: we kept having to drag you back on course.

But such determination! Whatever your little mind and will desired, you went after it with all your might. So many goals you have already achieved, but that was yesterday, there are so many more to run after today.

I am glad you do not fully realise it yet, but because God has given you so much, you can be a power in this world for good, a power beyond the ordinary. I am glad because this kind of weight is too heavy for you to bear just yet.

So just keep on the move, Hilary, and your mum and I will try to guide you. We will pray that you will be kept in the Way. Advice springs all too quickly to our lips, but we will try to hold back, try to let you run with the freedom you were born for. And as for those gifts which you are so busy unwrapping, we will ask the Lord that, in His time, He will allow you to discover with delight the purpose for which He gave them to you.

With love,
Dad

Compassion

This morning, upon awaking, I found a little plastic bag on my bedside table. It was full of coins. A note on a scrap of paper read: 'For Kalou'. I was touched, and slowly counted out the coins. Three weeks' pocket money! That was an awful lot for her to have given.

I recalled the conversation of the previous evening: I had been explaining to a friend how Kalou, our Kouya Christian colleague, was having a hard time financially right now. I had not known that my daughter was listening in. Not just listening to me, but to the feelings of compassion the Lord was prompting in her heart.

Then this afternoon, another daughter exclaimed: 'I'm really fed up with some of these social anthropologists I have to read! You'd think the people they're describing weren't real people! They talk about cultures and peoples as 'primitive'. It's sooo patronising. Why, those groups are probably miles more sophisticated than they are in some ways!'

She was leaping to the defence of the under-privileged peoples, the so-called under-developed nations. I could see that it was compassion in another form. Warmth spread round my heart.

I was proud of them both, happy in the knowledge that years with the Kouyas had helped create this tenderness of heart.

Wastefulness

My kids laugh at me over this. You see, when I am living in Northern Ireland, I can't pass a skip on the street, without examining the contents. Our daughters think that this is why I go out, regular as clockwork, for my midnight walks. It's not of course, and I prefer to call them 'constitutionals'. They think that I go to have a good peek, under cover of darkness, at what the neighbourhood is throwing out.

Perfectly good cupboards, doors, stained glass windows. Desks, dressing tables, wardrobes. I confess that some of these are now adorning our garage, waiting for the day when they will be re-instated with a shout of triumph from the one who discovered and rescued them. Rescued with permission from their original owners, of course. This is the bit that embarrasses the girls, and I do understand their feelings.

But, in my defence, let me climb on to my soapbox for a minute.

You see, I hate the wastefulness of our society. The abandoned, half-eaten burger left on the restaurant table. The perfectly intact wristwatch, which is not usable because the glass face is broken, and no jeweller in town, it seems, has a face to suit it. Machine after machine breaking down and being thrown out, because it is cheaper to buy a new one than to have the old one repaired. What we wear being determined by those who decide what is fashionable this year, instead of what is still practical, useable, without holes, even if it happens to be the wrong colour or shape.

You know what I mean. Moving in and out of the two worlds, the disposable society on the one hand, and the 'make-do' society on the other, just serves to aggravate the sense I have that something is wrong here. It explains why I take two 'broken' watches to Africa with me, and get them fixed at the 'Horlogerie moderne' ('modern clock shop') at the end of the track, for only a few pence. The half-eaten burger is given to a hungry child nearby. Not literally - I do not take the burger out to Africa with me! There, unwanted wardrobes are sawn up, and planed for shelving. Broken metal coat-hangers are twisted creatively to produce toy bicycles for eager children.

Now do you wonder why I hesitate as I pass the skips?

But I *am* making progress in adapting to this culture, and my family give me helpful pushes now and then. The first Christmas after our return, I remember asking: 'Where shall I keep this wrapping-paper?' (which had been used on a present received). The second Christmas, I 'went for it' in a big way, and threw the paper out, with only a few seconds of doubt and indecision. By the third Christmas, I was not only throwing out the paper, I was trying to dispose of everything else in the lounge that reminded us of Christmas! I became a giant human vacuum cleaner, sucking up everything Christmassy in my path, and I even felt good about it afterwards.

I am told this is progress.

Luke Published!

We were seeing progress in translation too.

At last, the Kouya Gospel of Luke was published! Gold covers, seventy-six pages, only a preliminary edition, but the process showed us what was ahead of us for the whole New Testament. I thought back over to the stages the book had gone through.

First there was the initial translation with the Kouya team. I had prepared the exegesis with Heather, and as the men translated, we checked for accuracy of meaning as well as for consistency of spelling. Next, we invited a few other Kouyas to read this first draft, and noted their suggestions for improvement. The improved version was then read out to larger groups in the villages to gauge reaction and understanding. The translators also used this version to preach and teach from Luke in the Kouya churches.

Then about a year ago, we invited translation consultant Dr Fritz Goerling to spend two weeks with the whole team, to examine the Gospel verse by verse. Backtranslators had been chosen to tell us what they thought the Kouya meant. These men were neither translators nor believers, and were therefore unfamiliar with Scripture. This was a deliberate choice on our part, as it would show us where we needed to make the translation clearer.

The draft of Luke, somewhat battered and bruised (constructively!), was then taken away to insert the necessary improvements and corrections. We consulted with other Kouyas on problem passages.

One copy came back to Britain with us last year, while others were left with the Arthurs' team and with each translator for comments. I read through the manuscript again here in Belfast, also checking punctuation. Then Emile and I met up in Ivory Coast in November 1997, and found further little details to change, especially in the hyphens and apostrophes by which we now indicated the tones.

Now Luke was ready, or so we thought! Heather met up with Sue, Didier and Dibert in March 1998 on her visit to Abidjan. They discussed key Scripture terms, such as 'repentance', 'grace' and 'mercy'. Most were easily agreed upon, though 'prophet' and 'shepherd' remained problematic. Together they decided to change the word for 'agape' love, because the previous choice had meant 'to need' and 'to want', as well as 'to love'. 'Zɛkalʏe' was better for a pure, unselfish love. When Heather returned to Belfast, we modified the 'love' passages throughout Luke, corresponding with the Arthurs by e-mail.

Now we had to print it out. Graham Lyttle helped us produce the final copy. A friend of John and Ruth Hamilton sponsored the publication. Child Evangelism Fellowship did an excellent job of printing it for us.

So many midwives to bring one book to birth! It meant pain at times, but the joy of holding Luke in our hands helped us to forget the pain. I guessed this was a foretaste of the feeling we'd have once the New Testament was complete.

I looked forward to travelling out with John Hamilton later that year, to distribute the Gospels around the villages. The most important thing was that Luke be read!

I've Started so I'll Finish...

I can't decide whether this fixed idea is the bane or the blessing of my life.

It seems to have been always present. The compulsion to complete assignments, repay debts, settle up, and settle for no less than finished.

It has meant that I could not leave the Kouya translation in mid-stream, when that would have been easier than to continue. A new life beckoned, which could perhaps be lived without that constant weight on the shoulders.

It has also meant not being able to really rest, really relax during the final stages of translation, for the next day's deluge of details would inexorably engulf me.

Am I a slave to it? In a way. I've started so I'll finish. Yet a willing slave mostly, knowing that no criticism would have come to us if we had left the project, especially when illness struck as it had done so often, but conscious too that we would have to live with ourselves afterwards if we had pulled out. We would have had to live on with the might-have-beens.

Now that it's nearly over, now that the end is in sight, I feel mostly a great relief. Soon enough, as day succeeds day, will come the bubbling joy. For now, it is enough to know that that joy will one day come our way. Disengagement will have to be gradual, just as engagement was.

Emile, Kalou, Didier and the rest of our Kouya friends may fear that we will abandon them after the translation. But this also will be a gradual disengagement, an agreed separation, never a definitive divorce. We are together for life, in some form or another, but we shall have to learn to live apart, they without me, me without them. This process is already underway, and it is a hard lesson, but an important one: the Lord is perfectly capable of looking after each one of us without the others' help.

Soon I will be finished and then, perhaps, I can make a new start ... but we are not there yet.

It's Dark, Lord

When there is no light, darkness can be very scary. When I fly over Africa by night, and peer down, it is a dark continent. The blackness below is complete, except for a rare cluster of amber lights indicating a village or small town: glowing embers around which men, women and children huddle, the threatening blackness at their backs.

Today was black for me in Belfast too, Lord. Black and bleak. Inside, not outside, for here in Ireland there are no real wild animals waiting to pounce.

Outwardly, we are safe, external fears are taken care of. But what is fearsome are the dark forces within, the inclination to sin and despair. I sigh when I know it will be with me till I die. Will I make it to the end of this translation? Will I have the strength? At these times, I feel so alone, and ask myself whether You will tolerate my weakness, and let me live to see the dream fulfilled. Or shall I remain like Moses in a place tantalisingly close, but still outside the Land of Promise?

And so I huddle round my own small fire, and gently blow on the embers with the little spiritual breath that remains, waiting, waiting for a faint glimmer of hope to return. Waiting, and hoping that some day my fire will flame and crackle and spark again, and basking in its glow and warmth, I will be able to forget the fearful, doubting darkness that constantly seems to lurk behind me.

I am waiting, Lord. *Breathe on me, Breath of Life.*

It was time for another trip to Africa. These were a great boost to morale. I would look forward for weeks to being back in the familiar tropical environment, back with colleagues all involved in the same purpose, that of translating the Word of God into West African languages. I would wake each morning with a focused purpose, knowing what I had to do that day, and that was a comfortable feeling.

Storms

A storm was coming! It was the noise of the wind that had wakened me from a deep sleep. Just in time! I ran to close all the louvre windows before driving horizontal rain penetrated the flat. Outside in the tropical night, the palm-trees bent and danced like dervishes, while the wind howled eerily.

Last window! Adrenaline pumping and heart pounding, I sank down on the cane settee to watch in awe the powerful forces of nature.

Waves of rain already hammered on the tin roofs; lashes of lightning whipped through the sky, cracking so close that I jumped! Now the supple palm-trees bent almost double, but I knew they would be the last to fall. A severe crack, a tinny answer somewhere, and the lights went out. For almost an hour, our puny electricity was cut off, while the power of the heavenly flashgun illuminated the wild scene.

Safe now, I began to enjoy it. I remembered how we had experienced our very first African storm in Ivory Coast, in this very flat in the Abidjan S.I.L. centre, so many years ago now, in April 1983.

Long periods of calm, and sudden storms. Storms in which we had witnessed the utter supremacy of God's power. This had been the story of our life and experience among the Kouya people. A story now reaching its climax. In less than two years' time, we should be sending the translation off to the Far East for printing. Would there be any more storms, any final twists in the tale?

Perhaps it was the knowledge that a chapter in our lives was drawing to a close, but on the regular visits out, I found myself just relaxing and enjoying this society where we had spent so many years.

Haircut

Today I had my hair cut by 'Mineral Water' in Abidjan (A dynamic translation: she was actually called 'Awa', after the bottled Ivorian water of the same name.)

As it was my first time ever in a hairdressing establishment in Ivory Coast, I confess I was rather nervous. I mean, our European hair is so very different, but when you are playing away from home, you don't have much choice. Heather has always done it, ever since we first went to Africa, and always claimed I owed her £5 after each cut. Such are the little rituals that go to make up marriage.

I needn't have worried. Awa was very good, and her carefree confidence as she attacked my weeks of growth must have been infectious, for my nerves disappeared and I began to look around me.

My neighbour was a rich Ivorian lady. I knew she was rich because she was plump. Flicking through a hairstyle magazine with one manicured hand, in the other she languidly cradled her mobile phone, and spoke in very cultured French to a friend who must surely have been a long way away, if she needed to speak that loudly. If she was not used to having a white European man beside her in the hairdressers, she did not show it. I was pleased I did not make her feel inhibited.

On the other side, however, I *was* being watched. This did not bother me too much, as I have to remove my glasses for haircuts, so everything is rather fuzzy these days in any case. Twice Awa asked my opinion on her work, so I had to grope for the glasses on the counter before nodding encouragement. This I feel I overdid a bit, but I felt there was less chance of disaster if Awa were confident as opposed to nervous, so I was determined to be appreciative whatever.

The girl on the other side was an apprentice. She sat at forty-five degrees so she could get a really good view of the proceedings, and mostly talked to Awa about how much did she think the boss would be paying her at the end of the day for being an apprentice. Again, I felt rather incidental to the real action in the hairdresser's that day.

However, when the glasses went on for a final appreciation, when the mirror was produced for a back view, it all looked remarkably similar to what I see during hairdressing finales down at the Arches in East Belfast. Well done, Awa.

Maybe it *is* time I had that eye-test after all?

'I will Build my Church'

Now I was back in Dema in the wooden village church, this time as a visitor. On my mind was Matthew 16:18:
> I will build my church, and the gates of hell shall not prevail against it.

I looked around me. The building was packed. The Lord was certainly continuing to build his church among the Kouyas. We regularly heard of conversions. The most recent was Victorine, a friend of Heather's from the early days in Bahoulifla, who had finally come through to faith.

In the Matthew verse, the Lord was talking about people of course, not bricks and mortar. But the Lord can speak through bricks too. He's interested in bricks, and He sometimes cements our faith in Him through them.

'*On prend les vingt-cinq francs!*' the announcer would cry out at the end of Sunday morning worship in Dema village. Even before we left Dema for Ireland, it was the custom to take in and record the contributions to the building fund. As so often, the hearts of two missionaries would rise and sink all at once. They rose, because we felt this was a great initiative on the part of the village Christians; and they sank, because we knew that the procedure of collecting the contributions would take another twenty minutes, and it was already stiflingly hot inside the little wooden building.

Slowly, and with dignity, individuals would rise to their feet, move across their row, and up the aisle to the shaky wooden table at the front. If they were on the tall side, they had to remember to duck to avoid the lowest crossbeam. When I moved around the church, I could often see palpable terror on the faces of the faithful as I approached that beam. And with reason, as at six feet one I had been known to almost knock myself out on it! I felt the whole church breathe out in relief when I remembered to stoop. 'Their missionary' - as they called me - was intact.

Stopping then in front of the table, the believers would produce their twenty-five franc coins from somewhere in their robes, and set them down with a clink in front of Emile Zola. Emile Zola, who you will remember was our gardener, our house-guard, policeman and general waker-upper of the sleeping saints in church, was also the man who kept the church accounts. With each new arrival at the table, he would glance up, then write down the names in a yellow exercise book with a picture of a pop star on the front.

Twenty-five West African francs are worth two and a half British pence, or about four US cents. This was the amount the church had agreed upon for each believer to set aside every week, if possible, towards the building of the new church. '*Petit à petit l'oiseau fait son nid*,' runs the French proverb. 'It's little by little that the bird builds its nest.' And so for several years, little by little, brick by brick., the new Dema 'temple' as it was called, was rising from the hard red-brown soil on the other side of the main road to Vavoua.

The mason was Honoré, a Christian from nearby Sébouafla, a tiny Kouya village. Now that five Kouya churches were under construction, Honoré was a busy man. Every Thursday was set aside by the Dema village Christians to help keep down the prolific undergrowth, and to assist with the heavy, non-technical side of the job.

As in due course the foundations were poured, and the walls began to rise, so the faith of the village Christians began to grow also, that one day they would complete the task. Emile, our translator and leader in the church, showed me round the site.

'You, see, Filipu, it's in the shape of a cross. The main hall here will hold five hundred people. The two side arms will be for storage, and for an office or overnight accommodation.'

I admired his vision. It was such vision that had led him, as a young lad of twenty almost twenty years ago, to start building his own village-house with every spare franc he earned from his shop job. He eventually completed that project, while so many of his peers had used up their extra funds on youthful pursuits. Then, as now, Emile's eyes were on the future, rather than the present.

The plan of the church was already clear, but it was still just a shell.

'The hardest part is the roof, isn't it?' I paused to ponder. So much money was needed all at once for the roof-timbers, and the corrugated metal sheets. Roofs, unlike walls, could not be left half finished, or else they would be whipped off in the next storm. 'I'll make the need known to our friends and supporters.'

I returned to Belfast, remembering my promise to Emile.

Though money was sometimes a taboo subject in prayerletters, we felt in this case it might be acceptable, in that we were asking on behalf of others! And so we wrote about the need in our next newsletter.

One morning, a gift for a thousand pounds came through our door, with the comment: 'Please use this for a Kouya church roof.'

I didn't know whose excitement was the greater, my own, or that of the Kouya Christians when they heard the news. I quickly wrote off to Emile to tell him, and worked out the best route to send the gift. It went through W.E.C. in England, to the W.E.C. school in Vavoua, and from the office there Emile could withdraw funds as required for the roofing.

We hear about God's perfect timing, and how about this? Emile wrote this letter back to me:

'We received your e-mail letter of 12th December, 2000, on Saturday 16th. Jonathan, our missionary, brought it out from Vavoua to us. At that moment we were all fasting and praying in the church about the subject of the roofing and other remaining work on the new church. Then we got your letter with the wonderful news.

Filipu, when I announced it, the whole church praised and applauded the Lord for a full hour! The Lord be blessed, and all those connected with this gift!'

There are no phone-lines linking Vavoua with Dema, but the timing of the letter's delivery could not have been better orchestrated! Once again, the Lord had provided. *Jehovah Jireh* – He always did.

Looking for Inspiration

Back in the attic, I plodded on. One day, immersed in a sea of details, I looked up through the skylight at the chimneystack. The sky was a hazy blue, rare for Belfast. Inexorably my thoughts returned to Africa.

I thought again of Baï Laurent.

The whole Kouya New Testament had now been translated, and translation consultants had checked every verse. There were over five hundred adult Kouya believers, and probably as many children again. Each Kouya village had a church, apart from the two smallest who could walk to villages next door. Some villages had several churches. Kouyas were learning to read and write their language in preparation for the Scriptures' arrival.

And what of Baï Laurent? His rusty green bike was parked now more often than ridden, though he still walked out to work his coffee plantations. A generation of younger Christian men had lifted the responsibility from Laurent's shoulders. His eyes twinkled as he watched them go purposefully about the Lord's business, with a set to their jaw. We prayed that the day the Kouya New Testament was dedicated, Laurent would be present. What a joy it would be to see him accept the book in his hands, now complete in his own language for the very first time!

As my eyes turned back from the chimneystack to the translation desk, I found them full of tears. Yes, Philip, don't stop now, just keep on going.

I resumed my search for the missing tone marks.

Prayer

Create in me a clean heart, O God, and renew a right spirit in me.

Lord, I come to this point so often. How I must exasperate You. Fondly imagining I can manage to sort life out by my own tiny understanding of it, I float from day to day, applying reason to what I see, and will-power to move towards the goals of our life. It works for a while.

And then, all of a sudden, my boat runs aground: its hull scrapes over submerged rocks, and it crunches to a halt. Yes, Lord, that's me sitting there, utterly stranded.

No, I can't make it on my own. What sadness! I can't measure up even to my own meagre expectations, never mind Yours, Lord. I have thought thoughts that should never cross a missionary mind. I so yearn to rise above these temptations, to be free of their crippling power, and on days like today, I can't do it.

Yes Lord, I come to this point so often. How I must exasperate You. In Ireland, in Africa. In England, the U.S.A. and France. I can't run away from it, for this weakness is within me, and it follows me wherever I go. Tears well up, tears of frustration, tension and remorse. I cry them before You: they are a cry for help.

And slowly, the flow of tears clears the decks. Eventually, their flow allows the boat to float free of the rocks where it had foundered.

You met with me there on the rock, Lord. There I confessed before You my pride and my sin. There I cried for cleansing, and You answered with a new filling of Your Spirit.

Once again, You have provided a way of escape. As promised. I can start to move into the future again, shakily, but depending on You.

Thank You, Lord.

Hugh

Early one morning, I was walking along to the Building Society in Ballyhackamore in East Belfast when a Kouya greeted me.

'-Na fuloo!'
'-Aoo. Kao -sa ...What?!?'

I jerked my head around in time to see Hugh McCormick's smiling face, then the back of his head as he sped away from the traffic-lights with a wave of the arm.

I grinned. Two worlds, and I was half in, half out of each of them most of the time. Not too many Kouyas in East Belfast, true. But comforting that at least some of our Irish friends knew about the other world, and had even been to see it for themselves. Hugh had visited Dema in January 1985. As I thought back, memories of his month in Ivory Coast came back to me vividly.

'I don't believe what I'm seeing'. Hugh's face had been a picture: a mixture of pleasure and amazement. 'This is a miracle!' I had to agree with him, it was. At that particular moment, we were witnessing a bulldozer flatten our building-site, achieving in an hour what would have taken our manual workers at least a week. 'Should help the construction flow-chart, Hugh!' I joked.

He had taken time out of his busy schedule as a surveyor in N. Ireland to come and help us build our new house in Dema. Dema was next door to Bahoulifla, only ten minutes up the track towards Vavoua. Earlier that day, we had come to make arrangements for the manual workers to start, only to find a road-grading machine parked in Dema market place. 'Where did this come from?' we asked. 'The sawmills' we were told. It gave us an idea. Would the wood-factory let us use their machine?

A quick visit to the wood-factory followed. 'Ja, ja. Kein Problem. I'll see he does it when he's finished the other job. Give the driver a tip!'

And so it was that the valleys were filled, and the termite-mountains made low. I reminded myself to be sure to lose the next international chess-match with the director!

My village-friends never saw a white man work so hard in the heat as Hugh, before or since. To this day they talk about it, and his muscles expand with the telling. He dug foundations, he lifted cement-blocks. He made heavy wooden window-frames with anti-theft bars running through them. And by the end of his month with us, we saw our new Dema house reach lintel height.

Psalm 127, verse 1: Unless the Lord builds the house, they labour in vain that build it.

Absolutely true. Cement-block houses, and spiritual ones as well.

Money

The temptation was great to worry about it.

Because we didn't know in advance exactly what would come in each month, from the very outset of the translation project, sometimes the dark fear lurked that insufficient would arrive! I wondered did Elijah ever have doubts about the ravens? Did he ever scan the horizon anxiously?

I admit that *I* have done so, and at such moments it was frightening to look forward, to future bills, to predicted needs. I'm sure Elijah hadn't a mortgage out on his cave. Water was free at Cherith, and there were no school uniforms to buy there! I would expend much energy thinking of ways to cut down, to do without, or to postpone. If things were good one month, should we go ahead in faith and decorate that room, or would we need those resources for next month's bills?

At such times, looking back was very comforting. Yes, Lord, you have brought us this far, our last regular pay-cheque was twenty years ago. You have built up a band of faithful, generous, praying supporters. You have prompted them to give when it was most needed, and some have given regularly for as long as we have been in this ministry. We look back and we say: 'Thank you, Lord.'

And He says: 'Remember the day you were in a

dilemma? You were wondering whether to go ahead and support Kalou in producing a Kouya gospel cassette?'

'Yes. We remember.'

'You trusted me then, didn't you? That's how I want you to trust me all the time.'

'In a way that was easy, Lord.'

'How is that?'

'Well, we needed four hundred pounds. A letter came that afternoon with a cheque for that amount. Even we could see it was ravens delivering our post that day!'

'Do you think I don't know how much you pay on your mortgage...??'

'That's right. You know, Lord.'

Manna. It had kept us going up to that point, and there was enough for that day. *Keep trusting, Philip!* I exhorted myself, *for tomorrow is really just another today in disguise.*

Risky Living

One morning, we woke to the news that two teenage girls had been killed. They were passengers in the back of a joy-rider's car in a town near Belfast. We asked ourselves: why did they do it? Why take such unnecessary risks?

I think it is partly because we were made for risky living. We grow through pain, but we become fat and flabby on our beds of ease. So when the normal risks that life throws up are taken from us and from our young people, when our environment is so anaesthetised that we walk surrounded by unseen pillows, then there is a serious danger that we become too soft.

Clearly, many are uneasy with this state of affairs. I see men and women go to such lengths to re-create all kinds of risk. It is even called 'recreation'. Bunjy-jumping, hang-gliding, white-water rafting, fast driving, rock-climbing, especially without a lifeline... all this and more to manufacture the pleasurable thrill of dangerous living.

For my African friends, the thrill is more easily come by, and much less expensive. Snakes and scorpions help. Having to watch your step at all times. Living far from a medical doctor, or hospital. Knowing that even the help at a hospital can sometimes be a hindrance to health. Violent electric storms that send heavy primeval trees crashing to earth. Rubbing shoulders daily with malaria, hepatitis, cholera and now Aids.

If my African friends were here, they would be amazed that we *choose* to put our lives deliberately at risk, for fun! Are we not just grateful to God for being so well off??

A few days ago, I watched a documentary about 'extreme modelling'. A young woman modelling a swimsuit was put in a cage and lowered into a shark-infested ocean. Cameramen circled in flippers, wetsuits and oxygen masks. Bundles of raw meat were also lowered to attract the sharks, and waved about appetisingly. All in a good cause: think of the great photo-shots, the novelty factor, not to speak of the money!

Sure enough, along came the predators. Sure enough, one managed to enter the cage somehow. The model almost lost her life, but presumably everybody got their adrenaline rush, and their money.

However, I think it shows something. Risk sharpens us. We were meant for it. Take it away from us - even from the best of motives - and we want it back. We crave it.

This is a plea for a tiny bit of disorder. Let us live, please, with a little bit of risk in our diets, and maybe some will think twice before they go on the kind of unnecessary adrenaline-binges that put both themselves and everyone else at risk.

Reflected Glory

On my next trip out, I slept under the same roof as the

President of the Ivory Coast!

It happened by chance. I was travelling up by car from Abidjan to Vavoua, and had to pass through the administrative capital, Yamoussoukro. Fifty years ago, Yamo - as we affectionately call it - was little more than a village in the interior. But it also happened to be the birthplace of the former, revered President, Félix Houphouet-Boigny. Today it is a small city, with state-of-the-art buildings, banks, offices, hotels, and a basilica of world renown.

The most impressive of Yamo's hotels is the Hôtel du Président, a giant mushroom with a restaurant at the top, offering views so breathtaking that you forget what you are eating. When you remember, you recognise that the food is excellent also. I usually drop in there for coffee and a break. 'Coffee with the President' I would add jokingly to friends. Perhaps today was as close as I would ever get.

That day, three hours after leaving Abidjan, after negotiating a bad stretch of road, I relaxed as the wide boulevards of Yamo came into view. It often occurred to me that you could easily land an aircraft on them. And soon the hotel appeared on the left-hand side, rising majestically out of mauve bougainvillaea and emerald golf course. As I parked the Peugeot, it was clear that something unusual was going on. International flags crowned the masts, black flashy limousines lined the car park, and tamtams throbbed from the direction of the foyer. I was curious. As usual the car-park attendant was my source of information.

'The President is in conference with the presidents of Togo, and Bénin. Lots of other *grands types* too.'

'Ah.' Would there still be coffee, I wondered? As far as caffeine is concerned, I am a creature of habit, easily put out by minor changes in routine.

'Would I do like this?' I asked him, looking down at my travel-weary clothes.

'Ah oui, pas de problème', he assured me.

I was relieved that at least I had got my better shoes on. When my feet are covered, I am told I am usually presentable.

There was a lot of coming and going in front of the hotel as I strolled in, swaggering just a touch. This is what everyone who is anyone does here, and the body-language is catching somehow. I did feel like an intruder, but my curiosity got the better of me.

The grand marble foyer was packed. When I come, usually only a few souls are braving the freezing cold of the air-conditioning - all is relative- and enjoying the chandeliered setting. I made my way over to my usual coffee-corner, noticing a couple of other white men, and some very expensive outfits hanging gracefully on dark bodies.

It was all very interesting. People meeting people. Suits and mobile phones. One young couple - two men - made their way sedately across the floor, fingers intertwined, with two mobiles pouched in their two free hands.

Attention focused on the lifts. Every so often the lift-bells would chime, and the doors would open to reveal dignitaries. Heads would turn. Groups in traditional Ivorian costume awaited their turn to ascend to the ethereal regions to meet the President. Others returned from the experience, their faces bathed in reflected glory, like Moses coming down from the mount. Friends reached out to touch them. 'Wow, you've been to see the *President*!'

Uniforms everywhere. Stripes and peaked caps. Shining white teeth. Bodyguards. Militia with guns in discreet corners.

I caught sight of myself in one of the mirrored pillars. Mm, not bad: I didn't seem too out of place. Like a gentleman on safari, I thought, if you stretched the imagination a bit. And the *café au lait* was as good as ever. Bonhomie took over, and I sank down a little lower in my leather cushioned chair to enjoy the spectacle some more.

Now whether it was the pounding music in the distance, the urbane hum of voices, the long car-journey or the flight from Europe catching up with me, I do not know, but I began to doze off. It was siesta time after all...

I woke with a start. Something was happening. Where was I? Should I be here? Around me all sorts of folks were rising to their feet, and making their way with increasing speed across the open marble expanse. '*Monsieur le Président arrive. C'est le Président!*' I heard from all sides. I found myself joining them, taking care not to be seen to rush.

And so it was that the Great Man passed before me. He *did* look well. How did he achieve that aura of importance? I guessed it was probably from being in the public view all day, every day.

I enjoyed my little moment of reflected glory, and yet, as he was whisked away from us to the waiting limousine and I turned happily to find my Peugeot again, I was glad that I was not famous. I was glad that I had the freedom to take a short nap undisturbed even under the same roof as the President!

But I did notice that the tip I gave to the car-park attendant was several times larger than I would usually give! Mm. Something was definitely catching.

Cross-cultural Lows

It seems to me that cultures are neither good nor bad, just different. But some differences are easier to adapt to than others. Fresh pineapple and a slower pace of life were not hard for me to adapt to, but it would be misleading to imply that over the years we had achieved anything approaching total cross-cultural adaptation...

It was the butter in the coffee at breakfast that made me lose it. I saw it floating there out of the corner of my eye, and couldn't even bring myself to look at the yellow on brown straight in the face. Call yourself a missionary, Philip?

As so often when I fail miserably, I keep on going down the slippery slope. That morning, as I shared breakfast with my Ivorian co-translators, the coffee experience brought to mind other low points. And these are lows perhaps for me alone: what turns the stomach is all very personal.

For me, it is that peculiar, protracted rasping as the bronchial passages are cleared in the bathroom, followed after a pause by the ejection of unwanted material through the mouth. This is slightly more tolerable after breakfast, a nightmare before it. The sound resounds round the building, out through the open windows, bouncing back off the walls to hit you a second time when you thought it was all over. Surely that effort was successful? You listen in hope and dread. Yes... no..., it starts again, and the perpetrator blithely repeats his performance. This time he does succeed, but leaves you a quivering wreck in the adjoining bathroom.

Mind you, our method of taking the offending material, carefully wrapping it up in a handkerchief, and slipping it into our pockets *to keep it* (imagine!) - this custom was always indescribably disgusting to our Kouya friends.

Then there is the Kouya crunch. Crunching the knuckles. You pull each finger, one by one, till they crack. This is apparently relaxing. Crack, crunch, crack. Fingernails on the blackboard is nothing to this. I roll in mental agony.

Crunching the fish-bones. 'The head of the carp is the tastiest, Filipu!' insist my Kouya friends, passing me the dish. 'The best taste is close to the bones, you must eat them to savour it!' Ah, there are limits to the extent to which this cross-cultural coward can identify with the people the Lord has called him to. Crunching fish-bones was not in the job-description.

The Village Film-show

This was the second time I had watched a Christian film being projected in Dema market place. What happened during the second show was a carbon copy of the first one. That it should happen once could be coincidental. For it to occur twice was a sure sign that God had been in it.

Jonathan and Becky Hacker were W.E.C. missionaries in Vavoua after the Arthurs and ourselves had left the area. They had a vital and effective ministry of encouraging the churches through Bible teaching, training, practical and medical help. Jonathan also projected films in the villages.

That particular night, Jonathan had taken us to Dema in his double-cab truck, to show two films. The first was the 'Jesus' film in the Gouro language. Many Kouyas speak and understand Gouro, because Kouya men like Gouro women, and often marry them: consequently, many children grow up understanding both Kouya and Gouro. Afterwards, we were to show a shorter one in French, *'La Solution'*, in which African actors portray the spiritual journey of a man looking for a solution to his life-problems.

Jonathan was used to setting up the equipment: we helped where we could. Soon the truck was parked behind the little timber church building, and the television set up in front of it. Using hoes, the local Kouya Christians had cleared a large area round about, and brought out the church benches to form rows in front of the main doorway.

It was on to these benches that the children were now arriving, jiggling and shuffling in their excitement. When all the places were taken, dozens more found a space on the red earth. It was seven o'clock and night was falling fast, so the set-up team had to move swiftly to make sure all was ready. Lighting was provided by rolling out a cable to a nearby electricity-point belonging to the one and only shop in the village-square.

In the gloom behind the church, Jonathan was starting up the generator, attached to his truck-battery. A splutter and a roar, and we were in business. The building effectively masked the drone of the motor. The music began, as a cassette of Kouya gospel music by Kalou Ambroise began to play over the speakers, giving notice to the village that it was time to start.

Emile took the microphone. Thirty years before, Emile had been one of these village children he was addressing. He told them that this was a special day. It was Good Friday, and on this day Christians everywhere especially commemorate the death of their Lord. The film they were about to see would show the life of Jesus, and explain why He died.

An expectant hush, and the show began. I sat, and marvelled that it should all seem so natural to me now. As if I were in my drawing room in Belmont Park, Belfast. Except, looking about me, this was Dema, and by now hundreds of village children sat around me on bench or dusty earth, a sea of unmoving silhouettes, intent on following the story on the screen. Behind them, sweeping round in a giant circle, stood their mums and dads, uncles and aunts, their second, third and fourth cousins, as if guarding their offspring from the threatening night beyond.

One television. Five hundred Kouyas. Five hundred souls hanging on every word. The day before, Emile had shown me the progress on the new church building. 'How many would it hold?' I had asked him. 'Five hundred' he had estimated. I recalled that conversation now as I looked at this crowd, and wondered was this the future congregation? Not for the first time, I was grateful for Emile's vision of the possible.

The Greatest of Stories ran its course. Three hours later, and no one had left. Children had been beckoned for bed, but begged to stay on! Older folks squinted or craned their necks to try to see clearly what was happening: spectacles were a luxury not many could afford. Some who knew the story had delighted in telling their neighbours what was about to occur.

I moved around the outside of the circle, greeting old

friends as they watched. But there was a change in the air. It had grown perceptibly cooler, and there was lightning about. Huge bright patches illumined the skies like an El Greco masterpiece. Village lights flickered, went out, and returned a few moments later. But our generator held firm, and the picture stayed steady on the screen.

The storm was coming closer. Wind gusted and howled. Dust swirled. The children cried out, rubbed their eyes, but kept on watching. Jonathan prayed, Emile prayed, I prayed, we all silently prayed that the rain would hold off until the final film-credits appeared. It was threatening, threatening...

But it held off!
Cables were rolled up, speakers packed away. The crowd scattered, the church-doors were shut. And then the huge drops of rain started to fall.

This had been the second time that a rainstorm almost ruined a film-show in that market place. But it didn't. It was as if God had allowed us all to watch right to the end, and had then once again poured down His blessing on the five hundred Kouya men, women and children now running for shelter to their homes in Dema village.

Milestones

By October 1998 every verse of the New Testament had been translated into Kouya. By September 2000 every verse had been checked by a consultant, many verses more than once, and the twenty-seven books were passed for publication.

However, in between these landmarks, something unprecedented had happened in Ivory Coast. On Christmas Eve 1999, this normally very stable West African state had undergone a military coup! Thankfully, there was little bloodshed, and although the President was deposed and fled the country, law and order were quickly restored after a few days of uncertainty.

It left many expatriates feeling uneasy. For ourselves also the question arose: could it possibly be that after so many obstacles had been overcome, the political situation might cause a further delay in the Kouyas receiving their New Testament?

The coup had the effect of dispelling any attitudes of complacency as we entered the final phase of the marathon.

THE LAST LAP

In April 2001, Sue Arthur and I travelled out to Ivory Coast for one last visit before the typesetting process would begin. Our aim was to have as much of the translation as possible read aloud in front of as many key Kouya Christians as possible.

We planned to hold the readings in the living room of our house in Dema, but first, we had to set out on a grand tour of the Kouya villages, to deliver personal invitations, and to explain the arrangements.

Enoch

Bahoulifla was one of our first ports of call, but Williams wasn't at home when we arrived to give him his invitation.

'He's at a meeting', explained his wife Prisca.

'Where?'

'In the church. He shouldn't be long.'

We sat down to wait.

Dusk was descending on the village of Bahoulifla, our very first home in Kouyaland. How strange the sounds, the smells, the centuries-old noises had seemed to Heather and me all those years ago, when we had first walked these dusty streets! And how familiar they all seemed now. The residents did not look twice at me when I visited. Now we had half an hour of that welcome cooler temperature before the blackness of the African night overtook us. Prisca, needing to make good use of these minutes for her cooking, excused herself and disappeared behind the mud-wall of the kitchen house, from which smoke drifted and pots clanged.

We were left in the entertaining company of Williams' old dad, Dogbo Kalou, and Enoch, Williams' two-year-old son. We had always enjoyed Williams' sense of humour, since the earliest days, when he had helped us start to live there in Bahoulifla. Looking now at his dad, with an impish smile always at the ready on his twitching lips, it was easy to see where the humour had originated.

I did not yet know Williams' little boy, Enoch. I tried greeting him in Kouya. He looked back at me, jumped up on to a plastic chair, and sprawled on it. His big, bright eyes stared at me without fear, sizing me up. I tried again, with all the addressing-a-two-year-old-boy-friendliness I could muster. I even tried to smile.

Still no response. His mum, who was passing in search of something, tried to get him to answer. His granddad had a go as well, for the white man's sake. But Enoch's mouth stayed firmly shut, he looked past me diagonally into the air, at a point several hundred kilometres away.

I smiled again, shrugged, and turned to his granddad for a reminiscing session.

'Remember the story you told us in 1983? We recorded it. Wrote it down. We play it sometimes. We hear you speaking Kouya to us in Ireland! Remember the one? "The rich man and the cat". How did it go now...?'

'Why is it that they never kill cats and eat them when a rich man dies in the village? That's what the story is about. Do you really listen to me in Ireland?'

'Yes, *Madame Esther* loves hearing you tell that story.'

The old man could hardly see now, his eyes were covered with a white film behind thick, scratched glasses. But his character and courage were still intact. Just then, a young woman crossed the courtyard.

'Evening, granddad!'

'Don't you "granddad" me! You're as young as you feel!'

'Huh!' She laughed as she swayed gracefully round the corner of the house.

My eyes returned to little Enoch, still sitting propped up on his chair, chewing a plastic bag, his big eyes still examining me. I stared back, trying to keep my gaze gentle. He still hadn't said a direct word to me.

He began making that clicking noise with his tongue, that Westerners think sounds like a trotting horse. On impulse, I followed suit, quietly. He stopped abruptly. I stopped too. He slowly began another type of clicking, out of the corner of his mouth. I copied him, stopping when he stopped. He gave me a long blink, then tried a sucking sound with his lips. This was harder for me, but I managed it.

And so the copycat session went on. He had me stretching, looking heavenward, singing Hallelujah choruses (not Handel), he even tried spitting on the ground, but there I drew the line. Always he returned to his favourite horse-click.

Throughout all this, Emile was seated beside me, engrossed in the spiritual book he always carried round with him for such occasions; granddad was thinking his own thoughts; Prisca was pounding banana *foutou* behind the kitchen wall; night was closing in, and we were all killing time until Williams would make an appearance. In Africa, you learn to wait.

Williams did eventually come. We knew he would, for banana *foutou* is the Kouya man's favourite dish. It was now dark. We exchanged news, and explained to him when it was that we had arranged for the Bahoulifla contingent to come to Dema for the New Testament read-through. Williams promised he would be there. We declined his offer of dinner, promising to come back another day for that purpose, and then we were all shaking hands and ready for off.

I slipped little Enoch my funny yellow torch, the one which can double as a lantern if extended, and he led us importantly to the car. There, somewhat reluctantly, he gave me back the Boots special.

As we waved goodbye, I reflected that Enoch and I had not exchanged a word in the two hours we had spent visiting.

And yet we had become firm friends.

New Testament Readings

At last all was ready to begin, and we started the readings on the appointed day! We stressed that we wanted honest feedback and advice, for this would be their last chance to have input. In four months' time, the final checking and typesetting process would be beginning in Horsleys Green, England.

Didier and Hippolyte shared the reading. Ezékiel listened for style, and Emile, Sue and I recorded suggestions and definite changes. On any one day, we generally had a dozen Kouyas listening in; the reading continued from early morning until dusk, with a break for lunch under the mango tree.

Ten of the twelve Kouya villages sent representatives. Kalou Williams was there with the Bahoulifla group, Séry Laurent came from Kouléyo. Prosper – tall and distinctive with his sandy hair - arrived from Bonoufla, and Barthe from Bouitafla also attended. Kétro Bassam, Dédiafla, Gatifla and Brouafla Kouya were all represented. Séry Emile cycled in from Gouabafla, followed by - who else but Baï Laurent of course! He wasn't going to miss the occasion! Kalou Ambroise was our minstrel, and he would regularly pick up his guitar to lift tired minds or flagging spirits with a song of praise.

Our remaining questions about key terms were resolved during these weeks. The group was happy to accept -Lagɔɔ gbʊgbanyɔ for 'prophet': it meant literally 'the one who speaks God's affair'. Then one day they tackled the thorny problem of 'shepherd'. It was problematic because Kouyas don't have herdsmen who stay with the sheep all the time.

Sheep wander freely round the village and its outskirts, and often a young lad will be detailed to drive sheep to another feeding spot. So the usual Kouya expression meant a 'driver of sheep', which would miss the idea of a 'nurturing' shepherd. 'A sheep nurturer' was possible to say, but it was unnatural in most contexts. The group came up with 'Bhlabhlɛɛ ˈyliyɔzunyɔ' which meant a 'A tender of sheep', that is one who keeps an eye on the sheep to make sure they are all right. All, including the translators, agreed that this was a most satisfactory solution.

These oral sessions were times of encouragement and affirmation, as we realised that, yes, this translated Word does speak with clarity. It was accurate, and it sounded natural.

Kouyas in Britain

It was great to see deep friendship and fellowship develop between our two Kouya translation teams during the final stages, as we combined our two translated halves of the New Testament. Our job was to harmonise and standardise the text, then run a series of checks for consistency on the computer, and finally to prepare each page in the desired layout and form, complete with illustrations.

Emile and Didier flew to England in August, 2001, and stayed for almost two months. In September, they were joined by Kalou Ambroise arriving from Switzerland, where he had taken the Child Evangelism Course at Kilchzimmer. Sue and I worked with the three men at the Wycliffe Centre.

They had opportunities to meet supporters who had prayed for them for years. Didier alone spoke English well. Ambroise understood quite well but spoke little. Emile spoke no English at all before he came. But they communicated, both through interpretation, and through love. They visited Above Bar in Southampton, the Arthurs' home church, as well as Long Crendon Baptist church close by, and Rock Baptist church, Cambridge, where they met up again with our friends

Gordon and Helen Dalzell. Gordon and Helen had been speakers at our Ivory Coast Branch Spiritual Retreat in 1997, and Gordon was now pastor of Rock. Helen had eaten with Emile and Juliette in Dema.

Before the Kouya men returned to Africa in October, I drove up to Preston with Emile and Kalou, stayed overnight with my sister Pamela and her husband Arnold, and crossed the Irish Sea at Stranraer. This was the Kouya men's first time in such a 'big canoe'. It was a rough crossing, but they loved it! Then Didier joined us in Belfast, and they all discovered what the Irish are like in their own village. The men certainly got a good warm Irish welcome at Brooklands, our home church! They are still recovering from the hugs from some of our ladies, who had prayed for them for years. It was an emotional meeting, one Emile in particular will never forget, as he has lost both his mother and his father. Now he could see at first hand how Christians here cared for him.

The Moonbow

It was 25th November, 2001.

I took a moonlight walk that night along Castlerock beach, my favourite seaside resort in Northern Ireland. It was a two-thirds moon, light enough to see by, not bright enough to be seen. Rainclouds passed swiftly overhead, chased over the hills from the north-west. Some spilled their contents, sporadically, on the wind.

As I walked, I thought back. It was almost nineteen years since we had first set off on this adventure, as a young couple with a toddler and a baby. It had taken us to Cameroon. To the Ivory Coast. To the Kouyas. Into Bahoulifla to live, and then into Dema. Into learning a language that had humbled us.

We had experienced marvellous encouragements. We had witnessed a new church being born. Then the serious obstacle of Rachel's sickness. Furlough, and back for more.

Highs and lows. Picking ourselves up, time after time. Then it was Abidjan, and Heather's brush with death. In all our years in Africa, it never got lower than then.

I walked further, profoundly moved by the memory, towards the mouth of the river Bann.

Leaving Thame in 1994 had almost seemed like starting out all over again. We had felt fearful, yet daring to hope. *Seven years ago now*. I pondered those years. *Thank you, Lord, I breathed, for seven good years.* How the project had accelerated! More language-learning to start with, then tentative translation, checking out the initial attempts. Gradually, more confident translation, then checking that out. Returning to Ireland in 1997, with seventy-five percent of the New Testament drafted between the Arthurs and ourselves. Soon the complete draft, then all the checking. Four years of trips to Ivory Coast, and finally the Kouya men arriving in Britain for typesetting.

And now, one month from Christmas, 2001, we had said good-bye, they had returned to Africa, and we could see the end of the translation project. Could it really be true? It had not sunk in yet.

Lost in these thoughts, I turned and looked back down the beach. There, across the sea, stretched a rainbow, a *moon*bow. Not a ring around the moon, but a silvery arc where a rainbow would be by day.

Maybe sailors know all about these, but it was a first for me. Rainbows spell hope, and promise. And this moonbow reminded me that there is hope in life, even when all seems pitch black. Following on from the despair of sickness, interruptions and apparent failure, the realisation of our hopes and aspirations during the past seven years had certainly proved the truth of this!

Right there and then on Castlerock beach, I bowed my head. My full heart sang out in gratitude to God.

At twenty past midnight on Saturday, 26th January, 2002, Wycliffe typesetter Doug Estabrook shook Philip's hand to mark the completion of typesetting. We now knew there would be 675 pages. The Kouya New Testament was complete. It was a moment of great joy, but little did we know that another ten years would pass before a dedication ceremony could be held for this book.

DEDICATION DAY

Life and bustle had returned to the Abidjan streets in recent months. Jay-walkers strolled across the carriage-ways as usual. The disturbing pictures we had seen of lines of ordinary folk hurrying to escape the mortar-bombs and bullets, hands and white flags above their heads, were a thing of the past. Only the tell-tale blackened wounds on the tarmac, or the burnt out shell of a car gave any clue as to the fierce battles that had waged on the city's streets when the New Forces army had arrived in the capital. The next day would be Wednesday 21 March, 2012, the day that the Kouya New Testaments were finally going to be dedicated in the Kouya area.

As we were packing our bags into the car the day before the event, dripping with perspiration in the Abidjan heat and humidity, we wondered what would lie before us in the hours to come, and for the remainder of the week.

How much would the country have changed during the eleven difficult years since we had last been up in the Vavoua area? There were stories of lawlessness up North and West. Would the celebration event take place? Would the authorities overrule it for some reason? It was with a sense of anticipation certainly, but with an optimism tempered by cautious apprehension, that we set out.

Turbulence within Ivory Coast had meant that a large upcountry celebration had only recently become possible - ten years after the Kouya New Testaments had arrived in the port in Abidjan. A mini-dedication had taken place on 5 November 2005 in the capital city, held in the Assemblies of God church in Yopougon, a northern suburb of Abidjan. Up to one hundred had been able to attend, the number including many who were not Kouya, but other interested friends based in the capital. As had become customary by now, proceedings were in Kouya, translated into the national language, French.

There were readings, preaching and scripture in song, all in Kouya. A limited number of Kouya New Testaments were given out, so that at least every Kouya village would have some copies for use in the churches; these had later been taken up to the Vavoua area during times of relative calm.

Much fervent prayer went up that these New Testaments would reach their destination safely, and be quickly put to good use. On that November Saturday, messages sent by Arthurs in England, and Saunders in Ireland were read out and translator Didier told us after the mini-event: "God be praised, because everything went very well."

Then, a couple of years later, Kalou Ambroise sent us some pictures by email from his home village of Bassam. We studied them eagerly. Imagine our joy to see one of a Kouya man standing to read out from his Kouya New Testament in the village church! A shaft of sunlight fell from an adjacent window on to the well-thumbed pages, red with village dust. So we realised that the New Testaments were gathering dust, but through constant use, not through being kept on shelves!

Now, though, seven years had elapsed since that mini-dedication, and at long last we were back to see for ourselves. We were stopped at the city limits by stern policemen dressed in black. They demanded to see our papers. This car had only recently been bought, and the previous owner's name was on some of the documents. No, none of us knew this person. Tension was mounting, until our national colleagues drove up hastily to explain. We were allowed to proceed, but as we pulled on to the motorway, we realised how on edge we were.

Knowing that many were praying for this journey was a great solace. It seemed there was so much that could go wrong. But for the moment, we relaxed on a good road out of town, happy to note the thriving rubber trees, the stretches of banana plantations, the odd farmer wending his way to his fields with his wife, machete in hand and dog in tow. Normal life, life as we had known it, continuing on in the Ivory Coast.

"This is a great road!" exclaimed Laurel, our American colleague and driver for the day. We had all heard about the potholes an hour or two ahead of us, but for now it was plain sailing.

It was funny how now, in context, memories of landmarks came back. We remembered that there was this village here, that pit-stop there, that soon the road would rise to present us with a beautiful panoramic view. Villagers or hunters hurried out to the roadside to try to tempt us to buy bush-rats, strings of mushrooms, even a long snake which looked like a python. Idly I patted my coffee flask, thought of the sandwiches and mangoes we had prepared, and said to myself yet again: *Let's just keep it safe and simple this week!*

If the countryside seemed fairly deserted, the towns were buzzing. It was as if folk had concluded there was safety in numbers, in extremity they wanted to be together. Goods and merchandise were plentiful, piles of yams, pineapples and tomatoes showed that the ground had not ceased to produce, in spite of what violent men had tried to do to wreck things.

Yamoussoukro appeared, with its wide roads, its grand Basilica, impressive street lights. Trappings of a not so distant affluence. The *Hôtel du Président* rose majestically to our left, and we wondered whether it was open for business? It was. Our two cars stopped outside, and we entered the marble airconditioning, feeling ever so slightly shabby. Still, we enjoyed the plush bathrooms, and the cool drinks in the foyer. It was *café au lait* for me, for old time's sake. For lunch we repaired downmarket for a *shawarma*, to a nice Lebanese place, within view of the presidential palace.

Yamoussoukro was about half way to Vavoua, but usually only an hour and forty minutes from Daloa, where we had arranged to stay overnight, at the Protestant Mission guesthouse. However, it very soon became clear that this part of the journey would be slow. It was hot by now, the airconditioning in the car was only working sporadically, and some of the ruts and potholes in the tarmac were enormous. We crept westwards towards our destination.

There was time to think in between the bumps. My mind began to run down a check-list of arrangements for

D-day (D standing for dedication and distribution). We had sent up the New Testaments in advance, a few packets at a time. Each box held either twenty or forty copies. They were sent by public transport, and the bus or taxi would stop off each time at Dema to offload to the local Christians. Since Emile had recently acquired a working mobile phone, we knew that the New Testaments had been getting through. Well, we surmised, if the New Testaments are there, and the Kouyas have not run away, a dedication of some sort can be held! Even if the guests and dignitaries from elsewhere don't make it! This was a comfort. We motored on.

Bai Emile had been busy for weeks with arrangements on the ground in the Kouya area: making sure everybody was informed, going in person round the villages, inviting chiefs, providing transport money for some of the widows and other people we wanted there but who could not afford it. He also delivered last-minute letters to the local secular authorities, who needed to be kept informed, whether they attended or not.

Then there were the huge open-sided shelters covered by tarpaulins, to provide shade for the guests. These had to be ordered, and erected closer to the time. A sound-system had to be organised, along with hundreds of seats, and covered armchairs for the VIPs. A cow would be killed close to the big day, and rice and cooking-pots got ready. The singing groups and dancing troupes would have their last-minute practices. Emile had a lot to think about.

Happily he would have some additional assistance, as well as that of the local Christians. Two good men – Touali Martin and Kalou Ambroise – would be there already, having come up to help from Abidjan a few days early. Touali had come to give Megavoice training: one or two from each village would be learning how to operate and run listening groups for the Megavoice players. These little machines were solar-powered, and played back recorded Scripture. As well as this, Touali would be organising some folk to read out Scripture passages from the Kouya New Testament during the dedication ceremony. I really looked forward to these readings.

Then Kalou Ambroise, the intended Master of Ceremonies, had travelled up in advance with his wife Ruth. We had heard, though, that he had fallen sick, and was flat out in recovery mode! Much prayer was being mobilised for him.

All of a sudden I was jolted back to reality! Our vehicle screeched to a halt and stopped on the brink of a particularly nasty-looking pothole stretched across the road. Some of us were confident, others dubious. In the end, discretion won the day, and we backed off, and took the by-pass.

As we worked up through the gears yet again, I peered through the dusty rear window of our companions' car in front of us. It was comforting to see the piles of special white celebration tee-shirts in the boot. We had bought four hundred of these, and one car would be taking them on to Dema that night. It would have been better to have sent them up earlier, but they had not been ready. On the front of the shirt, beside a picture of the New Testament, was Hebrews 4 verse 12 in the Kouya language: "God's Word is alive, and powerful", and underneath, in large letters in French – *"Dieu parle Kouya!"* – "God speaks Kouya!" On the back were these words: *"Dédicace du Nouveau Testament Kouya. Dema, 21 mars 2012."*

This reminded me that there were speeches to be given tomorrow. The Dema chief would start off, he should be already there in the village. Emile would be next up, and he was also in Dema. Then would come Didier, he was in the car in front. Next would be Sue, she was right behind me in the car. And last would be myself, as possibly the oldest in the group. A "veteran missionary", I had been introduced as in a church service not so long ago. *What a cheek!* had been my reaction, but then later on I had looked in the mirror, and wondered. I recalled a recent visit to the hairdresser's. When you start not to believe the colour of your hair on the barber's floor, you are definitely in denial!

Many bumps and jolts later, Daloa came into sight at

last. Daloa. Memories of our last two years as a family in Ivory Coast, fifteen years ago now. Memories of a final year of concentrated work in that large rented house with its leaks and dodgy electrics. Its lovely garden which the snakes also liked. Memories of the three girls coming home for their long holidays, and of outings to the French club. I would love to explore the town and the old haunts again, but there would be no time for that on this trip.

We turned into the Mission compound. It was familiar, though somewhat overgrown, understandable given what the town and its people had lived through over the past few years. But tall palms and mature trees afforded welcome shade to weary travellers such as ourselves. We felt glad to have decided to spend each of the next three nights in this quiet place.

While we settled in, worked out our water systems for washing, and how much bottled drinking water we would need to buy, the other car left for the Kouya villages, driven by Tiga Ambroise, our faithful now semi-retired services manager and friend from SIL in Abidjan. He was accompanied by Didier. They wanted to check out how arrangements were going for the festivities tomorrow, and would sleep in Gouabafla, Didier's home village.

The remainder of our party slept in Daloa that night. Yegbe Antoine, SIL translation co-ordinator and consultant; Sahi Josias, director of Public Relations for SIL based in Abidjan, who had grown up on this very mission compound; John and Ruth Hamilton from N. Ireland who had taught at Vavoua International school for eight years from 1989; Laurel Miller, who had helped with both the Kouya New Testament and the Megavoice project in numerous supportive ways; and Sue Arthur, who had double-teamed with husband Eddie, Heather and myself since their arrival in 1988.

With other work and family commitments, Eddie and Heather could not be with us. But we could count on their prayerful support at every stage of this momentous journey.

We were joined in Daloa by Hans-Martin Werle and

Gnaly Kpata. Hans had been the translation facilitator for the Guibéroua Bété New Testament, and had worked during the final stages of that project on this very mission compound. Gnaly was the co-ordinator of the Kru Initiative, overseeing ongoing work in half a dozen Kru languages. The next day Jonathan Hacker, former WEC missionary in Vavoua, was also due to join us in Dema. So it was wonderful to see how the Lord had brought all these folk together, representing so many sides of the translation and church planting work in Ivory Coast, and the Vavoua area in particular.

As I lay quietly on my sponge mattress that night, the crickets setting up their nostalgic refrain just outside my glass-less window, I was full of thankfulness to actually be here, so close after so long to the villages where so much of our lives had been lived. I reflected on how natural it all seemed, a million miles away from the concrete jungles of the Western cities I had passed through to get here. I reflected, though, that the next couple of days would be as intense as any I had ever lived through, as dozens of people would be re-surfacing from the past thirty years. With the adults I should be all right. Faces would be older, yet basically the same. But kids who had grown into adults in ten years, wearing different tee-shirts, how would I recognise them? Would their names come back to me? Would I be overcome with emotion by the immensity of it all? I was glad in those moments that sleep has always been a friend to me, and never too far away at the best and worst of times. I drifted off.

I have never needed an alarm clock in Africa. If it is not the crowing of the cocks, it is the local birds which do the job. It was the bulbuls' chatter that awoke me when daylight came next morning in Daloa. This was finally "it", I thought. The day so long awaited!

It is rare that I give more than two seconds' thought to what I will wear. Blue, grey or black, with the occasional break-out for a party. But for this special occasion, I had asked my wardrobe consultant for advice before leaving Ireland, and she had recommended either the check cotton long-sleeved number, or the short-sleeved black cotton article. Either way, Tesco's was the winner. Looking at pictures of important events in the Abidjan newspapers had convinced me that the darker the better. So the black number won!

After a quick bite to eat and hastily swallowed coffee, we were off on the road again, heading north from Daloa, and on to the infamous road to Vavoua, now tamed by reasonably smooth tarmac.

Daloa is Bété, and it was through Bété speaking villages that we first passed. Each one was a reminder to me of journeys past. Had anything at all changed here since I left, I wondered, as I looked out from the front seat of our car. The familiar luxuriant flame-trees still framed that clump of houses set back a little from the road. Now we were coming to the village where a police motor-bike monitored passing vehicles, but no one ever seemed to come out from the shade to stop them. And then, further on, not far from the giant termite-hill, yes, this was the place where a large green snake once slithered right across the track in front of us.

The memories flooded back. Soon it would be the first Kouya village, Bonoufla. Here Heather and I had slept amid cocoa bags and cockroaches on an overnight visit to the little Kouya church. This was where our WEC friends, Rodney and Hélène Gordon, had shown the *Jesus* film in the schoolyard... yes, the school was still there, with its primary schoolboys dressed in khaki suits, and little girls in their blue and white check dresses.

Why were there so many people here? Of course, it was Wednesday, which was market-day in Bonoufla. Each of the Kouya villages had their markets on different weekdays. The Bonoufla market seemed to have grown enormously, spilling over on to the main Vavoua road, and threatening to cut off the thoroughfare completely. People, noise, and goods on display on every hand. Plenty of smells, but no whiff of a depressed economy here. As we crawled through the crowd, our spirits were lifted to see normal trade clearly in such a vigorous state of health. This augured well for the country.

Leaving Bonoufla, I felt a quiet excitement, mixed with nervousness, for I knew that the next village – ten minutes further on – would be Bahoulifla. This was where we had started out on our Kouya adventure in 1983. Just a few kilometres before the village, where the road traverses an expanse of low wetlands and rice is grown beside the river Dé, we slowed down, and were confronted by a poignant sight. It was a burnt-out armoured personnel carrier, a remnant, apparently, of the civil war in 2002. That was a year which meant something else to me: it was the year that the Kouya New Testaments were printed in Korea, and transported by ship to the port of Abidjan. Grass was now growing up through the gaps in the shell of the army vehicle in front of us. War brings death and destruction, I mused; the Word of God brings life and peace.

Ten minutes further on, we arrived in Dema. The village lies in a hollow. You reach the brow of a wooded hill known as the "Carrefour", the Crossroads, where you may turn west again and head for the SIFCI wood factory, and then on down into the forest to the rest of the Kouya villages. So Dema is strategically placed, at the crossroads between the Kouya villages on the main road, and those down in the forest.

From the brow of that hill, we could look down towards Dema. There was no outward sign of anything unusual. But appearances were deceptive: we knew that the dedication event was going to be held in the grounds of the "new" Dema church building, just a little distance beyond the village centre, on the left hand side of the main road. I had never seen this building in its finished state. Eleven years before I had walked across its foundations, which were in the shape of a cross if viewed from above. Gradually, as the Christians saved up, and as some help came in from other Christians, walls had arisen and the roof had gone on.

Now the church was before us, and now there was activity everywhere. Our car found a place to stop, and it was greetings, greetings and more greetings. A special hug for Emile, whom I hadn't seen since he had come down to Abidjan two years ago. He looked older, but there was no mistaking the profound joy underneath the wrinkles. I found myself flanked by two young girls, who seemed to want to be in every photo taken of me. It was the same for John, for Ruth, for Sue, and the other new arrivals. Lots of the dedication tee-shirts were on show: how had they managed to sell so many since last night? I knew that this was a day when many, many questions would have to be stored until a later date.

As a group, we were escorted in a slow, dignified march around the outside of the church to the main arena. A natural theatre, set between trees, with long low tents for shade on four sides, full of rows of chairs. Noise grew in intensity as we approached: drumming, dancing, the general hubbub of people chatting to one another. I took a seat on the soft settee assigned to me, looked to see the others also sitting down, and settled back to look around.

Very quickly I started to relax. There is no awareness on such occasions of the spotlight being on oneself personally. Even though folks are free to look around, and they do, and discuss whom they see, there is in Kouyaland an informality about such occasions, which is at once personal, and yet respectful. Proceedings were yet to begin, so individuals came over to say hello briefly, let us know they were there, and express their joy at seeing us again. The feelings were reciprocal, and I was amazed that the personalities were just as I remembered them, though one or two had grown more frail. But there was no time to go too deeply into their circumstances, just register what I saw. I promised some I would be back the next day to speak at greater length, especially to those I knew had suffered bereavement.

Didier had reminded me of the need to publicly acknowledge in my speech the passing of three of our translation team in recent years. These were François and Dibert who had worked with the Arthurs, and Ezékiel, who had worked with us. Kalou now came across to finalise some details of the programme with me: we had worked on this together in Abidjan, but he had come up early after having some announcements made on Christian radio *Fréquence Vie*, and on the national network also. We had wanted to let Kouyas scattered around the country know what was happening, in case they were free to attend. I was pleased to see that Kalou seemed to be reasonably strong today, in spite of his illness, and praised God for that answer to prayer.

All of a sudden there was a problem! The loud speaker system was not working. With Kalou being below par, we desperately needed this to work. We thought quickly, and called Jacques from Dédiafla village over. Now Jacques has a superb voice, and can make it carry many a mile in a Kouya forest. If he could interpret into Kouya, then at least the assembled crowd would hear and understand, even if the French was lost on them. Jacques agreed to help out.

As it happened, they figured out a way to get the sound-system working again. How? – another question for later. But it was still a boon to have Jacques' assistance. Three hours later, as the ceremony was ending, he was still going strong!

There are moments from that day which stand out for me. The public warm welcome from the Dema chief, a man with a humble and sincere spirit. He mentioned how the villagers had always appreciated being taken in our car for a hospital emergency, or for a baby to be born in the Maternité at any hour of day or night! Then there followed Bai Emile's speech, in which he said, through tears, how he had wondered whether he would ever live to see this day. As emotion threatened to overcome him, Kalou and Didier came alongside and supported him, with one of the teenage girls - the "guardian angels" - providing a box of tissues! With their help, he got through.

Didier spoke in his capacity as SIL in-country director. But as well as outlining the work of the organisation, he told of his own personal involvement in the Kouya translation project. He had come to faith while translating the Gospel of John with Sue, and had bowed the knee and recognised Jesus as Lord of his life. To symbolise this, that morning of the Kouya New

Testament dedication, he knelt down on the earth in the centre of the arena before the entire company.

Then it was Sue's turn. What a hard language Kouya had been to learn! But what a rich language it was! She underlined God's faithfulness to the Kouya Christians, and to the Arthur family through many ups and downs. They had left family in Britain, but God had given them Kouya brothers and sisters, who had become for them a second, precious family. They could all rejoice together that God speaks Kouya today! Through His written word, He has come close to them. Sue finished with an invitation to all to accept this word, and find true life in Jesus.

Later, Sue was called forward to present a New Testament to several widows. One was Madame Bai Laurent, and it was touching to see her, an old lady now, walk slowly right over to the middle with the courage we had come to associate with her late husband. A Testament was given to representatives of Dibert's family, and to Adèle, François' widow. As Sue put her arm round her, and quietly prayed with her, interpreter Jacques conveyed the deep emotion of those moments to the crowd: "Des mots d'encouragement... quelle émotion ... que Dieu la soutienne!" I was given the opportunity to pray also with Ezékiel's widow, present her with a New Testament and thank her personally for her husband's wonderful contribution to the translation. We had known Ezékiel as *Mr Style*, because of his way with words.

My own time came to speak. I took the chance to thank the communities of Bahoulifla and Dema for their warmth and acceptance of us as a family so many years ago, and brought greetings from Heather and the three girls. I wanted especially to honour Kalou Williams, our first language helper. I had been delighted to see him again earlier that morning, so I now asked him to stand up and be recognised by all. Then I outlined the history of the project, and important events well before we arrived. Together with the older man Bai Laurent, young Bai Emile had met with the WEC missionaries in Vavoua in 1979 at the time of the Gouro Bible dedication. They had prayed together that a translation into Kouya would soon be started and eventually become available in their language too. Twenty-three years later, their prayers were answered.

At some point in my speech, there was a commotion several yards away to my left, with people jumping from their seats to hammer the ground with shoes and sticks! It was obviously a snake, and the words were given to me: "Just as they've killed that snake, the Devil is a defeated foe too! But today we are celebrating the arrival of the Word of Life, and a *living* Saviour Jesus!" Or words to that effect. Apparently, we heard later, a green mamba had slithered up on to the trouser leg of Didier's younger brother Fiacre, sitting near a tree. Shocked, he had stood up and shaken it off! After a few frantic seconds, it was struck with a stick, and lay dead.

Even as I spoke and witnessed this, I was impressed by the inner calm the Lord gives at such times. How often significant events in the Kouya New Testament's coming to birth had been marked by the appearance of a snake. If the danger were not so serious, it would almost be funny. Each time they had been killed, and each time the danger was averted.

The moment the boxes of New Testaments arrived in the arena, a surge of excitement moved through the crowd. The boxes were brought up from the village itself, balanced on the heads of the women singing as they arrived in a large procession. Then they were ceremoniously placed in the centre of the assembly. Heading the procession was a young girl of perhaps ten years old, carrying a large black Bible on her head. Babies swayed as they slept comfortably on some of the carriers' backs. The song the women sang told of the tears with which the seeds of this translation had been sown by Bai Emile, but today he was reaping with joy the fruit of his labour. We knew Emile would not have asked for this recognition, but we were glad on his behalf that his part was being honoured in song in this way.

There were readings from Scripture in Kouya; there

were readings from the Kouya reading book by women who had never been to school; there was a miming of the Blind Bartimaeus story; the Megavoice players were presented and an extract played over the loudspeakers; a copy of the New Testament was given to a representative from each village – a chief or his deputy; and prayers of dedication were offered by a circle of Christian leaders.

The large Bible carried by the young girl turned out to be a box with a lid, and towards the end of the ceremony, Kalou Ambroise opened it, and pulled out a number of objects. He had everyone's full attention, as he illustrated the power of the Word of God from these objects. This was a lesson for young and old alike: he let money fall from his fingers, he brandished a sword, he held up a tin of milk, a loaf of bread, then a mirror, then a lamp. "God's Word is a treasure," he explained, "it's sharper than any sword, it's like milk and bread – you can feed on it, and it gives you Life. It's a mirror too, and you can see reflected who and what you truly are, and it can be a lamp for your feet and a light for your paths!"

"Be prepared to come forward again!" Emile whispered to Sue and myself. What was this about, we wondered? It turned out that we were to be clothed in beautifully woven *pagnes*. There was so much material in mine, that I had a job keeping it off the ground as I wrapped it round my body. Sue managed hers much better. But as the chief of Dema gave me a final hand-shake, he pronounced me an honorary Kouya chief! I took that comment away with me, determined to milk as much respect from my friends and family as I could in future days. It was fitting therefore, that the Dema chief and I should sit down together to tuck into our rice and steak in the church afterwards: we were equals after all!

The whole event was a kaleidoscope of such moments. "How did it all flow so smoothly?" Jonathan Hacker asked me afterwards. I was sure of one thing: it was the Lord's doing. So much could have gone wrong: yet so much went right on the day.

As our group talked things over in Daloa that night, we agreed it had truly been a Kouya event. Led by Kouyas for Kouyas, in a Kouya way. And we rejoiced in the fact that it was not a show put on for outsiders.

Back in bed after a truly momentous day, I thought of the Kouya churches which had sprung up over the years in the villages, where there had been practically no Christian witness before. Back to my mind came the smiling faces of the leaders I had talked to throughout that day, who were still going on well. Séry Laurent from Kouléyo, Gondé Robert from Bassam, Jacques from Dédiafla, Jules from Gatifla, Barthe and his wife Eugénie (of royal descent) from Bouitafla, Emile and Tra Jules from Dema. Then there were Kalou Williams with younger leaders Jules and Magloire from Bahoulifla, and not forgetting Prosper from Bonoufla. These churches were in good hands.

Would I ever live here again? I did not know, but this place and this people group would always be close to my heart and in my prayers. Was this the last chapter? Perhaps yes, in some respects. But not in others. The New Testament has finally been dedicated, properly, in the Kouya area. But this is not the end of its life. It is only the beginning.

The Bible is, after all, an *extraordinary* book.

THE BOOK OF LIFE

One day He will hold a book in His hands
And He alone is worthy
To open it up

For He died, and by His death
He bought back for God
People out of every tribe and group,
Language and nation.

One day all books will be opened
And all will be revealed.
The thoughts of all men's hearts
Will be made known.

And one day He will take up a great book,
The Book of Life,
And He will read the names from it.

And we will weep with joy,
for we will hear
The names of Kouya friends,
A great number, many we had not known.
Saved by grace.

Names which our tongues could once not master
The Master will read out perfectly,
For all tongues are known to Him.

And when He holds that book in His hands,
The need to translate will disappear,
No more need for Living by the Book.

For in that great day,
when we meet Him in person,
Then shall we know
Even as also we are known.

APPENDIX A

Events between the Publication and the Dedication of the Kouya New Testament

Three days before civil war broke out in Ivory Coast on September 19th 2002, the consignment of Kouya New Testaments left Korea by ship bound for Africa. It consisted of two thousand copies packed into twenty-five large cartons.

Seven weeks later, on 7th November, these boxes were being off-loaded from a truck outside the S.I.L. centre in Abidjan, the very place where we spent our first night as a family in Ivory Coast, way back in March 1983. Kouya translator Bita Tra Didier was present to open the first box of books, and to be the first Kouya to hold the published New Testament in his hands.

The war had started in this way. On September 19th, northern elements in the Ivorian army had rebelled, and had subsequently been joined by elements from western Ivory Coast, who had also felt disenchanted and excluded by southerners from political power. If French forces, rushed into the country to reinforce government troops, had not intervened, the rebel faction threatened to take over the whole country. As it was, the northern half of the country was swiftly brought under the control of northern rebels.

A shaky peace agreement was brokered by France between the leaders of the rebellion, those forces which were loyal to President Gbagbo, and the opposition political parties. A Government of National Reconciliation was formed. Ministries and positions in the Cabinet were shared between Gbagbo partisans, opposition politicians, and rebel leaders. The French Foreign Legion, along with West African peace-keeping forces, endeavoured to maintain this tenuous agreement, by keeping the sides physically apart as best they could in a zone running roughly east to west across the middle of Ivory Coast. United Nations forces soon joined them in this effort.

However, big obstacles remained in reuniting this country of 16 million. On 3rd May 2003, rebels and army signed a total ceasefire bringing an end to months of bloodshed in western regions. French and West African troops secured a ceasefire line on 24th May. By 4th July, army and rebels declared that the war was over, but the country remained split between the rebel-held north and the government-controlled south.

And what about the Kouyas? The country was torn in two, and the Kouya territory lay along the divide! How could we ever have imagined that the Kouyas would become refugees in their own country within a matter of weeks? When hostilities first broke out, they found themselves squeezed between rebel forces sweeping down to Vavoua from the north, and Government troops desperately defending Daloa to the immediate south. Many fled to set up temporary homes in their plantations. Others braved increasingly difficult conditions in their villages, until forced to leave.

Translator Zebli Baï Emile had to walk for two days and nights through the forest with his wife Juliette and their four young children. They eventually arrived shell-shocked, and gaunt with fatigue at a relative's compound, comparatively safe behind government forces' lines. Kalou Ambroise's courtyard in Daloa became a haven for his fleeing Kouya relatives: as many as seventy-five ended up seeking safety there. Kalou held Christian meetings morning and evening, using the Kouya New Testament which Didier had managed to bring up to him from Abidjan. There were conversions. A Kouya literacy class started up in that courtyard too.

While much of the overt fighting ceased after 2004, there were sporadic outbursts of violence. Many attempts were made to broker peace deals and power-sharing, both locally and through international intermediaries, but with little lasting effect. The rebels, under leader Guillaume Soro, remained in control in the north; Gbagbo, with the Ivorian army behind him, controlled the south.

Gbagbo partisans insisted he was the constitutionally elected leader, and some even felt he had a divine right to be in power. Opponents saw him as clinging to office by all means possible, and unwilling to allow a free and fair presidential election.

After repeated delays, elections aimed at ending the conflict were finally held in October 2010. The results were too close, though, for either side to admit they had lost, with accusations of widespread vote rigging, despite international scrutineers being present in the country. So the vote simply ushered in more unrest when Laurent Gbagbo refused to concede victory to the internationally recognised winner, Alassane Ouattara. For a time there were two "Presidents" in the country. Ouattara was almost a prisoner, holed up in the lagoon-side Hôtel du Golf, protected by United Nations peace-keeping forces. This was the hotel where many missionaries used to enjoy a cool swim in happier times.

There was a stand-off between the two factions lasting for four months. This was only ended when Mr Ouattara's forces overran the south of the country, amid much bloodshed, finally capturing Mr Gbagbo in Abidjan and declaring him deposed in April 2011. Ouattara has been President, and not only in name, ever since.

It was clear to neutrals that in such a war environment there would inevitably be atrocities committed by both sides. The events of the past ten years have left a terrible sense of numbness. Healing will take time, and it was in this atmosphere that the Kouya New Testament was dedicated in March 2012 in Dema village, near Vavoua. This gives the Kouyas the chance as a people group "to live by the Book".

It is our prayer that lasting peace and stability will return to all peoples of the Ivory Coast.

APPENDIX B

Landmarks in the development of the Kouya Church

1. Brief history of the Kouya church

Before 1980:

- Baï Laurent of Gouabafla, converted mid-1950s, keeps the faith despite much opposition.

- A handful (perhaps a dozen) Kouya Christians dotted about the country.

Early 1980s:

- The only regular meeting in Kouya was an evangelistic one, in the village of Dema, where the Gospel was explained to children. A little wooden hall was built here by Tra Jules and Zébli Baï Emile.

- WEC missionary David Williams taught Bible lessons in French in four or five Kouya village schools.

Late 1983:

An initial discussion was held with the three recognised Christians in Bahoulifla. It was suggested we meet for worship in Kouya, after the pattern of First Corinthians 14 verse 26.

2. How it developed from there: our (Saunders') role as translators

- The first public Christian event in the Kouya language involving the Christians in Bahoulifla was a baby naming ceremony. The baby's father, Suzan, asked the Christians to pray in his courtyard.

- *January 1984*. The first Sunday morning meeting in Bahoulifla.

- Regular meetings began on Friday evenings.

- A few months later Christians decided they should have an offering.

- Williams told us they had decided to have three days of prayer and fasting for the evangelisation of the Kouyas. By this time the group was growing and other villagers were becoming interested.

- *March 10th 1985* The first Kouya Christian funeral (15 months after they started to meet on Sundays.)

- Evangelistic Bible studies in Bahoulifla - informal translation sessions where the Christians, with a few Catholics and unconverted neighbours all had their input.

- W.E.C. missionary David Williams, whose time overlapped with ours for two years, strongly advised us to stick to the Kouya language in our meetings. Why? Reason given: other Christian groups had sprung up in Ivory Coast, where the majority were immigrant Mossis from Burkina Faso, and where the trade language Jula was the language in common. These often became Mossi churches which used the Moré language, and the Assemblies of God took over. While many of these churches were strong and effective amongst the Mossis, there was a problem in that once the church was composed mainly of Mossis it was usually ineffective in reaching Ivorians, apart from a few isolated individuals.

We could see the sense in this. There already was a thriving Assemblies of God church for Mossis in Bahoulifla village where we lived at the time, but it was not touching the Kouyas at all.

- The Kouya Christians began meeting at a different time in the same building. Because our grasp of the Kouya language was so limited we could only take minimal part. - *Our strong desire was to see the Kouya Christians develop their own gifts and leadership.* It was wonderful to see how the Holy Spirit led the Christians. There was great variety in the form of these meetings.

- At the same time, Philip was regularly attending general village meetings with chief and elders and noting the way they conducted their business. They sat in a circle. When a serious matter was under discussion, each one involved would stand up to state his point of view, both men and women, with the elders giving the final words of wisdom and direction. We thought this an appropriate pattern to encourage when the Kouya believers came together. The form that existed among many other churches in the area was of a trained pastor directing the whole service from the front, with little participation from others in the congregation, who sat passively in rows.

We were able to see the benefits of encouraging many to participate right from the beginning, rather than the worship and growth of the church depending on the presence of one or two people. At the time, many of our churches in Britain were discovering the importance and richness of a team ministry (priesthood of all believers), and it seemed right for the Kouya churches to have this emphasis from the very beginning. Since none of the Kouya Christians in Bahoulifla at that time had much knowledge of the Bible, there was no one person in particular who could be responsible anyway, but gradually gifts began to emerge.

Week by week the growing number of Christians were each contributing in their own way, in prayer, or requests for prayer, testimony, exhortation, singing, composing new Christian songs, or - for the one or two who could read - a reading, translation and application of some part of Scripture, using a French version. We perceived that because it was the responsibility of each Christian to bring his contribution, no one was able to hide behind a wall of silence, and spiritual growth was more rapid.

Even after only a year the W.E.C. missionary commented that this group showed considerable maturity. This was not always evident amongst new Christians who had been overly dependent on the Vavoua Church, running to the mother church for even the smallest of problems.

- By 1987, there were small churches in seven Kouya villages, perhaps 150 Christian adults in all. The monthly preaching rota instigated by David Williams was continuing, with eight Kouya preachers visiting other churches each month at this stage. There was a dual purpose for these exchange visits: firstly for evangelistic outreach, and secondly for teaching the Christians. The programme helped to inculcate a sense of corporate identity. At the same time, secondary-school students (collégiens, collégiennes) and officials (fonctionnaires) from big towns who had been converted through other churches and missions, were now starting to attend village churches in the holidays, making a most valuable contribution.

Evangelistic motivation was high, both among secondary-school students and farmers. Many regularly made visits to believers in nearby villages, and loved to encourage the different groups by attending their services.

- A yearly conference rotated around the different villages. These played a vital role in mutual encouragement, intensive Bible teaching, sharing joys and sorting out church problems.

- Bible College students: the first two were Jonas, son of M. Robert the Vavoua postmaster, and Zébli Baï Emile, our translator/co-worker. They attended the W.E.C. College at Zuénoula.

- Quarterly leaders' meetings began, to decide policies, and to resolve the most complicated matters.

- *1988:* Eddie and Sue Arthur arrived, joined the Kouya language project, and set up home in Gouabafla, where they were strategically placed to relate to forest villages, and encourage the new churches which sprang up there.

3. Relationships with other churches, and our role as expatriates.

There was pressure, undoubtedly, to conform to the pattern of some other churches in the area, where lay participation was minimal. The idea of the central pastor being "the expert", or big chief, was paramount. Yet if small problems could be sorted out by the village churches themselves, then this more experienced pastor could be freed up to help resolve the really complicated cases, should outside help be required.

It was expected that the tithe from each church should be brought to the central church, though some Kouya leaders were beginning to grumble about this, and would have preferred to use the money towards new church buildings, or for sending different members of their fellowship to Bible school for training. The main Vavoua church contributed towards our translator Emile's expenses at Bible College. They would also probably have helped, as they were able, to provide funds for a new village church building. But how much should this have been the responsibility of the village Christians themselves? A healthier situation might have been for the Kouya village churches to have a measure of independence and responsibility for managing their own affairs, while maintaining close links of fellowship with the church in town. This was the old thorny question of church government. Our experience in Ivory Coast was that less dependent churches were freer to develop their own forms and flavour, instead of automatically reproducing a pattern found elsewhere. But accountability was also important. It was clear that neither the extreme of over-independence, nor that of total dependence were particularly healthy. And yet there were pulls in both directions by persuasive individuals. Our personal aim was to encourage inter-dependence with accountability.

Even in our short time in Africa, seeing a church come to birth, start to take shaky steps, then gradually grow and move forward with confidence, we had witnessed how it was possible even for a new church, at times, to go mechanically through learned and lifeless forms of worship. Happily we had also experienced, in the great majority of new Kouya churches, an expectation and a knowledge that the Living Lord was present and would be active amongst His people as they met together.

The Issue of Authority

So how was the authority structure to develop? We did not feel personally that our role should be in *overt* leadership. We did not make any decisions for the group regarding their finances or funerals, but discussed any issues that they asked about, and tried to draw their attention to Scripture passages which were relevant to the particular issue at hand. Our aim and prayer was that they and we would view the Scriptures as our final authority.

In Bahoulifla, Williams evolved as "leader" *(dirigeant),* Lucien was later appointed elder by the Vavoua church. Williams and his old aunt, Old Anatole and Lucien were the first to be baptised, in Vavoua, by the church elders there. The first village baptisms took place in Dema dam.

Another important aspect of our supporting role in developing church life was to encourage the Kouya Christians to look to the Lord to guide them, to follow what they believe He really wanted them to do in each situation, and to have confidence in themselves. The Holy Spirit would direct them as they grew in their understanding of Scripture, including what to do about the issue of the authority of the central church. Our attitude seemed to be a strengthening factor, and the new Christians recognised that *we* had more confidence in their ability to discern the Lord's voice than they did themselves at times. So we tried to keep asking, "What do you really think is best in this situation and what does the Bible have to say about it?"

We owed a great debt to Wayne Dye's "Scripture in Use" principles here (as explained in his book *"The Bible Translation Strategy"*), and found them to be extremely effective in our situation. They also helped us to define our role as cross-cultural translators within the developing Kouya church.

APPENDIX C

Short Glossary of Terms

Animism – A religion which holds the belief that natural effects are due to spirits, and that non-human objects (for example trees) have spirits.

Charlatan – Medicine man.

Fetish – Object endowed with spiritual power through incantations of a religious charlatan.

Foutou – Staple food made by thorough mashing in a mortar with a wooden pestle. Yams and cooking bananas (plantains) may be mashed in this way, with water continually added during the process. Banana *foutou* is one of the most popular dishes in the forest region of Ivory Coast.

I.P.A. – International Phonetic Alphabet.

N.I.V. – New International Version (of Bible).

Pagne – Wrap-around cloth.

Scriptures – The Bible.

S.I.L. – Summer Institute of Linguistics, or *Société Internationale de Linguistique.* Sister organisation of Wycliffe Bible Translators.

Sorceror/sorceress – Witch doctor/witch.

W.B.T. – Wycliffe Bible Translators.

W.E.C. – Worldwide Evangelization for Christ.